Other Titles by Susie Bright

How to Write a Dirty Story

*Full Exposure: Opening Up to Your Sexual
Creativity and Erotic Expression*

The Sexual State of the Union

*The Best American Erotica 1993, 1994, 1995,
1996, 1997, 1999, 2000, 2001* (editor)

*Nothing But the Girl: The Blatant Lesbian
Image* (with Jill Posener)

Herotica, Herotica 2, Herotica 3 (editor)

Sexwise

*Susie Bright's Sexual Reality: A Virtual Sex
World Reader*

Susie Sexpert's Lesbian Sex World

www.susiebright.com

The best American erotica 2002

edited by

Susie Bright

A Touchstone Book
Published by Simon & Schuster

New York · London · Toronto · Sydney · Singapore

TOUCHSTONE
Rockefeller Center
1230 Avenue of the Americas
New York, NY 10020

Touchstone and colophon are registered trademarks
of Simon & Schuster, Inc.

Designed by Lauren Simonetti

Manufactured in the United States of America

ISBN 0-7394-2201-4

Acknowledgments

This edition of *The Best American Erotica* is brought to you thanks to the care and attention of many people besides myself. My special thanks to Bill Bright; Jennifer Taillac; Jon Bailiff; my agents Joanie Shoemaker and JoLynne Worley; my editor at Simon & Schuster, Doris Cooper; and all the editors, publishers, and fans who helped bring the stories in this volume to my attention and pleasure.

The Best American Erotica 2002 is dedicated to the memory of Kris Kovick, 1951–2001.

Contents

Introduction   13

Talk About Sex: An Orientation
Jamie Callan   21

Joe
Maggie Estep   34

In Deep
Simon Sheppard   44

The Lesson
Debra Boxer   62

Penny Candy
Andi Mathis   67

Cowboy
Adelina Anthony   74

A Clean Comfortable Room
Pam Ward   87

Mer, from *Nymph*
Francesca Lia Block   101

Driving Lesson, from *Sarah*
J. T. LeRoy   108

Orange Phone
Laurie Sirois   113

On the Dangers of Simultaneity,
Or, Ungh, Mmmm, Oh-Baby-Yeah,
Aaah, Oooh . . . UH-OH!
Robert Devereaux   118

When to Use
Stacey Richter   126

Champagne Tastes on a Crystal
Budget
Gary Rosen   128

Stiletto
Lucy Taylor   141

Ropeburn
Anne Tourney   151

From *Horse Heaven*
Jane Smiley   164

Backhand
Ernie Conrick   169

Night Train
Nell Carberry   184

Ganger (Ball Lightning)
Nalo Hopkinson   189

Homewrecker
Poppy Z. Brite   210

Two Years
Paula Bomer   214

Trolls
Michael Stamp   220

Reading *Lolita* on the 9:25
Tsaurah Litzky   229

From *Lofting*
Alma Marceau   237

The Whole Bloody Story of
My Life from Beginning to End
Shaun Levin   245

Contributors   253
Reader's Directory   259
Credits   265
Reader Survey   269

Introduction

Erotic lit has been a lot of things during the past couple of decades: a renaissance, a political football, the best conversation piece you ever left out on your coffee table. It's transformed itself from publishing shame to book business savior, from militant manifesto to supermarket special.

But for those of us who've been enjoying (or criticizing) the modern heyday of erotica, it's also been something else: one of the most compelling soap operas around. There's always a new character threatening to take over the room—the Gothic babe, the safe sex mensch, or the cyber-amazon—which one will be the star this year? In addition to the new kids on the series, we've got such stalwarts as the sensitive macho, the rebellious virgin, and the notorious diva who never dies—the Whore with the Heart of Gold.

In the 1980s, erotic lit revived itself in rebellion, as the horny battle cry of the outcasts and the invisible. On one side, there were the pro-sex feminists who thought the best way to kick a double standard in the ass was to create their own juicy alternative. It was the erotic version of "I am Woman, Hear Me Roar," and this time the girl was in ecstasy, unapologetic and orgasmic.

The queer side to the new erotic wave was the spectacular growth of gay and lesbian publishing, which was much more outspoken. Again, it was all in the vein of "I Am (Name Your Label Here), Hear Me Roar, Sweat, Come, and Whisper Dirty Somethings in Your Ear."

Much of this early writing was first-person, confessional, and triumphant. This style did not make it as the darling of the literary fiction world, which considered the whole trend to be adolescent raving. You weren't about to see "Lesbian Coming-Out Stories" heralded as best genre of the year by *The New York Review of Books.* But like many genres that are disdained by the literary establishment, coming-out stories were a huge hit among everyday readers.

I look back at my first collection of erotica (*Herotica,* in 1987) and it's like looking at my teenage self—so precocious and poignant at times, so ridiculous at others. It's a remarkably popular book even today, and I think that's because, for many readers coming into their sexual identity, it's still the perfect welcome wagon. These coming-out stories invite the reader to join a community that proclaims, "Yes, we're sexual, we're healthy, we're the future leaders of tomorrow, dammit." If you're someone who has heard only the dirtiest and most shaming messages about sex all your life, this is the enlightenment.

Nevertheless, as more and more talented writers explored erotic fiction, a bit of backlash began. It was a reaction to the sunniness of the coming-out formula, and I called it "porn noir." This was the attitude of the writer who said, "I don't want to be a role model, I don't want to be wholesome—I 'came out' ten years ago, and it was hardly the highlight of my sexual career."

Porn noir peaked in the mid-nineties, and we started seeing a lot of dark stories, parables with erotic antiheroes, ambivalent endings—and yes, bad sex. Yet they were still arousing—the storytelling was irresistible. Authenticity was their watchword, and "keeping it real" meant not putting a cherry on top of every cum shot.

In this edition of *The Best American Erotica,* I'm seeing a new trend that goes beyond reaction or rebellion. Instead, it has to do with a changing viewpoint, a new authorial attitude.

The hallmark of the coming-out story was that it was told in the first person; it was autobiographical. When the porn noir craze hit, even though the author was not as optimistic as we had become accustomed to, s/he was still telling "his or her own truth," as it were. The "I" was still the most popular viewpoint for telling a sex story; the implication was still largely confessional.

Writers being the great liars that they are, no one wanted to "be themselves" for very long . . . how dreary. That confessional "Look Ma! Look Pa! I'm Fucking Myself!" thing was exhilarating at first, but it was a dead end after the early generations. Some writers are very private about their personal lives, and their own sexuality is often quite a departure from their protagonists'.

There are seven stories in this edition that portray a male point of view, in which the "I" is a man, or the third person is employed to show a decidedly masculine perspective. Six of these stories are written by women. It's the same on the other side; I have men who are writing lesbian and female-centric work as well. One of the "gay male" stories is written by a woman. Of course, since I'm sworn to secrecy, I can't even tell you how many of the author names you see on the stories are actually the gender they appear to be. Just keep guessing.

Now I realize that this wouldn't be big news in literary fiction. No one says to Joyce Carol Oates, "My god, it's incredible the way you write men's dialogue, how can you bring yourself to do it?" But in contemporary erotic lit, this is pretty racy. When Pat Califia first wrote *Macho Sluts* in 1989, she trailblazed this cross-gender viewpoint, but it's taken until now to become part of the erotic writing mainstream.

Not only is it a leap of writing sophistication, it's also been a departure from political correctness. Many women erotic authors have always been perfectly capable of writing male viewpoints and vice versa. But because modern erotic fiction has been so feminist in its roots, there was always an unspoken peer pressure to write as a woman, to show the woman's point of view, to interrupt the male monologue that seems to dominate every other part of the media.

Men who wrote erotica were discouraged writing female

viewpoints because there was resentment there, in the spirit of "What the hell do you know, you patriarchal windbag!" After all, so many patriarchal windbags had already gotten published that the guilt trip worked as an effective shushing.

What's interesting now is to see women taking on male characterizations to make their stories come to light—or gay authors using heterosexual sex to make a homosexual point, and so on. It brings to mind the words of filmmaker Gregg Araki, who once said, "I was so sick of directors who made gay-themed movies for a straight audience—so I decided to make a 'straight movie' for gay people."

This flexibility in viewpoint has made erotic lit a lot more complex and unpredictable, which is the flavor of any good yarn. It's been satisfying to see women's stories where the argument for why women are entitled to have sexual feelings is not rehashed for pedagogical benefit. Instead, the characters *do* have sex, they *do* have emotions, but the story unfolds with all their contradictions building up our anticipation. The gay stories, in particular, are often so far away from the legend of "how I became queer" that when I find one of those coming-out confessions today, it brings a tear of seventies nostalgia to my eyes.

One character that's been particularly shaken up by this new candor and creativity is that old whore with the golden heart I mentioned at the beginning of the introduction. The fastest-growing erotica this past year has been the explosion of writing by artists who work in the sex business.

The obvious reason for the burgeoning number of sex-work stories is that so many people now count some sex work as part of their résumés. If you're living in Southern California, I would lay odds you've either worked a sex-related job, or you have a relative who does. We're not just talking porn stars here, but rather everyone from the warehouseman who trucks your dildos, to the sales manager for the printing press that delivers hardcore box covers. There are the doctors who work in clinics that cater to prostitutes and adult actors, and the lingerie manufacturers who wouldn't exist without strippers as their biggest customers. And that's all aside from the "talent": the models, the phone-sex operators, escorts, dominatrixes, and so on.

The peculiar American prejudice against sex work is that, first, it's for dumb people, and second, it's for the chronically horny and hard-up. Yet if you take a look at any of the books, plays, and films created by sex workers, you'll see that they're as articulate, educated, and outspoken as any group of nonconformists. They have the same highs and lows of libido as any civilian.

One of the best anthologies I read last year was *Tricks and Treats,* edited by Matt Bernstein Sycamore. The theme is sex workers talking about their clients. Once again, the "I" is used, it's intended to be autobiographical, and a few of the stories recall how the authors came into their trade.

Yet as the editor says in his introduction, "These stories are written as if we are talking among ourselves." He goes on further to explain the risk he took in showing a warts-and-all view of this world: "The media's most common portrayals of sex workers are of sex-crazed perverts or trapped victims. . . . In a world that still views sex workers as primarily vectors of disease (literally and figuratively), counternarrative is crucial. Sometimes, however, sex-worker spokespersons end up oversimplifying sex work by showing only the positive sides. To me, this is as inaccurate as the talk-show host and the social worker who call us depraved or deprived."

Oversimplifying—the great sin of the do-gooder, the sex-positive cheerleader, the optimistic assimilationist. Truth be told, it's the cry of someone who would just like to be understood and appreciated for a minute before the next tidal wave of sex-shame barrels up. And yet look where it gets you—there's the initial applause for trying to play to the crowd, but it's only a matter of minutes before your façade is unmasked, and the calls of hypocrisy are thrown into the ring.

Fiction has always been the most transformative place to tell the truth. Storytellers aren't running for office; they're simply here to suspend disbelief. Writers don't have to take one side, because if they're any good, they'll make you step into multiple pairs of character shoes. Authors don't have to "do the right thing," because their most appealing hero can be the one who never does anything right. It's this empathy that arouses our convictions and sways more minds than a thousand stump speeches.

Erotic lit is getting messier every day, much to my approval. I'm relieved that the new erotica writers don't expect me to love them, or to become them, just because their story turns me on. Give me the soap, the lather, and all the dirt, because I'll stick around for the next episode, and the one after that. Coming-out stories have finally come clean and grown up, like all good genres should. I don't know what's going to happen next, and that's the biggest thrill of all.

—Susie Bright
February 2002

The best
American
erotica
2002

Jamie Callan
Talk About Sex: An Orientation

The little room has a purpose the way Puritanism has a pur-
pose but we don't want to go into it & talk about sex, we
don't want to pay someone to sit on a bed & talk about sex.
—Lewis Warsh, "Elective Surgery"

All I'm going to do is talk. That's right—you're going to pay
me to sit here and talk to you. Let me explain—I come to your
hotel room, I always wear something nice, maybe a jacket and
matching skirt, or a simple dress, pearls, always stockings, always
heels, always tasteful. I sit on your bed, cross my legs, smile, and
then I talk about sex. You're not allowed to touch me. That
would be breaking the rules. I talk for exactly forty-five minutes.
I always finish on time. I charge three hundred and fifty dollars. I
accept all major credit cards and I am completely discreet. If, for
example, I bump into you on 58th Street, and you are going into
the Paris Cinema, I will not acknowledge you and I will not talk
to you. That would be breaking the rules. Yes. The rules.

There are seventeen rules altogether.

The most important one is that you do not touch me. I know I
already said that, but it's worth repeating, don't you think? The
second most important one is that you do not touch yourself. And
the third most important rule is that you appear and remain completely dressed. You don't have to wear a suit or tie, but a nice

sports coat and a pair of khakis or well-pressed chinos are appreciated. You may not eat during the session. This isn't actually on the list of rules, but it's common sense. Obviously it's hard to talk about sex when a man is chomping on a pastrami sandwich. And there's the smell to consider as well. It gets distracting. So no eating. However, you may drink. Cola, orange juice, bottled water, and beer or wine—in moderation—are all acceptable. No hard alcohol. It dulls the senses, and you just won't get your money's worth—not that I care, but you might. I provide none of these refreshments. It's up to you to keep them in the fridge, and if your hotel doesn't supply you with a fridge. . . . Actually, if you're not staying in the kind of hotel that supplies you with a completely stocked fridge, then I probably won't be visiting you.

I will not accept any beverages, so please don't offer me any. However, if my throat becomes dry after talking for a time and I need a glass of water, I will get up and fetch it myself. You don't need to bother yourself; I will take care of getting it and work the interruption seamlessly into my conversation. You will not even notice a change in tone, so don't imagine that you can get an extra five minutes at the end for lost time. There will be no lost time.

Now, the "menu," as I call it, is extensive, updated weekly, and includes not only the classic favorites such as the man who gets caught in a rainstorm and must seek shelter at the home of three nubile teenaged girls who have been abandoned by their parents and are living in a woodshed on the side of a deserted highway in Minnesota but also five or six daily specials. For instance, on Fridays I might offer Catholic schoolgirls in plaid jumpers and knee socks who forgot to put on their underpants that day, playing hopscotch on the sidewalk in front of your enormous split-level house in Mamaroneck, eating pork chops on a Friday, when Father O'Leary comes along and must find a way to teach them a lesson and punish them. This one takes place in 1967 and it's a favorite with fifty-three-year-old Jewish men from Westchester County.

Of course the list is computerized, alphabetized, and on the Internet. I do have a website, and you can access me at www.hoteltalk.org. This does not mean I will respond to inquiries, and I seldom answer e-mail. But please feel free to send a message. Just don't expect an answer.

Rule number four. After I leave, you must never pretend you are very preoccupied and get on the phone as I've closed the door, only to jump up, stand by the door, and spy on me while I punch the elevator button for the lobby, and then quickly run out of your hotel room the moment the elevator doors close, race down the stairs, follow me out of the lobby, and then dart and dodge through traffic, almost getting run over, trailing close behind me until I get in a cab, and then grab a cab yourself and tell the driver to follow my cab, giving your driver a hundred-dollar bill to do so, all the while trying to restrain the enormous erection that has been forming in your trousers as you descend the streets, 51st, 50th, 49th, 48th, 47th, wondering where the hell I am going to get out, nervous it might be 42nd, relieved in Chelsea, then sweating again through Tribeca and Chinatown, getting stimulated, too, imagining that I live in a loft apartment on Walker and Lisbernard with a poet boyfriend who beats me, and that I am not at all the hardened businesswoman that I appear to be but instead a victim, bringing home my ill-gotten gains and handing them over to a drunken poet named Raoul who hasn't written a decent line of verse in the last twenty-five years and hasn't shaved since Friday. Whatever you do, do not get out of the cab and follow me up the five flights of stairs and stand in the doorway, watching as he grabs at the cash still hot from your own hands, presented to me only minutes before, having nestled in your pocket for an entire afternoon. And do not feel tenderness for me when Raoul screams at me that I am a whore, a bitch, and knocks me about the filthy kitchen, throwing pots and pans, as he continues to get drunker and rail against the New York literary scene, harping on the difference between the experimental poets and the language poets, and how the hell John Ashbery got to be so darn famous, when he suddenly lifts up my skirt, kisses my thighs, begs me for forgiveness as he pulls at my garter belt, brings me closer to him—me standing, while he sits at the kitchen table, wearing only boxers and a T-shirt with tomato sauce stains—rubbing my legs, pushing them apart, poking his fingers inside, deeper and deeper, while he talks about going to Tuscany to live for a year, renting a villa and maybe even having a baby and changing citizenship, while you stand there just out-side the open door, and suddenly our eyes meet and you believe in that moment that you can rescue me. Then you watch as I close my eyes, and you are not sure whether I saw you or not, or whether I am thinking about Raoul. About how, despite the fact that he is a dreamer and we will always be stuck together in this godforsaken heat, with him pressing his dirty, unshaven face up against my soft chin, taking me there on the kitchen table, and me moaning as he forces his way in, as I concentrate on the knife on the counter and the beer bottle in the sink, while you stand outside the door, witness to all this, wondering if there are any sublets available in this roach-infested building and how you might leave your wife in Cincinnati for me.

Rule number five. You must never leave your wife for me. I know. This is a difficult one. More difficult than remaining dressed or not touching me. Right now you don't think it will be a problem, but you're wrong. This problem always crops up, pri-marily because you don't see it as a problem so you don't prepare for it, and then one day you find yourself cleaning out the attic, packing away photo albums, deleting names and addresses on your Rolodex and opening up a mailbox number at the Canal Street Post Office.

* * *

You're probably wondering how I got started doing what I do, and you're probably wondering exactly why I do it, and if there's any possibility that I do anything more—perhaps for a bit more money—than simply sit on your bed and talk. The answer is no. I do nothing more than sit on your bed and talk, and I am not going to tell you why I do what I do or if I have any plans to do more. But of course you might not care one iota whether I tell you what I do when I'm not here sitting on your bed. You may be the type who wants to tell me about what you do when I'm not sitting on your bed, you may be the type who wants to sit there for forty-five minutes and tell me all about your fantasies, how you really like the idea of you and two women together and how you like to imagine that I have a sister named Candy, who's still in high school even though she's nineteen and a half because she's been held back two years in a row as a result of an undiagnosed learning disability and a penchant for playing hooky. You may want to tell me how Candy's morals are skewed because she hasn't had much parental guidance and her father abused her, and that at fourteen she fell in love with Mr. Swann, her geometry teacher, and he began to explain an especially difficult proof one afternoon in the back of his eighth-grade classroom, and as it got to be about four o'clock and the room grew dimmer and dimmer, he noticed how Candy's delicate white ankles led up to a shapely calf, which led to a girlish knobby knee with a little flesh-colored Band-Aid pointing upward to Candy's supple thigh, which she crossed and uncrossed, and crossed and uncrossed, pressing her wool plaid skirt, the green and blue and yellow lines crisscrossing over and over again, creating a kind of geometrical pattern that rises and falls according to her breathing and the movement of her hands across her lap, and her hands across her lap, yes, resting right there, on top of her pubis, so soft and furry, you imagine that you—because you are now Mr. Swann, the geometry teacher, don't deny it—cannot help but lean forward and put your hand on top of Candy's and press it down, comforting her, saying, "There, there, now the Pythagorean theorem is not so very hard to grasp." And in that moment, your eyes meet and she leans forward, slowly closing her eyes, almost as if she has fallen asleep—suddenly decided to take a nap in the middle of your classroom, in the middle of the afternoon, because geometry is just so wearisome, and she falls

into your arms, kissing you full on the mouth, and you, support-
ing her slender frame, kiss her back, and back, and back, and
then her father walks into the room and says, "What the hell are
you doing to my daughter?"

Hah! You didn't expect that, did you? I apologize, but I just
couldn't help myself. Rule number seven—I have every right to
start off telling a story about a ménage à trois and then suddenly
switch gears and tell a story about a geometry teacher getting
brought up on sexual harassment charges and losing his job and
being sent to prison, where all sorts of dreadful things happen,
and if you'd like I'd be glad to tell you all about them in lurid
detail. No extra charge for that.

Did I mention what rule number six is?

No? Oh, that's too bad.

Rule number six, then—you must never criticize anything I
say or do. I think this bears repeating. You must never criticize
anything I say or do. I know what I'm doing, and even if it seems
like I've lost all control and I really should not be out talking
about sex to strange men in hotel rooms, rather that I should be
home in bed watching soap operas with all the doors and windows locked and a thick blanket wrapped around my body, and
my psychotherapist's telephone number poised on redial, you
must not say a word about it. You must behave as if everything is
as it should be. Even if I were to suddenly begin sobbing in the
middle of a story and tell you that someone in my family died this
morning, someone quite close to me—my mother for instance.
Even if I were to suddenly begin discussing how much I loved her
and how I am completely lost without her, and how I am really
psychopathically sad, and this whole sex-talk business is simply a
reaction to a repressed childhood and an overbearing mother, and
now that my mother has died I no longer feel the urgent need to
rebel and I don't know why the hell I'm in your hotel room because it all seems so futile and idiotic, and just plain bad.

The main reason you are not allowed to criticize me is
because I am extremely sensitive. I know I might not seem it, but

the truth is, I am. It might seem unlikely to you that I go home and think about you and all my other clients, the millions of men I've seen in my many years of business, but in fact I do. I think about each and every one of you. I keep a file on you. I carry this file wherever I go. You probably want to know what I have in this file, but I'm not going to tell you. That would be breaking the rules. That's rule number nine, perhaps. I'm not sure. I'm losing track. But I will tell you a few of the things I keep on file about you. For instance, if you prefer domineering women, if you loved your mother too much, if you think all women are whores and that only your mother is truly good and pure and clean, and that if you keep yourself pure for her she will finally see your goodness and kiss you on your lips, take you to her bedroom—the one with all those pink woolen blankets and lace, and pictures of the children, the one with your father's ties hanging limply in the closet, smelling of the 9:07 P.M. train from Grand Central Station, the vanilla-scented bedroom where the secret of procreation is kept, the origins of your very own DNA, and there, there, finally knowing that you have been good, that you have saved that little corner of your brain, your heart, your soul for her alone, she will take you back to whence you came.

You see, I keep track of these things. Plus what's your favorite color, ice cream flavor. What your pet peeves are, whether you prefer blondes over brunettes, if you take cream in your coffee, if you've ever had a fantasy involving the laundromat and a millionaire businessman who walks in because he's lost, busy on his cell phone when he sees a young girl wearing only her underwear because that's all she's got and the rest of her clothes are in the dryer, and she lives in Santa Cruz, and you, movie mogul from Hollywood, think, wouldn't she be good in your next picture? So you eye her there, in the middle of the laundromat, sitting there on top of the vibrating Westinghouse Superspin in nothing but a pair of slightly tattered thong bikini underpants and a white lace bra that barely covers ample brown breasts straining to burst out of the thin latticework of fabric, and she smiles at you, whispering, "Hi, my name is Cherise. Would you like to know the ins and outs of doing your laundry here at the Suds and Gossip? Believe me, I know the ins and outs because I've been doing my laundry here since I was a little girl about seven years old, with my mom. She used to be this exotic dancer in San Francisco until she moved me and my three brothers and two sisters here to Santa Cruz. She said we'd have a healthier lifestyle, but now she's cut her hair, dyed it green, pierced her navel, and joined some weird religious cult."

You, movie mogul that you are, all the way from Hollywood, are not thinking about the Westinghouse or the spin cycles or the Fab with Fresh Lemon-Scented Borax, but instead you are concentrating on her thighs, so brown and firm, and her ass, perched there—just *perched* there—and how dry your mouth feels and her blond ponytail, all sun-bleached, and the tension growing in your belly, and how you could get her to Paramount Pictures, talk to her about a career, about how she would be beautiful on the screen, but what's the point really? It would be too much of an effort, and after all, here you are in the Suds and Gossip, and the universe is demanding that you seize the day, so you move to the table, lean against the folded, freshly washed shirts and faded work pants, jeans, and towels that belong to someone else who has gone across the street to the 7-Eleven to buy a pack of Camels and a Bud while the rest of his wash tumbles in the dryer. You lean against the table and suddenly find yourself in front of her, the brown girl with the ponytail, worshipping at the shrine between her legs, licking up the last juices of a ceremony you don't quite understand, while she pats your head and says, good boy, that's a good boy, although you are not sure whether she is saying good boy or good dog.

You feel a little excited about that. The dog part. Don't be embarrassed. I know these things. It's my job. I'm a professional. I'm absolutely attuned to all the nuances and subtleties of my work. I'm completely intuitive and psychic. I read minds. I analyze handwriting. I know the zodiac. I know your sun sign, your

moon sign, your rising sign. I know when Mercury is going ret-
rograde, and when Jupiter is entering your sun sign, and how
you become so sensitive whenever Uranus gets anywhere near
Pisces.

I know what you had for breakfast this morning. I know
when you've had too much sodium, when you should cut down
on the caffeine. I know what you did in the bathroom of the
lobby. I know what you called your mother's sister when you
were twelve years old and didn't know better. I know you feel
guilty about the day you called your father a big fat jerk. I know
when your moon is out of phase. I know about the lie you told
when you wanted to get out of that engagement. I know when
you last saw your psychotherapist. I know about the thing you
did on the side of the garage when you were eight and you
thought no one could see. I saw you.

And I know when you haven't called for your weekly
appointment because you're sitting in the corner of your kitchen,
crouched between the refrigerator and the stove, wearing nothing but your Calvins, shivering and shaking. And I know about
that week you did nothing but watch Hitchcock's *Vertigo* for
twenty-four hours a day, staring bleary-eyed at your television
set as Kim Novak plummeted from the bell tower again and
again and again.

Rule number ten. You are not allowed to buy clothes exactly
like mine and then go out and get a wig and walk around New
York City as if you were me, buying flowers in Chelsea, a latte in
the Village, and a coffee-table art book at Rizzoli's in Soho. You
are not allowed to pretend you are me and you are having a nervous breakdown, a kind of *Vertigo* remake with a little sexual
identity confusion thrown in, where I become Jimmy Stewart and
you're Kim Novak, and I follow you all around town while you
buy flowers and visit an ancient graveyard and act very, very mysterious, and I slowly fall in love with you because I am heartbro-
ken from accidentally falling off the roof of a very tall building,
and I have lost my nerve, and you have lost something too—not

exactly nerve, but the same thing in a way—you, a woman-slash-man hired by a faithless, murderous husband to do away with his wife, making me the fall guy, through my own cowardice the unwitting murderer.

Rule number seventeen—I will not murder for you. I will not commit a crime for you. I will not die for you. I will not pay your bills, get you out of debt, steal a brand-new car for you, talk to your mother, get your twenty-three-year-old daughter to move out of your house, and I will not, absolutely not, poison your wife for you. So don't even ask me.

Now, you're probably growing a little discouraged, thinking, all these rules—where's the fun? What's the point? Why am I paying these kinds of prices to be with a woman—and not even a movie-star type, but an ordinary woman—if there are going to be all these rules?

Here is my answer to that: these are the rules. And there is no fun. So get the hell out if that's what you're after. Get out! Hello? I said get the hell out!

Why are you still here?

I know why.

I know exactly why.

Yes, I do. Come closer.

I'll tell you why you're still here.

It's because you've been bad.

And you know it. And I know it. Remember? I know everything about you. I even know you like to make a squeaky grunting sound when you're in the throes of orgasm. That only the thought of a small mouse nestled inside a chunk of Swiss cheese and the cat, Sylvester, poised atop the refrigerator with a cartoon anvil, waiting to drop it on the unsuspecting Tom and Jerry, will get you in the mood. That when you are rubbing yourself up against a woman, you are thinking about Chips Ahoy chocolate chip cookies and Bosco-flavored milk on a TV tray, about that afternoon in February when you stayed home from school sick as a dog and your mother leaned down to kiss your steaming forehead and you inhaled the fragrance of day-old Chanel No. 5 as your eyes were glued to *Looney Tunes,* and your little boy heart went *thump-thump-thump* from the heat and closeness of your mother's breast.

By the way, I've talked to your mother.

In fact, your mother is waiting outside the door for you, and she's got a big paddleboard and bottle of castor oil.

Just kidding. I mean, about the paddleboard and the castor oil. Not about talking to your mother because I did talk to your mother. Would you like to know what she said? Of course you would. She said: get on with it. Get over it. Grow up. She told me she's gone to Tahiti to live out the rest of her life among the natives, like Gauguin.

Now don't go and imagine your mother prancing naked among the palm fronds. That's called regression. No, instead imagine this—she's gone. She's happy. She's dancing among the orchids and lilies, wearing a nice little modest floral muumuu. She's drinking a daiquiri with a little paper parasol stuck in it. She's writing a novel. She's taking up singing. She's painting pictures. She's scuba diving. Collecting sea shells. Making pottery. Writing a screenplay. She's bought a video camera. Become a lounge singer. She's taken up with a hotel manager named Maurice. She's happy, laughing. And she's not thinking of you. She's forgotten all about you.

She's not watching you. Therefore, you are free. Free. Yes, free. You don't have to make love to a clone of yourself. You don't have to have sex with a rubber doll, a pinup girl, a cyberspace babe, a voice on the telephone, an Internet surfer girl, a dominatrix in leather lederhosen, a girl in a fancy apartment on East 92nd Street who only wants you for your money because that's all you have to give since your heart belongs to Mommy. You don't have to look for a woman who is so different from Mommy—a different race or religion or height or hair color— that looking into her eyes at night will not send you into Oedipal Shock Syndrome. You don't have to run the moment someone mentions marriage because marriage means Mommy and Mommy means death.

I know, you panic as soon as a woman is nice, as soon as she kisses your steaming forehead, as soon as she coos in your ear. You think of mice and cats with an anvil poised above their heads. You want to kill. You don't want to kill. Or you want to watch the Super Bowl for twenty-four hours or read a 1,500-page science fiction novel, or take your weed whacker out and mow down innocent dandelions, their little yellow heads severed and lying lifeless on the edge of your driveway waiting to be flushed down the sewer with one burst from your big, long garden hose.

I never orgasm. Don't ask me why because I'm not going to tell you. But it's good for business, don't you think? If I were in the middle of a story, talking about sex, and I suddenly found myself aroused (I do occasionally get excited, but I can control myself), but suppose I was overcome by excitement and threw myself down on the floor, ripped off my panties, spread my legs and began fingering myself, frantically searching, groping, trying to locate the button that releases all this pent-up emotion and passion, and I were to scream as the rivers crash through the barriers of my psyche and pour down through my head and breasts and legs and the center of my being as I writhe and moan for a full twenty minutes about how *good-good-gooood* it feels to finally—*fi-nal-ly*—let go, twisting and screaming on your hotel room floor, clawing at my own breasts, pummeling my center, tasting my own juices, as I press my fingers in and out and spread my own creamy substance over my thighs and breasts and stomach, my eyes rolling backward in their sockets as I speak in strange tongues and scream out my mother's name, to *stop-stop-stop. Please.*

My mother died this morning.

Did I mention that?

I said I wasn't going to reveal anything personal, but I thought you might like to know, since we're on the subject of mothers anyway. Everybody said to me, "Go to work—it'll take your mind off of it." So here I am. I loved my mother. I can imagine her in Tahiti right now. She taught me about sex. I probably have my professional life to thank her for. *Sex,* she said, *is like ice cream. It tastes good for a while, but when all is said and done it's a sticky liquid mess and it gets all over the sheets.*

I wish you had known her. I wish she had taught you about sex instead of me.

Kiss me.

Now.

Please. Kiss me.

I know it's against the rules. I know I said *no touching,* but my mother died today and your mother is in Tahiti. Do you remember the tune for *Tom and Jerry?* Would you sing it to me? Please.

That's right. Sing to me, and get me a drink. Make it hard—vodka on the rocks. And then, come here. And kiss me.

Oh, I'm sorry. Time's up.

Maggie Estep
Joe

One day Joe woke up with a headache so violent it made a red curtain hang in front of his eyes. He blinked several times, but it wouldn't go away. He sat up. He moved his head. He opened the newspaper, even though trying to read any of its print made the red curtain throb.

> LOS ANGELES (AP)—Children were greeted with hugs, love, and performing clowns today as they returned to the Jewish community center that was a place of terror just six days earlier.

Joe was glad he didn't live in Los Angeles. He lived in Chicago, near Rogers Park. The neighborhood was home to rehabs, furniture moving companies, people on SSI, gangs, and women who worked for tips.

Joe thought about the performing clowns cavorting around the murder scene. Which made him remember Susan's clown outfit, the one with bright red suspenders holding up a red garter belt and white fishnet stockings.

Thinking of this gave Joe a hard-on in spite of the now-blinding headache. He dialed 911. Joe briefly marveled over having a hard-on in spite of the fact that something was obviously very wrong with his head. This was the last thought he had for a long time.

When Joe came to in the hospital three days later, a nurse was there at his bedside, emptying a tube full of his urine. "They removed the tumor from your brain. It was the size of a grape-fruit."

Joe wondered why it was that tumors were always compared to fruit. He wondered if the nurse liked to have sex with fruit. Susan did.

* * *

Joe met Susan at the rehab where he worked as a janitor. No one really knew how Susan had gotten to the detox. She'd been left in the waiting room, sedated, with her hands bound behind her back by a handkerchief.

She was half Iranian and had a beautiful nose. She wore lots of cheap jewelry that turned her skin green. Her hair was so long it touched her ass.

She suffered severe withdrawal from heroin. Three days off the stuff and her hormones were raging.

Counselors at the rehab caught Susan trying to have sex with virtually all the rehab inmates, male and female. One day, Joe found her in his broom closet. With his mop. She was leaning forward against the Band-Aid–colored wall. She had inserted the mop handle into herself from behind. She had her long black skirt bunched up over her ass.

When Joe walked in, she froze. Then she turned her head and looked at him. Her eyes were black hot coals and impossible to read. Joe slowly backed out of the closet. He went down the hall and into one of the counselor's offices, where he mechani-cally started emptying the trash, paying absolutely no mind to the counselor who was in there.

About ten minutes later, Joe went back into his broom closet. He knew she wouldn't be there anymore. He carefully picked the mop up and licked its handle. It tasted like sugar.

Joe had been raised in a motorcycle gang in Oregon. He was first laid at age twelve, by Martha, his half brother's common-law wife. She was four feet eleven inches with kinky blond hair and facial tattoos. One night she just crawled inside Joe's sleeping bag and started sucking his dick. Once he was hard, she hoisted up her denim miniskirt, straddled him, and rode up and down on him so vigorously he was sure she was going to break his dick off. When Joe tried to kiss her, she slapped him so hard his lip bled. He was so afraid of her he couldn't come. But she did, making a horrible sound like a wounded moose. A few minutes later, as she was crawling out of Joe's sleeping bag, his half brother came over. He made a clucking sound in his throat and then laughed. Joe thought maybe his half brother would kill him. But he didn't.

The next day Martha fell off the back of Joe's half brother's bike and rolled under a truck on the highway.

"You killed her," Joe's half brother accused that night.

How Joe had killed her, he wasn't sure. And it was never mentioned again.

When Joe was sixteen, there was a massive raid of the motorcycle gang, and most of its members were indicted on murder and narcotics charges. Joe fled. He started hitchhiking east and got off in Chicago. Some guys jumped him and stole his shoes. One of them put his dick in Joe's mouth and came on his face. Joe went to a Salvation Army and slept there one night.

He ended up in a detox and was ultimately given a job as a janitor there. One night, he got picked up by a tiny stripper at a bar that some of the detox workers frequented. She wasn't stripping there, just getting drunk. She didn't even talk to Joe before putting her hand on his crotch. She took him home and told him to shut up and turn over, and she rammed stuff up his ass. First a finger. Then a hair brush handle. Then she ripped the arm off a smiling plastic doll and rammed it up his ass. Joe didn't protest. He watched her jerk off. She didn't put anything up her own ass.

Her name was Jolene.

He saw her a few times a week for several months. Then she was murdered. The cops never figured out who did it or why. She was found stabbed in the bathtub in her apartment.

Now Joe hadn't had sex in two years. Every time he fucked someone, they died.

The day after the mop incident, Joe found Susan in his broom closet again. She was completely naked but didn't have anything inserted inside herself.

"What are you doing?" Joe asked.

"Nothing," Susan said.

She stood up and turned her back to him. She was so skinny her shoulder blades poked out like razors, but she had a nice shape, hips rounding out slightly from a miniscule waist.

She bent forward and smashed her cheek against the Band-Aid–colored wall. She had extremely long straight black pubic hairs that parted to reveal the pinkness between them. She turned her head and looked at Joe with hot coal eyes. Joe didn't move. He didn't even put his hand to his dick that was so hard and distended it hurt.

"That's a really bad idea," Joe said to her after eternal seconds.

"Yeah yeah yeah," Susan said and then arched her back and wiggled her hips slightly.

"Do you need a place to live?" he asked.

Susan straightened up and turned around and her face turned little girl.

"Yeah."

"Okay. You can live with me," Joe said.

* * *

An hour later, Susan had packed up her plastic bag of belongings: two pairs of panties, a black T-shirt, and a bra.

The moment they set foot inside Joe's small two-room apartment, Susan lay down on the floor and fell asleep. After sitting there watching her sleep for a few hours, Joe gently scooped her up and put her on his twin bed. An hour later she woke up and went back to the floor. She was still asleep in the morning when the phone rang and one of the counselors from the rehab called to tell Joe he'd lost his job. Consorting with the patients was strictly against the rules. But Joe didn't care. He had Susan in his apartment.

When Susan woke up she was horny. She didn't even brush

her teeth or take a piss, she sat up on the floor and reached for Joe, who was sitting in the only chair he owned, a plastic armchair the color of avocados. She put her hand on his crotch and Joe made a face.

"What, baby?" Susan said.

"Don't do that."

"What's the matter?"

"I don't wanna."

"Yes you do," Susan purred, feeling the big lump in his pants.

"No," Joe said.

Susan peeled off her shirt. She had an orange bra on.

"I got this in France at Tati," she said, running her hands over the bra. "Tati is this amazing cheapo store they got over there. Kind of like our Kmart or something, only the underwear is nice cotton. You can't find nice cotton underwear at Kmart," she said, defiantly, as if expecting Joe to contradict her.

"I realize that," Joe said, even though he didn't. "Why were you in France?"

"Come *on*," the girl said, taking off the bra and teasing her dark brown nipples so they stood up like angry blueberries.

But Joe wouldn't do anything.

Over the next few weeks, Susan tried a lot of things. She got outfits. First just run-of-the-mill things like vicious red teddies and garters and stockings and fuck-me pumps. She would dance in front of Joe in his tiny apartment and Joe would watch but he wouldn't touch. She got a nurse's outfit. It was starchy and hard when she rubbed up against Joe's skin while he tried to sleep. It gave him a hard-on but he still wouldn't fuck her. He didn't want Susan to die. He thought maybe even telling her about it, about the curse of the women he fucked, could kill her.

Then Susan got the clown outfit. It was the stupidest, craziest thing any girl had ever done to or for him. The tenderness of that stupid crazy gesture almost melted his resolve. But not quite.

Not even when he came home from work one day—he'd gotten hired on as a housekeeping aide at the seedy Heart of

Chicago Motor Court not too far away—and found Susan in bed with another girl, a chubby Spanish girl with a lascivious red mouth, and the two of them relentlessly ate each other and inserted fingers and vibrators into each other. Joe just made eggs. He and his hard-on.

And then Susan started shooting dope again.

Pretty soon she had gone through all Joe's money buying dope. She would shoot up all over her body and Joe would just watch. He locked her in the bathroom one day to try and make her kick her habit but she just jumped out the third-story window.

A few days after jumping out of Joe's bathroom window, Susan resurfaced.

She was at least ten pounds thinner and her eyes were huge and full of pain.

"I'm sorry, baby," she said when Joe opened the door and let her in, and he folded her into his arms and felt her bones poking into him.

"It's all okay," he reassured her, but after a minute she grew fidgety and then Joe went and sold his stereo to get her some dope.

In a week, Susan had pawned everything Joe had, which wasn't much. When his apartment was completely barren, Susan left. The next morning, Joe woke up with the headache.

After the surgery, as he lay in his hospital bed reflecting on what life would be like now that he'd had the grapefruit taken out of his head, Joe glanced at a newspaper and saw that the singer Carnie Wilson was having her stomach taken out and having a new one put in. This one would be the size of a peanut.

Carnie Wilson was quoted saying: "I am so obese I could die."

Maybe the grapefruit from Joe's head could try shoving itself inside the peanut in Carnie's stomach. Thinking about it gave Joe the first hard-on he'd had since Susan had left.

When Joe got out of the hospital he didn't want to go home. Home would remind him of Susan and of the grapefruit. He wandered the streets for nearly twenty-four hours straight and then, completely exhausted, he went home. There was an eviction notice taped to his door. He would have to find a job soon.

Two days later, when Joe was walking and wandering as he'd taken to doing, he bumped into a woman on Wilson Avenue whose hands were smeared with tattoos of the motorcycle gang who'd raised him. She was stocky with brassy blond hair. She had on a Black Sabbath concert T-shirt with the sleeves cut off. Her arms had loose meat hanging off them. She noticed Joe staring at her tattoos and she started talking to him.

"I ain't running with them anymore, though," she said after Joe asked her about the motorcycle gang's Chicago offshoot. "I got a good job. I'm a lifeguard. Lotta old people come in there and dog paddle and I sit there. They let me smoke too. No one says shit. Sometimes my husband comes in and we sit there and get fucked up and the old people don't care," she said.

"I'll hook you up if you want," she told Joe after a while.

"What's that?"

"They need a weekend lifeguard. I'll hook you up."

"I can't really swim."

"I'll teach you," she said.

* * *

A week later, the woman, whose name was Denise, let Joe pass the lifeguard test and then hired him as part-time lifeguard. Five days a week, Joe sat in his room watching the little black and white TV he'd found in a Dumpster on Astor Street. On weekends he was a lifeguard.

Denise started hitting on Joe. One Saturday, when he came in for his shift and went into the tiny office where he was to sit for the next nine hours watching old people dog paddle, he found Denise sitting there, smoking a Kool. She was wearing cut-off shorts and a tank top. She had enormous breasts. They seemed to have a life of their own. He reflected that if Denise were to travel, a separate passport would have to be issued for her tits.

"You wanna come over tonight? Stewie's out of town," Denise said to Joe, taking a languorous pull on her Kool.

"Oh," he said, frightened.

"Oh? I make you an offer and 'Oh' is all you got for me?"

"I can't."

"You can't what, boy?" Denise hissed through her very small teeth.

Joe thought about how her teeth were so tiny and her tits so huge. Her maker had clearly been having a bad day when her number had come up.

To quell any more nastiness, Joe agreed to come by her place that night.

When he got there, she was wearing nothing but skimpy mesh underpants that rode up her strange flat ass. When Joe didn't instantly grab her and throw her down and fuck her, she flew into a rage. She looked horrible when she was angry.

Finally, as she was calling him a cocksucking pussy, Joe reached down inside the panties and put his finger inside her. She shut right up. He pushed her down to the floor. He moved the crotch of the panties aside and stuck his dick in her. She said: "Baby, baby, baby" and her hips wiggled and her eyes rolled back in her head. The moment Joe came, he pulled out of her, hoisted his pants back up, and left. He figured her death was imminent. He didn't want to see it.

The next day Joe didn't show up at the swimming pool. He didn't want to be hearing about Denise's death. He stayed in for a week straight.

He pulled the phone out of the wall. He cooked up a big batch of rice, the only thing in his cupboard, and subsisted on that.

On the eighth day, he went by the detox where he had once worked. The detox people agreed to hire him back. Patients came and went and sometimes Joe wondered if Susan would appear again.

One day, Joe was walking home from the detox when he saw Denise coming down the street. She was with another older woman. A short woman.

"Joe, babe, what's up?" Denise said.

"Hi," Joe said, and his heart stammered.

"You look pale, what's wrong?" Denise asked.

"Joe?" the other woman said, scrutinizing Joe.

Joe looked nervously from Denise to the other woman.

"Joe, did you used to live in Oregon?" the woman demanded.

"Yes," Joe said tightly. The woman was Martha, his half brother's common-law wife, the first woman whose death was on his head.

"I thought so. How you doin' kid?" Martha said, and she pressed her short squat body up to his.

Joe stood frozen.

He didn't understand.

Just a day later, watching a movie on TV, he saw the stripper, the ex-girlfriend who'd turned up murdered. She was playing a nurse on a TV movie that had been filmed just a few months earlier.

Joe consulted with one of the counselors at the detox, who then hooked him up with a shrink.

"I thought I killed everyone I slept with," Joe told the shrink, a small man with close-cropped dark hair and an extraordinarily long nose.

The shrink was fascinated and told Joe he ought to come in three times a week. He then had many colleagues talk to Joe and take pictures of his brain. They concluded that the grapefruit's position inside Joe's brain had triggered an extreme sexual guilt complex. Now that it was gone, so was the complex. Joe needn't think he killed everyone he fucked anymore.

The detox hired Joe back. Eventually, Susan did come back through. At first he didn't recognize her. Her hair was shorn short and she was dressed in vivid colors. But she still wore the cheap jewelry that turned her skin green.

She pretended not to recognize Joe. He cornered her in the hall when she was heading to the bathroom.

"Come live with me. It'll be different this time, I promise you that."

Susan just laughed at him, a hollow lifeless laugh. She wordlessly walked ahead into the bathroom. Joe left her alone for the rest of the day. He tried again the following day.

She just laughed again though. She wouldn't speak.

One night, when all the other patients were in the TV room, catatonically staring at the big screen TV, Joe ran into Susan in the hallway. She was sadly shuffling down the hall. She was wearing a limp blue bathrobe.

"Susan," Joe said, planting himself in front of her.

"You sent me off the deep end, Joe," she said, looking up at him with her lifeless eyes.

"It's all a terrible mistake. I had a grapefruit in my head. I loved you. I didn't want to kill you."

"You're insane."

"No. It was the grapefruit."

"Joe, you need help."

"Let me show you," he said and he forcefully took hold of Susan's bony arm and led her toward the broom closet.

"You have to leave me alone," Susan protested when he'd gotten her in there.

"Look," Joe said, putting his hands to his head and parting the hair there to show her the scar. "There was a thing in my head. A tumor. I can explain everything."

She just looked at him with those hollow eyes. He put his hands on her shoulders and forcibly flipped her around. He leaned her forward so that her cheek pressed against the Band-Aid–colored wall and her ass arched out. He bunched her limp blue robe up over her hips. He parted the incredibly long straight black pubic hairs and kissed her and licked her. He put his fingers inside her. He rubbed his painfully distended dick against her ass. She finally turned her head and looked at him and a fragment of life had come back into her eyes.

Simon Sheppard
In Deep

Utila's just a flyspeck on the map of the world. It lies right off the Honduran coast, one of the Bay Islands, a place settled by pirates who braved the seas for gold.

These days, the island's wealth arrives with young divers who come to explore the coral reef. These days, visitors don't arrive by frigate; they fly in from La Ceiba on small planes, planes with warning signs written in Russian, decommissioned junkers from Aeroflot or someplace. Every time the plane dips its wings toward the Caribbean's blue, the passengers hold their breaths and pray. I know I did. Except for the praying part.

I'd been to Guatemala already, spent a full-moon night amongst the pyramids of Tikal, communing with ghosts, getting over a love affair I never should have allowed to drag me down. I'd submerged myself in Kate, her desires and her life and most of all her needs. And after two years of misery, I'd discovered it was a mistake. She was a mistake, my job was a mistake, my life was going nowhere. I decided to skip the worst of a Philadelphia winter and head to Central America to lick my wounds.

The flimsy little plane managed to touch down on Utila's grassy airstrip, just beside a crystal-blue harbor. It was only a short walk to the main street. Quaint as hell, wooden buildings, tropical paradise. Dive shops. Restaurants. Lots of small hotels. Hotels without a single room for rent.

Semi-exhausted from dragging my backpack up and down the street in a fruitless search for a place to stay, I collapsed into a tattered wicker chair in the lobby of Lucie's Hotel.

"Hey. You look exhausted."

I looked up. He was dark and slightly stocky, Greek background maybe, wearing shorts, flip-flops, and a raggedy T-shirt.

"I am. You know of anyplace to stay? I'll be damned if I can find a vacant room."

"You should have caught the earlier flight over."

"Now you tell me." I grimaced.

"Listen. There's a second bed in my room, if you don't snore. You'd be welcome to spend the night. I'll just have to check it out with the management."

"Lucie?" I asked.

"There is no Lucie. Never has been, I hear." He extended his hand. "My name's Aaron."

"Thom," I said. "Pleased to meet you. How long you been here?"

"A while. Great place to dive."

"So I hear."

"Water's so clear you can always see the bottom. All the way down."

* * *

I spent the afternoon settling in, exploring the little town. Half the families in town had the same surname, Harrison. And half the businesses were dive shops.

It was a great place for scuba, all right. Or at least a bargain; prepurchasing ten boat dives brought the price down to a third of what it would have cost Stateside. I found a likely looking dive shop, the Neptune, checked it out, and paid for ten dives, enough to keep me busy during my planned week on the island.

I was at the far end of the main street when the sky began dumping rain. Everything was getting that wet-tropics smell as I jogged back toward the hotel.

I made it back, soaked to the skin, and went to my new room

and changed. I was sitting on the porch overlooking the harbor, listening to the rain hammering on the corrugated metal roof, when a blond woman came up the stairs. She wasn't bad look-ing—a little plump, maybe, but she had nice breasts, and her nipples showed through her rain-damp T-shirt.

"Hello," she said, her accent Scandinavian. "You just arrived?"

"Yeah, this morning." I was thinking about how one of those nipples would feel in my mouth. I hadn't had a woman since Kate had left me.

"You stay at this hotel?"

"Yes," I said, "I'm doubling up with a man named Aaron."

She made a strange face.

"Anything wrong?"

"No, it's just that I've heard . . ." Another mysterious look. "Never mind."

We chatted for a while about approximately nothing, the way that strangers on the road do. I kept glancing at her tits, I guess.

I finally decided to pop the question. "Are you doing anything tonight? Want to go for a drink?"

"I should tell you," she said, "that I am a lesbian."

And that was that.

* * *

That night I went for dinner at a restaurant down the road, the food tasty but served at a snail's pace. It was Saturday, so the town's two discos were cranking up their sound systems, blatting bad music into the balmy tropical night. I popped into one, and by the time I'd finished my first rum and Coke, had decided it really wasn't my scene.

I headed back to the hotel and curled up in bed. I'd had to get up early to make the trip from the mainland of Honduras, so I drifted off quick.

Something woke me up.

I looked around. In the dim blue moonlight, I could see that my roommate Aaron had returned. He was sprawled on his back in the other bed, a few feet away in the small room. The sheets were tangled around his feet. His hairy body was naked, and he was jerking off.

I hadn't watched guys jack off since Boy Scouts, and I was kind of curious. Careful not to draw his attention, I watched Aaron as he stroked and squeezed his dick. His technique, I noticed, was very different from mine; I tend to really pound away. He was more poetic, slow, like it was happening underwater.

I felt, to my surprise, my own cock getting hard. Not embarrassment, not shame, just surprise. I would have reached down to my crotch, but I was afraid he'd see me. So I lay there scarcely breathing for three, four, five minutes as he played with himself. Every once in a while he'd take his hand away to get more spit, and I could see his cock was very hard, not very big, and gleaming wet.

Eventually he started writhing and arching his back, moaning loudly enough to wake me up, if I'd been asleep. With a muffled groan, he oozed a big load of cum on his belly, then wiped it up with his hand and licked it off his palm. He pulled the covers up, rolled over with his back toward me, and seemed to go to sleep.

* * *

The next morning I woke up in a sticky little puddle. I never had jacked off the night before, but my cum had made an escape anyway.

Aaron was already gone. I was up early enough to go on a morning boat dive. I grabbed a cup of coffee and a slice of coconut bread at a nearby bakery. I thought about the night before, then tried not to. I figured it wouldn't happen again. I slurped down the last of the coffee and headed for the Neptune Diver Shop.

Even without reservations, I had no trouble getting a place on the morning boat. I pulled on the rented dive gear, the wetsuit tightly hugging my body, grabbed my two full tanks, and headed for the dock. There were four other customers on the boat: a Canadian married couple, and a dreadlocked blond surfer from Southern California with his purple-haired girlfriend. The divemaster, Berndt, briefed us as we headed southwest of the island to Stingray Point.

The Canadians had just been PADI certified, so we took it fairly easy on the first dive, only heading down to thirty feet or so. The water was glorious, the coral beautiful, the reef fish streaking colorfully around our group.

It had been months since I'd last been diving, and now I remembered why I loved it so: the astonishing peace of the liquid world, the feeling of being where people weren't meant to go, the cold isolation of breathing the air of life through a mouthpiece gripped between my teeth. The beauty of the reef system, which in Honduras is pretty damn overwhelming. Lettuce coral, brain coral, pillar coral, elkhorn, and star. And the schools of angelfish, parrot fish, chromis. The second dive, at Jack Neil Point, was just as nice, even nicer as big sea turtles swam amongst our little group. When Berndt led us back to the boat, I was sorry to leave the water. I was sorry to get back to life.

But it was time to head back to shore.

Two dives a day are usually plenty for me. I had a lunch of fried fish at a little place run by two sisters, then went back to sit on the hotel porch and read and catch up on writing postcards. People came and went, sometimes making small talk. I wondered where the Scandinavian lesbian was; I would have liked to ask her more about my roommate, but she never appeared.

It was late afternoon before I saw Aaron. He headed up the stairs and climbed into the hammock suspended from the porch.

"Having fun?" he asked.

"Yeah, went on a couple of dives this morning."

"Explored the island yet? Out by Pumpkin Hill?"

"Nah," I said. "I figure there'll be plenty of time for that. I'm feeling really lazy today."

"We should go out there sometime," Aaron said, "you and I."

"Uh, okay," I agreed.

"Thought about dinner yet?"

"It's early."

"Yeah, but the service is so slow. And sometimes if you don't get to a place early, they run out of whatever you want."

I looked out at the Caribbean, ripples glistening in sunlight. "That's the thing about coming to a place like this. You gotta remain flexible. How long you been here?"

"I'm going to go lie down in the room. Come get me when you're starting to get hungry. After dinner we can go get drunk at the Bucket of Blood."

* * *

Dinner was good, the conch soup excellent—though, as Aaron had warned me, the service was glacially slow, even worse than the night before. By the time we'd paid the check, it was well into the night. Over at the Bucket of Blood, we drank rum and Cokes till I had trouble seeing straight. The dreadlocked surfboy was there, looking glum. I wondered where his purple-haired girl-friend had gotten to. For someone who'd been on the island a while, Aaron didn't seem to know anyone there. Which was okay; he was friendly enough, friendlier as the night wore on and we grew drunker. I kind of liked him.

When I'd had enough of cheap rum, strangers, and endless replays of *Bob Marley's Greatest Hits,* I suggested we turn in.

We staggered down the street, along with a lot of other soused tourists and a few semi-sober locals, and stumbled up the stairs to our room. Aaron threw himself onto his bed.

"Oh man," he said. He pulled his T-shirt over his head. "I'm ready to pass out," he said. His torso was fleshy, generously covered with dark hair. He began to unzip his khaki shorts.

"Want me to turn out the light?" I asked. "So you can get some sleep?"

"No, leave it on." He was down to his briefs now. He began rubbing his crotch through the white cotton. I just lay there watching him as he peeled off his underwear and started stroking his cock. He'd thrown his near leg over the edge of the bed so I had a view of his balls and the hair between his legs.

"Oh man," he repeated. His dick was hard.

And so was mine.

I looked him in the face. He looked back with deep, dark eyes and nodded.

I reached down and unzipped my shorts. I wasn't wearing underwear; the flesh of my swelling cock was hot to the touch. I pulled my shorts down and my shirt up, grabbed my dick, and started playing with the foreskin.

We lay there side-by-side, a couple of feet apart, two almost-strangers, masturbating.

I kept glancing from his eyes to his cock, then back to his face again. As interesting as it was to see him jacking his dick, it was more intense to watch his face. I'd seen women get off, of course, but I'd never watched another man while he had sex. I submerged myself in his eyes as he slowly brought himself close to orgasm.

I wanted to touch him, to feel what another man's cock was like, but I couldn't bring myself to do it. And I was half-afraid and half-hoping he'd get up, come over to me, touch me. But he didn't. So we just lay there, hands working our own hard-ons, until he nodded and said, "Now?"

"Now," I said.

He looked so beautiful when he came. I wondered if I looked that way, too. I glanced down; the hair on his belly was strewn with ropes of cum.

"Goodnight," he said.

"I've . . . I'm . . . gonna go clean up, take a shower."

"Don't move," he said. He swiveled himself out of bed, knelt on the floor beside me. He leaned over my torso and gently lapped up my cum, his tongue moving over my belly and chest. I wanted to grab his head, part of me did, and guide him down to my dick. But I didn't.

When he was done, he wordlessly got into bed and curled up under the thin bedcover, his back toward me.

After a while he spoke. "You can turn out the light now," he said.

* * *

The first thing Aaron said to me when I woke up was, "Fuck the boat dives. Let's go snorkeling out by the airport."

"Sure," I heard myself saying. We slipped into Speedos and T-shirts and, grabbing our fins and masks, headed out.

It was a shortish way down the street to the landing field. As Aaron and I wordlessly walked side by side in the morning sun, I kept thinking back to the night before, the sight of his cock, the feeling of his mouth on my flesh. I looked over at his face, then down to his hairy legs. Despite myself, I felt myself getting hard. I shifted the fins to in front of my crotch, but Aaron caught on and chuckled.

"Don't worry about it," he said. "Happens to the best of us."

Beyond the rocky shoreline, the warm Caribbean stretched forever. Nobody else was around. We adjusted our masks and snorkels, pulled on our fins, and walked backward into the gently lapping waves.

Even in the shallows, the waters were alive with riotously colored fish. Careful not to cut ourselves on coral, we swam a little ways out, breathing through our little plastic tubes. The ocean bottom receded with every stroke. Sea anemones wavered in the currents, feeding on things too tiny to see.

I felt Aaron's hand stroking my side. For a second, I wanted to push it away. Instead I hung there, floating on the surface of another world, while his touch explored my flesh. His fingers moved down to the waistband of my Speedos, then over my ass. Kate had never touched me that way, no woman had. He slipped his fingers beneath the thin fabric, touched the flesh of my butt. His fingertips moved toward my ass crack. With a kick of my fins, I jetted myself away from him.

I wanted not to be feeling those things, I wanted my cock not to be throbbing in my bathing suit. I wanted to look at the pretty coral and the pretty fish and forget that I'd ever known Aaron. Instead, I floated in the crystal-clear embrace of the water until he caught up with me. I let him touch me again, touch my chest, my belly, run his hand across my crotch, my hard cock, peel down the front of my suit, grab me, my flesh, my dick. He tugged my suit down to around my thighs and dove down beneath me. He pulled at my feet till I was vertical in the water, then surfaced for a breath and dove down again. Looking down, I saw him spit out the mouthpiece of his snorkel. Exhaling a trail of bubbles, he wrapped his mouth around my dick, his tongue even wetter than the water. The vagaries of buoyancy dragged us upward till I was on my back, Aaron floating between my thighs, his face now above waterline, breathing through his nose, his mouth still in possession of my cock.

"Jesus, Aaron, somebody might see us," I said, and as if on cue, the drone of the morning plane came over the horizon.

He took his mouth from my hard-on, which flopped onto my belly, little waves lapping at my dickflesh.

"Let's go back to the hotel room, then. Unless you're afraid."

"Let's just go back. Go back and do nothing," I said. "Give me time. I've gotta think."

* * *

The walk back was awkward. When we got to the hotel, Aaron kept on walking down the street. I went up to our room, took a cold shower, then went out to stare at the sea.

As I sat on the porch, the Scandinavian girl came up to me.

"You've been spending time with him?"

"Aaron?" I asked.

"*Ja,*" she said.

"Just what do you have against him, anyway?" I was sure she could see into me, my dirty secret. I was sure she *knew*.

"He's no good. Dangerous."

"How the hell would you know?"

"He used to be my boyfriend." Her voice was tired, resigned.

"But you're a *lesbian*!"

"Yes, mostly, but Aaron and I lived together in Chicago. We came here to Central America together, last month. He used to be my boyfriend."

"Until?" I asked.

"You'll see," she said.

* * *

I was lying on my bed, beneath an open window. There must have been a power failure. The electricity didn't work. The fan didn't move. Even with the window open, it was hot and stifling. I didn't care. I lay there, thinking about the shipwreck of my life.

Aaron still hadn't returned when the wind picked up, blowing dark clouds over the island. And then, with that suddenness of tropical rainstorms, it was pouring, coming down in sheets. I could have reached up and shut the window. I didn't.

The rain blew in, soaking me, my clothes, the bed. I didn't care, I didn't give a fuck about anything. I didn't have Kate, I hated my job, I hated my life. I was forced to admit it: the only thing that had given me real pleasure for a long while—well maybe not pleasure, but was interesting at least—was Aaron, being with Aaron.

"Enough time?"

Aaron was standing in the open doorway, sopping wet.

"Huh?" I said.

"You had enough time to think about things, to *decide*?" There was the slightest trace of a sneer.

I nodded. He walked over to my bed, stood in front of me, and pulled down his wet Speedos. His dick wasn't hard, not yet, and somehow that made it all the nicer. I could understand now how a woman could see a threat in a hard-on. I could understand how nothing matters, really. I reached for him.

Our wet bodies slid over each other. His dick was hard now, and mine was, too, and we kissed, the first time I'd ever kissed a man, our tongues like dolphins or something, our breaths intertwined. When our faces parted, I asked a question. "Now what?"

Aaron slid down, over the rainsoaked sheets, as thunder drummed outside. I expected him to suck my cock. But he pushed my legs up and slid his face down to my ass. His tongue dove inside me. I was ashamed. But my penis was stiff.

Am I a faggot now? I wondered, as he licked my ass, kissing, tonguing, like some strange fish swimming where it didn't belong. I heard a moan, my own, above the thunder. And then lightning. And his mouth moved to my balls, licking, sucking till I began to ache.

"My cock, please. My cock," I begged him.

"Suck me," Aaron said.

"Me suck you?"

"Who else?"

"Yes," I said. "I will," I said, then was sorry I'd spoken. But he was already moving over me, twisting his body so his crotch was against my face. The head of his cock, a deep, angry pink, darker than mine, was inches from my mouth. What the hell. I opened wide.

It wasn't bad, sucking cock. A little strange, maybe, but then it got good. I was hungry for Aaron, for his small, hard cock jutting from a bush of curly black hair. I was hungry for him and I gulped him down, as far down my throat as I could without gagging. He pumped into me, rocking back and forth the smallest bit, never leaving the back of my mouth. Rain was hitting my face. I grabbed his ass, held on tight. Rain was hitting my face.

I couldn't breathe. I tried to, through my nose, but it wasn't enough. I wondered if anybody had ever choked to death sucking cock.

"Let me loose, Thom. Back off, you fuck," Aaron said.

And he pulled his dick out of my mouth and slid down till he was lying on top of me, two men's bodies, wet, face-to-face, dick to dick. He kissed me. Harder, longer than before. I felt his hands go around my neck. If lightning had crashed just then, it would have been too melodramatic. Lightning crashed.

His lips were still on mine as he squeezed down, gently on my windpipe, harder on the arteries on the sides of my neck. I should have been scared. He squeezed harder. I was all of twenty-eight years old, maybe about to die, and I didn't mind. I wanted him to keep squeezing. Harder. Harder. He did.

I was straining to breathe. Trapped blood was throbbing in my brain. I was still aware enough to feel our two hard cocks rubbing together, wet. I wanted him to fuck me. He wasn't going to; he was going to choke me. Things looked darkish red, little spots dancing before my eyes. I was out of air. I reached for his wrists, intending to pull his hands away. I grabbed them, all right, but I drew them inward instead. The thunder was close now, rattling everything. I was making little mewling noises, hoarse, tiny gasps. My mouth opened wide for his tongue. I wanted to unhinge my jaw for him, a boa constrictor swallowing poisoned prey.

Things became even darker, dark as night. It was nice. I could feel my eyes bulging out of my skull. I threw my head back, gave my throat to him.

"Oh, yeah," he said. "Oh *man!*"

I thought of the blond dyke with the big tits. I had been warned.

Everything went black.

* * *

When I came to, struggling to the surface of consciousness, Aaron was lying beside me on the wet bed. My belly was spattered with ropes of cum.

"I been unconscious for long?" I asked.

"No, not long."

"And whose cum is this? Yours? Mine?"

"Does it matter?" Aaron asked.

"To me it does, yeah." Though I'm not sure I could have put into words just why it was important.

"Both of ours," said Aaron. "You came while I was strangling you."

"Really?"

"Yeah, and so did I." He didn't quite smile.

I wish he'd have fucked me, I was thinking. *At least then I'd know for sure what it feels like.*

"I guess we should close that window now, let the room dry off," I said.

But my bed was still damp when nighttime came around. When it came time to go to sleep, I crawled into Aaron's bed and lay there shivering beside him. He didn't say a word, just wrapped his arm around my neck and gave it a squeeze. My cock got hard.

It was still hard when I woke up.

* * *

The previous winter, Kate and I had gone cross-country skiing out West. I'd gotten hold of some cocaine, and we decided it would be fun to ski while we were buzzed. We skied five or six miles to the rim of a valley; the last few hundred yards to the overlook was an icy mess. On the way back, the coke started wearing off. We were in the middle of nowhere when a snow-storm hit. One of my gloves had started coming apart; the snow made its way through the unraveled fingertip, bringing a cold that led to numbness. The storm rose to near white-out conditions. I was exhausted and lost and all I wanted to do was give up. I started to whimper. I told Kate that all I wanted, all I could do was to sit down in the snowy field and wait to die, to freeze, to melt in the next spring's thaw. But she, unsympathetic, had skied on ahead and I had no choice but to follow. Somehow we made it back to the lodge.

I thought about that ski trip on the boat the next morning. Aaron had decided to come along and dive, and as I looked at him I remembered that snowy, helpless feeling.

The boat was heading to the north side of Utila, to the dive site near Blackish Point. The seas were a little rough, so to take my mind off the sway of the boat, I decided it was time to ask.

"I was talking to this blond girl, says she's your girlfriend. Is she?"

Aaron's handsome face battened down. "She's a bitch. A crazy cunt."

I kept quiet after that.

We reached the Point and the boat dropped anchor. The other divers on the boat weren't very experienced, so Aaron and I had talked the divemaster into letting us go off on our own. We double-checked each other's equipment, let some air into our BCD vests, held our hands over our masks, and launched ourselves backward over the side of the boat.

There's something about the shock of first hitting the water that never becomes routine. It's the feeling that your equipment, so heavy on land, has become effortlessly light. The sudden submersion, the bubbles rising from the regulator, the commitment to enter a whole other world for a while.

We made the "OK" sign to one another and let the air out of our vests, sinking down into blue space. Everything was beautiful down below. The choppiness of the surface subsided into a deep, wet calm. We swam side by side, Aaron and I. Schools of fish swam this way and that, reversing direction en masse. The reef was alive, all around us. There was nothing to break the silence but the bubbling sound of my own breath. Everything was beautiful. Everything.

I looked over at Aaron, made the "OK" sign again and got one in return. He gestured to go deeper down. With every exhalation I sank a little further, till we hovered over a patch of sandy bottom. The usual feelings of diving—being far beneath normal existence, somehow free of gravity, totally in my body yet really nowhere at all. I looked at my depth gauge: ninety feet.

He gestured me to sit on the bottom. I couldn't see a reason not to, so I knelt on the sea floor, stirring up a little sandstorm. He came over and knelt in front of me, so close that our knees were touching. He laid a hand on my shoulder and we stared at one another through our masks. I could feel my dick getting hard inside my wetsuit.

Then Aaron grabbed my air hose. I took a big gulp of air. He tugged at the mouthpiece. I let him. I let him pull it out of my mouth. I held my breath.

I could die right now, I thought. *It would take so little. Just allowing my mouth to open, letting the ocean rush in.*

Why was I doing this, trusting him, letting myself believe he'd give the regulator back to me and let me suck in life again?

Letting go. Right here, right now, my last moment. The end.

My lungs began to ache for air.

Relief. The salty water, salty as my blood, bringing an end, a darkness, maybe peace.

I thought of the moment when he'd put his hands around my neck and squeezed. The girl with the big tits was right. Aaron was bad news.

His face would be the last thing I'd see. He would watch me shoot upward into blue shafts of sunlight, only to thrash, relax, and come to floating rest.

I looked upward. The surface was so far above. It might as well have been as far as the stars.

I should do it, I thought. *It would be so easy.*

My body was rebelling. I needed air. Fuck this shit, fuck Aaron and the places he took me and my hard dick and Kate and my life. Fuck it all. I needed air.

I could die right now.

I grabbed for his hand. He let go of the regulator, which floated upward, out of reach. Through the glass of our faceplates, our eyes conveyed some primal, elemental message. Older than civilization: animal trust and betrayal. I made the "Out of Air" sign, fingers slashing across my windpipe. I was going to die. He would never let me breathe.

It would be so easy.

He blinked once and reached down for his spare mouthpiece, the "octopus." Gently, he held the back of my head with one hand and guided the octopus toward my mouth with the other. I opened my lips, he placed it between my teeth, I clamped down, greedy, breathing again.

He gestured to rise. I could have grabbed at my regulator hose, replaced my own mouthpiece. Instead, I remained breathing through his spare, the two of us sharing the same air as he put his arm around me and, locked in a wet embrace, we rose slowly toward the surface. When it came time for our decompression stop, he put both arms around me and hugged. Then he reached for his mouthpiece and his octopus, gently pulled the regulators from both our mouths, and kissed me, parting my lips with his tongue just enough for a trickle of salt water to rush in.

The he replaced his mouthpiece, I got my own regulator into my mouth, and we rose toward the surface, toward life.

* * *

I needed to go for a walk. I'd come to Utila to escape. To escape my life, but my life had followed me, hitched a ride with me on that Russian plane. If I'd come to Utila to simplify my existence, I'd come to the wrong place. Somewhere out in the middle of the sea, I was walking down the same small street again and again, wanting there to be somewhere to get lost.

I figured I'd finally hike out to Pumpkin Hill. I never got there. The Scandinavian girl was coming up the street, a bag of groceries in one hand. She placed herself in my path.

"The supply boat has come in, and the grocery store has now more food again. Look." She held the grocery bag toward me.

Jesus, I thought, *is this woman everywhere?* And then I realized it wasn't just her; since I got to Utila, I'd been seeing the same faces again and again. Only Aaron was hard to find, always disappearing.

"So what," the girl asked, "have you learned?"

What a fucking weird question. Or maybe she'd been reading my mind.

"Huh?" I asked.

"About Aaron. Have you found out?"

"Found out what?" I didn't want to talk about it. I didn't want to think about it, about Aaron, about me. I wanted to relax, let the currents carry me, watch my thoughts swim off like a school of bright, mindless fish.

"How do you think someone gets that way?" she asked, an odd look in her very blue eyes.

Fuck you, I wanted to say.

Instead I said, "Excuse me. I've got to go." And I turned around and headed back to the hotel, before she could catch up. Maybe Aaron would be there.

* * *

When he fucked me that afternoon, he didn't use a condom.

"I'm okay," he said.

"Trust me," he said.

I did.

It didn't feel quite like I expected. A little pain at first, which was to be expected, and then just a funny, full feeling. Once he got going, though, once I relaxed, once he was all the way in, it all changed to pleasure. Sweat was glistening on his chest, dripping off the hairs of his belly.

I wanted him to choke me again, but I didn't dare ask him. I lost my hard-on, from all the new sensations, but that didn't matter much. His pleasure was all that counted. I wanted to be nothing. When he shot off inside me, I hoped I could have been anyone. Even the girl from Scandinavia.

"Stay inside me," I gasped. "Please stay inside me." And I jacked off, getting hard fast, feeling an intense longing, a need to spew salty cum everywhere. It didn't take long for me to shoot. Jism arced all the way up to my face.

We showered. There wasn't much to say. I went off to find us a snack. In the heat of the late afternoon. Utila's main street was nearly empty. Walking felt strange; I could still feel him in my ass. It was as if my body was carrying some barely concealed secret, something about being looser, more open. I was glad there were so few people out; discovery would be less likely.

When I returned to the room, every trace of Aaron was gone. No note, nothing. I felt resigned, then curious. I ran from the hotel, heading for the airstrip. As I got there, the last plane of the day was warming up on the runway, pointed toward the mainland. As it taxied down the field, I thought I saw Aaron's face at a window, looking toward me, but I couldn't be sure. I stood there, stupidly, until the sputtering roar of the plane faded away over the deep blue sea.

* * *

When I got back to the hotel, there was a boy with a backpack at the front desk, kind of scrawny, but cute. His neck was thin.

"You look exhausted," I said to him.

"Know of anyplace to stay?" he asked. "Every hotel seems to be full up."

"There's a second bed in my room," I told him. "You'd be welcome to spend the night."

I looked down at his legs, fuzzy with brown hair, then back up at his face. It would be so easy. "You'd be welcome to spend the night," I repeated.

I caught a trace of motion from the corner of my eye; the Scandinavian girl with big tits was standing there, staring straight at me.

"Hey," the boy said, "that'd be great." So easy.

"This way," I said, and we headed up the stairs.

Debra Boxer
The Lesson

Everything is fine until the oysters come. The waitress sets the silver pail in the middle of the table and leaves us alone.

I look at you and squint slightly.

You laugh back at me in reply. "I'll teach you how to eat oysters."

I think to myself, so stealthy in form with those granitelike shells, they look like they'd rather be uneaten, undiscovered—undisturbed. They seem rather content in their inchoate state.

The waitress brings us tools: a flat, dull-tipped knife, a small fork, thick cutting board, a plethora of cloth napkins, melted butter, and four wedges of lemon. You eye my confusion and warn me how juicy these oysters are. You assure me I'll need these napkins.

You move the pail to the floor. You pick up an oyster and hold it high to demonstrate. You tell me to find the dark sliver of space waiting to be wedged open. (I notice you have no trouble finding that clandestine slit.)

You ram the dull blade into the crack and twist with vigor. You pull apart the halves and out pours a small rush of clear broth.

"See, I told you," you say.

I see the fleshy nub that fused the two sides together. You throw away the empty half and focus your attention on the one still holding fast to its slick, fleshy mound—the color of city smog. You quickly wrench it free with the tiny fork and toss the shell into the pail. It lands with a loud clunk.

All that shell, I think, for that little piece of meat. Is it so special, so sensitive, it needs all that rough armor?

You douse the nub with lemon then drench it in butter and finally offer it to me fully dressed. With all the juices dripping it glistens like a jewel. I take it and slip it whole inside my mouth. It mixes with the juices that have already mysteriously appeared there. Its texture is something impossible—a soft marble. It makes me smile.

You tell me to try opening my own now. I try but I feel like if I force it too hard I'll hurt it, so I end up holding back.

You guide me through.

"Try holding the knife sideways. Grab it like a tool. Like a hammer. Don't be afraid. Ram and twist. You'll know when you've opened it. You'll feel it give."

And I do.

Give.

"Now, pull apart."

Even though I know it's coming, the juice pouring out startles me as it soaks my hands—my fingers now slick with evidence of this oyster's thalassic birth.

You take the treasured half from me, poke your fork into it and then hold it up for inspection. I think to myself, impaled little oyster flesh rescued from the maw. What now?

"Look," you say separating the miniature folds with your finger. They flutter like blinds like eyelids. "A woman's genitalia," you say smiling proudly like a child who knows he has the right answer.

I am amazed. It is an exact replica shrunk down and enshelled. What sly god did that?

You say it reminds you of a conversation you had recently with a girl about the clitoris. I love how you say the word so articulately and without hesitation. Your eyes are the color of wet bark.

I'm no longer looking at you. I'm struggling with my own oyster. I feel the warm broth soak through inches of cloth napkin to the skin of my wrists.

I shiver like a compass needle.

"She says guys have no clue about the clitoris. No clue at all. They don't know what they're doing."

"Is that true?" I ask.

"Some guys," you answer.

I'm afraid to ask where you fit in. I'm afraid you have a clue. I'm suddenly nervous thinking of you with that oyster in your mouth so soft and newly sprung. I eat mine delicately as if it's a tiny bird egg that I don't want to crack.

"This feels like cannibalism," I say.

I feel tender between my legs. My clitoris descends.

Opening another, you ask, "Remind you of the gynecologist? Spread 'em." You laugh.

"I've never been," I say tossing you a clue. I've never been. I've never been spread opened rammed discovered. You're too engrossed in oyster meat to notice. I want to leave, but there's nowhere that I'd rather be. I look longingly out at the river. Could I drown my passions for you there, or would I have to drown my whole self with them because I can no longer differentiate between the two?

You ask, "Have you ever had female genitalia in your mouth?"

"No."

"Well, I've never had a guy's."

"Then we have something in common."

"Yes." But do you really understand what you're saying yes to? Do you really mean "Yes, I know, I know that you, too, have never had a man inside your mouth."

You tell me oysters are an aphrodisiac. I'm squirming long before you tell me this from the juice and the slickness and the folds and your hands—one on the oyster, one on the knife—ramming it into the black crack and twisting. How do I ask you to stop doing that? Or if you could take me home and do that to me?

Something begins pulsing steadily between my legs like an expired clock suddenly rewound. Crossing my legs only intensifies the beat. It'll go like this for hours now.

Everything we say is drenched in innuendo. I, too, am drenched. Aqueous. I want to shut up but can't. I fear I'll start to caterwaul. God help me.

You can't pry one oyster open so you toss it.

"Is that what you do when they're tight?" I ask.

You cast a furtive glance my way.

"Be gentle," I advise.

You smile too slowly and without looking at me.

I force open another. I close my mouth, so my tongue doesn't leap out—my tongue that wants to lick the two dozen vertebrae of your spine. I rub it instead against the roof of my mouth wishing it were the roof of yours.

You ask me if I'm ready for other new things since these are my very first oysters.

"This could be the start of something."

"Yes. New things." I say. And I smile too slowly and without looking at you.

I've had nothing to drink but water. I've inhaled nothing except the smell of you, oysters, and the river. Still, I sway. Drunk on the droplets of lemon butter and oyster juice glistening at the corners of your mouth.

When the rest of the food comes, and the oysters are taken away, I try to return to myself. (Or am I already too much with me?)

You order each of us a beer. You tear me a piece of French bread and tell me to dip it into the warm blanket of fishy soup set before me. I love how you don't hesitate to tell me how to do these things. And I do them because I know you're trying to show me pleasure. And I want pleasure. I wonder if you're like this in bed. I hope you are. And I would follow your instructions there as I do here so I could walk that heady path of pleasure. You have a gentle, yet confident way of instruction. If I were a nation, I'd follow you.

You dip your bread into my soup and proceed to finish it for me at my insistence. You drink my beer as well. I close my eyes a moment no longer able to watch you put food into your mouth. I am dizzy with the satiety of shellfish, soup, your body. I try not to look at you (as if it would help to forget what you look like). I am afraid to speak my desire to you even as my clitoris bangs against its shell like a fist against a wall.

You say, "That was the best meal I've had in ages." You lean back to stretch your long body out even further. It is a world without end. You pull your shirt up and pat your stomach to show me how full it is. But I'm more interested in that dark line of hair there that matches your eyebrows—so much darker than the hair on your head.

I lower my eyes as if I've just touched you where I shouldn't have and writhe beneath the table. You make a casual comment about me lifting up my shirt to see my stomach. I refuse. (There's too much skin around this table already.)

"I don't have a pot belly, if that's what you're thinking. You'll have to trust me on that."

"I wouldn't guess that anyway by looking at you."

The way you're looking at me now is as if you're looking without the intrusion of clothes. My clitoris seethes. I inhale sharply.

I'm spinning in a heightened state of restive awareness. I suddenly see and feel everything at once. Drunk on my own precision. I am wholly tuned into you. Plugged into a socket of purely carnal thought. Prickly, pleasurable, yet painful, sensations caress my skin like a cat kneading my thighs with its claws.

My legs are squeezed together so tightly, I think they'll meld into one. The clock ticks. So loud I'm afraid you can hear it. What if the alarm was inadvertently set and it goes off in public? Everyone will turn to stare. And here I'll be with oyster juice running down my legs.

Andi Mathis
Penny Candy

The one-cent piece is one of the most maligned of American coins. It weighs in the pocket, and can't—like it used to—buy you gum, parking, or sixty seconds through a Rocky Mountain viewer. It collects in little trays in convenience stores where the clerks can't be bothered to deal with the taxman. The penny still clogs up sink drains, and remains the most frequently swallowed coin of the American toddler. Not surprisingly, along with a clothespin and a poker chip, my sister found three of them in her broken VCR.

Once, minting pennies really was making something out of nothing. But now, inflation has transformed penny manufacturing into making next to nothing out of nothing. Strangely enough, however, people still flock to Denver to see Lincoln's head handily embossed on a round of copper, as if the minting of money was like watching water being turned into wine.

"Hey, Mickey!" A paper wad hit me in the shoulder. Instantly I turned and conveyed my disapproval to Jameson. "A coupla your kind on Channel One . . ."

Instinctively, I lowered the volume on my radio and turned my eyes toward the sidewalk monitor. It was one of the six screens I was responsible for. In its infinite wisdom, the U.S. Department of the Treasury had commissioned me to protect America's diminishing supply of pennies at the U.S. Mint in

Denver. In general, tourists are a trustworthy lot, but around money, nefarious minds are always at work.

Levon J. loved to tease me about all the dykes on the security cameras, and over the years he'd gotten almost as good as me at spotting them. The women were just about to step out of frame, into the dead space between One and Two, but the admission line had slowed. On the control panel, I toggled the zoom lens for a closer look.

Pia Sheppard was suddenly in front of me in high relief. I recognized the layered brush of her graying blonde hair, since I've watched her a lot from the back, playing darts at Joker's on Thursday nights. Her biker jacket was open and she was laughing, and unself-consciously holding the hand of a woman I didn't recognize.

"Bingo," I muttered under my breath. I knew all of Pia's friends, I thought. "Must be an out-of-towner."

She was shorter than Pia, but not by much, and her dark hair was cut in a blunt pageboy. She was wearing dark glasses and a long trenchcoat. It was precisely the sort of disguise we'd been warned to watch out for at security school. I'd have suspected a sawed-off shotgun under the khaki had she not had both hands where I could see them. The two women were at the end of the tour line and I knew they wouldn't be joined by any other curiosity seekers for the day. They'd caught the last tour, the 2:45.

Over the stairway to the gallery in the stamping room, Channel Two picked them up again, lingering at the rail and pointing at the machines. Despite the absence of audio, I recognized from the sway of their shoulders that the rhythm of industry was having an effect on them.

They stood away from other tourists, and Maggie Holowaczyk, the docent, was preoccupied with the questions of some precocious eight-year-old triplets at the head of the small crowd. But they got my attention.

Even with their backs to the camera I could see that Pia had her arm inside the stranger's coat, perhaps jammed down the back of her coffee-colored cargo pants, fingering an elastic band of underwear, tracing along a hip, already wet herself. The girl-friend had her head turned slightly, and I caught the warning, impish gaze that asked, *Just what do you think you're doing?*

"Yo, Jameson," I said loudly.

I heard my buddy twist in his chair. "What?"

"Check this out."

Pia Sheppard is the most frustrating and exciting lover I've ever had, and I've had plenty. It's not that I'm loose, but fucking is an art, and I've got a creative side. I like the chase, the seduction, the tease, the bite.

It's not serious between us.

It started about three months ago, one night after my team was routed by hers at the dartboard; I bought her an Anchor Steam. That was the first clue that she had some class. At first I had my doubts about whether or not I was really attracted to her—she's not my usual type. She shoots darts in silk blouses and sexy heels; her skirt usually matches the jacket she's discarded. But it's just drag for work, she assures me. She's a tour guide on one of the buses that run out regularly to the foothills of the Rockies.

She didn't resist my invitation to come home with me that night, and I fucked her for hours, with my mouth and hands, on top and underneath and from behind. She came in copious, creamy shudders, biting her lip, or mine, or gasping a throaty, "Don't stop," until she passed out in the breaking dawn. I hadn't let her reciprocate. I'm a patient sort, and a little too butch to let down my guard early in the game.

In the succeeding weeks, however, she got more assertive and I let her, but I couldn't orgasm to save my life.

Channel Three caught them in the stairwell between stamping and sorting. They'd fallen a good ways behind their group, and Pia took advantage. She glanced furtively over her shoulder to make sure there was no one behind them. The lover's coat was open, and the front of her shirt unfolded over two of the most spectacular breasts I had ever seen. With a lascivious slowness designed to torture, Pia lowered her open mouth to a sallow nipple and hungrily stuffed the softness in. Pia pressed the woman's shoulders against the wall and sucked at her like an angry stoat, denied enough. A hand raked through her hair, and her head moved to the other breast.

"Damn," breathed Jameson. He was standing behind my chair. He dug his hands deep into his pants pockets and fingered his change. "Is she going to do her right there?"

What the fuck was she doing? Maybe I shouldn't have been jealous—like I said, things between us aren't serious. But somehow, as I watched her saunter in the shadow off Camera Three, leaving her sweet young thing buttoning up and panting and saying something, I wondered what her agenda was. Then she was there again, grasping the woman's arm with an assured swagger, and once again, disappearing into the darkness.

There's dead space between Three and Four, a two-minute passage through the stacked pallets of coin bags and copper rods, down from the gallery and then onto the shop floor, where the sewing machines zip up five-dollar pouches. The tour group was already three minutes into the lecture by the time Pia and company emerged from the hallway. Pia had positioned herself so that the camera caught her dead on, but if she knew it was there she ignored it. Her back was turned three-quarters of the way away from her group, and she leaned in to whisper in her friend's ear.

Then she looked up, straight at the camera, expressionless, as she dropped a hand into her crotch, and she slowly massaged the inside of her thigh, as if she was packing. I watched her mouth the words: "I'm going to fuck you hard. . . ."

Behind me, Jameson groaned. "Damn, this works for me." I heard him unbuckle his belt and quickly slip it out of his belt loops.

I rolled my eyes, but gestured toward the door. "Don't look at me to help you out, partner," I said. "Lock up if you are going to get off."

I had to admit, I was pretty fucking horny myself.

I looked back to the monitor. Pia had stepped in close to her new lover, as if a conversation of deep importance was about to take place. From my vantage point, I could see that she had unzipped her jeans, and that she was guiding her girlfriend's hand into her panties.

That's when I lost it, to be honest, because Pia has large hands. I find that moment—when my partner's finger just brushes the crease of my dripping vulva—to be excruciatingly erotic, and I could see that Pia was getting exactly such treatment. Pia likes to be in me, with one finger or four, teasing and tugging, pushing hard and slow, especially when I am standing. I like it, too, until I can't stand anymore.

Jameson had had the decency to position himself a few feet away and behind me, and I heard his breath start to deepen and huff as he started to whack himself off. I have little interest in cocks, so I ignored him. I heard him mumble, *Shit, she's in her pussy,* and speed up his own action.

I moved to the edge of my own chair and unzipped my khakis and jammed my hand into my slippery slit. I wasn't going to waste any time, so I started my rhythmic thrum and felt my heart start to rev.

Pia's gal pal looked nervous. The look on Pia's face was hard, determined, and she shifted her weight on her feet, and I felt the squeeze of her pelvic muscles on my own fingers. A hand found an upper arm, a grasp I knew. Then the girfriend withdrew, holding her sex hand awkwardly until Pia lifted it and licked her own juice from her fingers.

The tour group had started to move again, the collective rumble of slow walkers turning in unison, and Pia zipped up. She was shaking a little, not with any kind of nervousness, but with the anticipatory kind of tremor that lets you know there's more to come.

At Channel Five I was hot, but Pia was nowhere to be seen. In shipping, the tourists crowded around the forklift track, as pallets of coins were stabbed and lifted, until the little trucks were nearly tipping over. Sweat ran down the nape of my neck and behind my ear. I was on the plateau, abuzz with hot engorgement, taking my strokes in practiced, long pleasure, not wanting to rush.

I scanned the screen, wishing I could see Pia, as if she might also be able to see me, and know what I look like on the veritable edge of coming.

The night before, with her tongue inside me, I had been begging, willing my cunt to swallow her, hoping that the pull and suck would never stop. But it did, and I hadn't finished. Pia had dressed in the semi-darkness, silently.

"Don't be angry," I'd said.

"I'm not," she'd answered too quickly. "I'm not sure why you're holding back."

"You can't really think that."

She shrugged. "Maybe it's me." A moment. A stare that could kill. "But I've never had this problem before."

What could I say? She slammed the front door as she went out.

I'd lost all sense of caring where she'd gone when Six picked them up in the lobby, lingering over the souvenirs and display cases of Penny Anomalies: Coins Gone Wrong. There, some penny sculptures and paper-thin coins made up a sort of Ripley's Believe It or Not of the weird and wonderful of Centiana.

I was solidly perched on my own three fingers, mixing and churning and waiting.

Pia looked pissed. She gestured at her girlfriend, sullen and threatening. The crowd had pretty much dispersed, and the lobby guard was trying not to listen in to whatever angry words were being exchanged.

I was seconds away from coming. If only Pia knew.

But suddenly, the girlfriend had hold of Pia's jacket, jerking it, and Pia reeled, turning toward the camera, and her hand went back, calculated her aim, and smacked the stranger's jaw in a hard, open slap. The girl staggered back a pace and jostled a display, knocking a jar of pennies to the ground in a shattering rain of copper.

The camera caught Pia in a sly smile, and I came all over myself.

Adelina Anthony
Cowboy

I am, to my father's dismay, more like the passive women in my family than the men. The women form a long chain of paper dolls, and I am half a doll at that. But I am my father's only child—his miracle one. When I think about it, he was more of an embarrassment to la familia than I ever was. Hell, I saved his reputation. Impotent, they would whisper at fiestas. Shake their heads and say, Chingao, what a waste. I get the same reaction from the girls. They see my sculpted body, the Spaniard complexion—you know the one, beetle-black hair against ivory white skin, the kind Don Juan must have had, and the girls go ga-ga. Girls and their locuras . . . I see them eye me discreetly and sometimes not so discreetly.

Tonight, as I saunter past the Crockett Hotel, the girls gaze in astonishment. They've spied the huge bulge my black leather pants try to contain. El viejo used to show me his chorizo in the baño and say, "Ya ves, mi'jo, when you grow up, this is what you can thank your papi for. It's gonna drive the viejas crazy." Gracias, Papi, because you were right, a man is nothing without a big dick, especially in jotoland.

But why think about that culero now? Maybe because my balls are shriveling from this chilly breeze while I wait to dance my buns to warmth inside the Bonham. Old historical Bonham, the only decent thing about San Anton' on Saturday nights. How many nights did I freeze my ass off that Thanksgiving el viejo kicked me out?

At least three, before my great tía Tita took me in like her own son. I grew up hearing la familia whisper about her, saying she would never get married and have kids because she was "one of them." A tortillera. Back then I didn't understand what eating tortillas had to do with her not getting married. My mom ate tortillas and she married my dad. It seemed the whole fucking town of San Anton' ate tortillas, even the gringos. It wasn't until Tía Tita showed me albums of all of her "comadres" that I got the picture.

Almost twenty years ago, and I still remember el ataque de corazón my parents had when it was my turn at the table to be thankful and I said, "I thank Jesucristo for letting me know so early on in my life that I think men are groovy." Thinking it was a joke, Abuelo Rufus laughed aloud. Almost choked on the turkey leg he had shoved in his mouth. But when I looked at our neighbor Jim Stonewall, a closeted fag, and said, "Tell them, babe"—a battle bigger than the pinche Alamo transpired. And just like back then, Mexicans were fighting Mexicans, and the pobre gringo got pulverized.

Ten more vatos to go and I'm inside. I hate it when the line gets stalled; you'd think they could card the jailbait a little faster. The music is already pumping so loud I can hear my dreamy Ricky blasting through the speakers. Tasty. N'ombre, I was into him when he was just a Menudo boy. And even now that his star has waned, I'm still his biggest fan. You see Junior, you can be loyal to a man. He's just gotta look like Ricky or George.

Not like the average joto I see standing out here. Carajo, I don't see anything worth a stroke. Just the regular faces. I think every guy in this line has already given me a blowjob. That's the daddy's girl in me. I still let the men do the picking-up. But it doesn't mean I'm a bottom. And that is definitely the macho in me.

Regardless of what el viejo said about me back then—that I'm a long-haired sissy joto who will never be a man or his hijo

'cause you like to take it up the ass like a pinche vieja!—I've discovered it's really not my style. It's like no one ever tells you that
if you take it up the ass you can't really enjoy it the first few
times. How? The whole fucking time it feels like you're gonna
crap. That grosses me out. They can blow me, give me a handjob
and I'll gladly fuck or suck them, but those are my boundaries. I
don't think it makes me less of a joto.

The only one who ever did me doggie style was Orlando, and
that's just because the puto was stronger than me. If the struggle
hadn't turned me on so much, I would've called it rape. After
Orlando, I've always made sure to only let smaller putos pick me
up. Too many psychos out there.

Speaking of locos, ay, mi virgencita, I don't believe my eyes,
pinche Gerald is here. Qué apropos, here I am going down memory lane and the only cabrón I let treat me like his perra is here.
At least, he's at the end of the line. Maybe I can avoid him.
Damn. I thought he moved to Irving five years ago when he
started dating that Dallas Cowboy player. He must be here visiting his sister Gweena.

That must be his boyfriend hanging on him like a sweaty
workout towel. Gerald always enjoyed being worshiped. I wish I
could say he looks like shit, but he doesn't. For a brother, his style
doesn't change much though. Black slacks and a white tank top
to show off his Olympian chest and arms. Delicious, but my
worst relationship. What did I expect from a gym rat? I mean, I
work out, but chingao, I got a life, too.

Now he's looking arrow-straight at me. I don't think he recog-
nizes you, Junior. How could he? I was in my blond ambition
stage when we dated. He never saw my natural look, well, except
for my nest where the pajarito sleeps. C'mon Gerald, get a good
look you pinche puto, because your slutty hands will never touch
me again. Look at him grinning, what a flirt, always on the hunt.
He's definitely got that guy dick-whipped.

Hello, honey, are you going to give me the regular special?
C'mon, give me the smile, papi chulo. Stamp my hand. In I go

for free and in return a nice squeeze to the ass to keep him caliente the rest of the night. Since Edward started manning the door, I can't remember the last time I paid to come in.

Ay, music throbbing, I can barely hear my thoughts. This is nice. A packed house and it's not even eleven yet. I love the holiday crowds: out-of-towners and their fresh faces. I should write a book about playing the game at clubs.

First thing any professional clubber does is cruise the entire scene as soon as he enters. Even if he's a drinker, the cerveza can wait once you get an idea of what kind of house it is. Actually, I rarely ever buy my own drinks, so I don't even worry about stopping at the bar. Tonight it's a rather eclectic crowd. I should have no problem getting laid.

Let's see, we got the young freaks who wear nothing but Hilfiger, Nike, and Adidas in the video hip-hop room. This is usually where I run into my ex-students. I used to get embarrassed and terrified the first few years this happened. "Coach Rodriguez? What are you doing here?" No, I should be asking you that, quarterback Joe, lineman Johnny, or running back Ricardo. Tough baby jotos. I let them squirm with vergüenza and then say, "Your mama asked me to find your joto butt and take you home." Their mouths opening with fear, just wide enough to take my cock, I think. And then I laugh my ass off and grab their balls.

And the truth is, if they are over twenty-one, I usually do take them home, or at least to my car. Any teacher who says they've never been turned on by a student is a liar. But with the new law San Anton' passed about teachers and students involved in sexual relations, I'm going to have to start checking their I.D.s. Make sure it's been at least seven years since I last spanked them.

It's not like I think teachers should be sleeping with their students, especially, if a kid can come back up until the age of twenty-one and sue your culo. Just gotta be more careful. Gotta be cool in the young face of temptation. I feel sorrier for the straight teachers. Some of those young girls are serious putitas. If

Coach Hernandez isn't careful with the third-year flunky, Melissa Gallegos, he's going to have some major problems down the road. Everyone says she keeps flunking eighth grade to stay in his P.E. class. Girl is way past the training bra stage. But there you have her, jumping jacks in the front row, where Hernandez can see her chichis jiggle like Jell-O.

Luckily, it takes my boys longer to figure out their sexuality. They're too busy trying to get pubescent panocha to prove their studliness. They overlook the fact that they're really in love with their own chorizos. Once they get past the societal bullshit, they realize a gay man's life is ideal. Dick whenever, from whoever, no questions asked. Well, at least that was the case in my early days; now everyone's freaked out about la pinche SIDA. But like I say, I have no problem with a complete stranger sucking my dick.

Like, who's that guy in the pool room? Now see, the pool room is where your older guys hang out. Men who could be as old as my father. My father probably looks like this hombre here. Good-looking tejano type with a small beer belly over his Wranglers. Yep, my dad would be wearing his ass-kicking boots, too, and, of course, the Stetson. But my father never smoked like this guy, my mama hated it. Made her asthma worse. And if this vato is the one who put Gloria Gaynor in the jukebox, he's definitely not el viejo. Dad was Texas Tornadoes day in and day out. Conjunto or nothin'. Ay, if there's nothing interesting on the main dance floor, I will definitely come back here, because the way this papasote is looking at me, he wants to burn his mouth with my chile.

Well, Junior, look who finally got in. Princess Gerald and his frog. I hope they stay at the side bar. I don't want to deal with diva shit tonight. And there's Randy, or is it Rudy? I don't remember, but he does have the cutest asshole, all salmon pink and precious. I'll just nod at fish-ass. I like to be polite. Just because I do a guy doesn't mean I have to be a cabrón and not acknowledge him. Just hope he doesn't follow me, because I'm not feeling like Jewish tonight.

Maybe it's all the reminiscing, but what you need, Junior, is an all-out Hispanic faggot with a Catholic complex. The kind that is always praying because he feels guilty about everything, so it's natural for him to be on his knees. Those are the men who usually indulge themselves with my body. Maybe it's all of those years of taking Christ in their mouths.

And now we get to the end of our cruise and what do we have on the main floor? Some biker boys, some pain-in-the-ass queens, a decent mix of lesbians, a couple of corporate types, lots of beefcake and, oh my—Junior, your eyes have landed on paradise. If Emilio Navaira ever had a twin brother, that is him over in the corner. He's everything that was back in the pool room only twenty years younger. And I am of the Hollywood mindset: younger is definitely sexier. I've never seen this one. He must be visiting from Laredo; he looks bien bordertown.

Okay, Junior, time to move to the second and most essential clubbing step. Parking. I'll just take my fine ass to the bar where my cowboy is stationed and make myself look available. Did someone just grab my ass? Oh no—the pink princess is shouting in my ear.

Hey, Zorro, you got that nifty sword of yours handy?

I'll just smile and pretend I can't hear him. Gotta keep dancing my way to Emilio.

It's Randy! I forgive you if you forgot my name, we didn't exactly do much talkin' last Saturday!

Just keep moving, Junior. No, I can't be an asshole. Fuck my Catholic upbringing! You're looking good, Randy, but I came here with someone! So, are you alone again? Shit, he didn't hear me. Okay, you've been nice enough, Junior, Emilio is going to get away if you don't drop this mosca. Oh, thank God, the YMCA song. I'll run away when he makes the em. Even better, let's bump hips with these bikers and pray one of them takes an interest in fish-ass. Chingao, I hope Emilio isn't watching all of this; I don't want him to think I'm cheap. Yet. Bingo, there go Randy and Mr. Harley Davidson himself. Cupid should pay me a commission.

I can't believe I've been standing here for over three minutes and my Emilio hasn't even made a move. I've already thrown him the eye, step number three. I throw it any harder, I'll be left with two empty sockets. Chingao, maybe he's hitched. Let me see if he's looking at anyone in particular on the dance floor. Nadie. So what's wrong, papasito? He may not be interested—nah, impossible. Dio, don't tell me I'm dealing with the shy type. Maybe he's straight and this is his first night out. Oh, well, Junior, you can move on. Mexican Marlboro Man is waiting in the pool room. But this Emilio is extremely cute. I'm getting a hard-on just looking at him. No mustache to tickle your cock, an authentic baby face. Ah, fuck it—be a man and make the first move, Junior.

"Hey, what are you drinking? Can I buy you another one?" Uh-oh, he looks nervous, maybe he is here with someone. Maybe he can't hear me through the Gloria Estefan dance mix. Wait, is that a smile? And he's holding up his Lone Star. Aaajuuua! I'm at the bar.

"Hey, Javier, will you get me a Lone Star and a Corona?"

"Oh my God, you're going to, like, actually buy someone a drink?"

"I guess you don't want a tip?"

"I'm just kidding, her royal highness. Here you go. And by the way, I love the eye makeup."

"It's just eyeliner."

"Oh, but it's so you."

I hand my soon-to-be loverboy his beer and sit on the stool next to him. Oh, he's so kissable. I don't want to jump to conclusions, but my vibe says he's a maniac in bed. It's like mama used to say, Watch out for the quiet ones, mi'jo, they don't talk 'cause they've got the most to hide.

Nice nails. Trim and clean, says a lot about a man. I wonder what he does for a living? I'll ask him later, maybe between sessions. Best thing about picking someone up at a club, no need to talk. Oh, look at him chug that beer. Ay, Junior, this one definitely swallows. Just thinking about his mouth around my cock is working me up. That's what I need to do, just get him up and off that stool so I can take a peak at his package. Those jeans are tight enough to give me a sneak preview. Well, I've taken the lead so far, no sense turning femme now.

Jesus, Junior, if Gerald could see the butch in you now. Don't let go of Emilio's hand until you're bumping and grinding to the groove. Soft hands. Gracias a la virgencita I wasn't born during that waltz era. How the hell would you get close enough to a man's body and figure out if he's really into you? Really. Well, this is a pleasant surprise. My Emilio isn't too tall. I'd say about five feet eight and since he's wearing boots, maybe that makes him only a five-six or five-seven at best. Who cares, the boy has got some serious Latin rhythm going on. And from what I can tell in these flashing pink and blue lights, he makes up for size in other areas.

And he's not that shy. He's letting me rub against him like I'm cloth-shining his boots. If he's not careful with that sexy look of his, it's going to turn into a spit shine pretty quick. Ay, virgencita, are those his hands around my ass? Junior, I think he likes you. This has got to be the best part about dancing to techno, it's sex with your clothes on. And the way he's letting me buck against his ass, carajo, I gotta get him into a bathroom pronto. "Do you want to go to the bathroom?"

Oh, my God. I feel like such a dick. Did he just shake his head and reject me? No one has ever told me no. Who the fuck does Emilio think he is? What is he pulling out of his pocket? Keys. Keys? Keys! Oh, yeah, cowboy, let's go.

The back of his van. I thought he'd be driving a Chevy pickup, but he's got a Dodge van from the early eighties. Tinted windows, of course. And a bumper sticker that reads AUSTIN in rainbow colors, no wonder I haven't seen him at the Bonham. I gotta go to the capital more often. Doors open—and I thought I had seen everything, but this shit is amazing. There's so much leather in here we could piece together a cow. He nudges me inside. It's just too wicked to stop now.

The doors close behind us. I can barely see the club through the windows. He parked his van too far away for us to hear the music. Cold. Our breath is still coming out in clouds, until he puts his mouth to mine. It's obvious both of us are naturals. Sluts, that is. His tongue and mine wrestle the way our bodies are gonna. Oops, his hat just fell off. I put one hand against the back of his head—ooh very soft hair—and the other on his ass—very tough—and suck-suck his beery breath. Curl my fingers around his biceps while he pushes me onto his mattress. I move my hand to touch his dick—his pelvis pulls back. I guess he wants to be in control. Short man syndrome? He's chulo enough to have me play along.

I love the way he respects silence. No need for having to think of something sexy or sweet to say on the spot. It always comes out sounding so corny, or I feel like shit because I know I'm lying to the guy. I dated this writer from Colombia once and he wouldn't let me touch his dick unless I came up with a metaphor. That didn't last long. What would I tell Emilio if he started talking? If he'll be my wetback, I'll be his border patrol? He starts unbuttoning my shirt, I close my eyes and listen to the stream of traffic rushing on the I-35 nearby. I place my hands behind my head so he can strip search me.

Smooth tongue works down my chest like he's licking an envelope. Then it lingers at the edge of my pants like a truant kid walking back and forth along the school fence waiting for his chance to jump it. There he goes. Emilio doesn't unzip me though. He's play-biting my dick and it likes him. I must be eight inches now. I wonder if he didn't let me touch him because he's smaller than me. I swear, machos can be so sensitive about those things.

Ay, yes, that's it, Emilio, unzip me and kiss it with those fideo-thin lips. He's really good at this. No teeth. Just his tongue massaging my dick in warm circles. A little moth dancing around my pole. My stomach muscles are getting tighter, gotta start holding back the juice. Ay, it's that good kind of hurt. The kind that makes the coming tingle in my tummy. Chingao, I can't wait to reciprocate the favor, whatever size he is. Wait, why did he stop?

Carajo, this is too much. He's dangling a pair of handcuffs. But what the fuck? Are you going to go to your grave without the experience of at least one guy tying you up? Lose control every now and then, or why be fucking gay? And I don't know what it is about this vato, but I feel like I can trust him. Like he's got something nurturing about him. Or maybe it's just my taut chorizo doing the feeling and thinking for me. I nod my head, sit up and hold out my hands. I am an offering. He grabs a piece of black cloth hanging from the window and starts—blindfolding me? Well, they do call me Zorro. Click-click-click goes the first handcuff around my wrist. Freezing metal teeth. Emilio moves quickly behind me and kisses the back of my neck. Ah, chingao, how did he know that was my weak spot? I'm Jack Frost in a microwave. Hold on! No fucking fair! How did he do that?

"Hey, chulo, hold on. I don't mind being handcuffed, but not from behind."

"Shhhh!"

Ah, shit, Junior. You better pray this guy isn't a homophobic killer. Dumb ass, of course he was going to handcuff you from behind. Vulnerable. Breathe. Just relax. This is part of the juego. See, your dick is still into him. All part of the fun. What's life without a little danger? Shut up idiota, you're a joto, you're always in danger. Now what is he doing? I could resist. Ah, fuck it. Whatever happens happens. A gag? Okay, this is beyond cliché. All he needs to do now is throw me on my stomach and—there he goes. How did I know that was coming? All right, Emilio, now I'm all yours. What are you going to do, kick my culo for being such a trusting faggot? Ah—he kisses my neck again. His touch is all gentle. I guess he feels he can be nice again, now that he's utterly in control. Hands massage my back. God, his hands are so silky. This ain't too bad, I should've tried this sooner. Okay, Emilio knows he's got me hot and bothered, I'm rubbing myself so hard against his mattress, he's got to know I want to be inside his mouth again.

Ay, yes, he's a mind reader. We are so connected. That's it, baby, take my pants off. I'll lift my ass up in the air so you can un-zip me. He's having problems. See Emilio, if we had just done this the old-fashioned way I could've helped you with my chaps. Now what? Where is he going? He can't leave me like this. What's he opening? A door? No, I would have felt a chill or something. Glove compartment? He's back but what's he trying to do to my leg? Tie it? No way, man. Now I'm going to make him earn his little masochist thrill. Where is the motherfucker? Just keep kick-ing in the air, Junior, you're bound to give him a good chingazo. Hey, where the fuck is the parking attendant when you need him? Carajo, I'm dealing with a real vaquero here, he's sitting on my knees and tying my ankles to who knows what. All right, Emilio, you win. I'm splayed like the fingers of the peace sign. Peace, brother, ever heard of that?

Hey! Did he just cut my pants? Cabrón, these cost me three hundred dollars! Hold on. Is he using a knife? Jesucristo, get me alive out of this one and I'll—I'll—Oh, wait a second, false alarm. That's more like it, Emilio. He knows he's got me scared shitless, so he's kissing my ass—literally.

Ssshhh! Another deep kiss between my butt cheeks. Ssshhh—ssshhh—yeah, easy for you to say, Emilio. I wonder how turned on he is by all of this? Not that I'm one to talk, my chorizo gets any harder I'm going to bruise my stomach. I hear a popping sound. Now what is he grabbing? A zipper. Well, I know how I'm getting it tonight, that's no surprise. A jangle, and it ain't fucking Santa. Must be some belts. I hope he doesn't spank the shit out of me. I have to work Monday. He's squeezing a bottle. Ah well, at least we know he's considerate. He's rubbing plenty of cold lube around my asshole. It's gotta be that brand called WET, rub it and it gets hotter, 'cause that's what I'm feeling.

See, Junior, he's definitely not a cabrón. He could just ram it inside of you. But he's actually being very sensitive about his entry. I knew I could trust him. Ay, he's coming inside of me inch by inch. I don't know what he was worried about, he's got a hell of a package. I think I've met my match. His legs are starting to sweat between mine. He grabs on to my shoulders and I can feel every thrust vibrate inside of me. I extend my fingers and they reach the edge of his pubic hair. It's the softest pubic hair I've ever touched, like a newborn's head.

Ay virgencita, there's nothing like a tejano. He rides like a thousand cowboys are in his veins. C'mon Emilio, baby, take me on your Chisholm Trail. God, I'll be your saddle any day after tonight. What was I scared of? Why does this guy feel so fucking good from behind? There he goes, coming so fast his tiny shrieks sound like an eagle or a boiling teapot. And me, I'm coming right along. Hold on, Emilio. Hear the hooves beating along the path? Or maybe that's just my handcuffs scraping against each other. Who cares—all I know is that we're both riding into that fucking sunset. He bellows and all I see is tiny lights. The blackness gives way to red, orange and then yellow spots. The pinche sol envelops us. I feel its warm rays all over my body—virgencita, I think I'm in love.

I wish he would at least take off my gag, my nose pressed upon this mattress makes it difficult to breathe. He's fallen on top of me and I can smell his sweat. Like cumin. My stomach is all wet from my juice, but that's a small due to pay for the pleasure. Hold on. I just realized something. He's still inside of me. Hard. How is that possible? Chingao, Junior, have you really met your dream man? Now that's he's removing the gag with his teeth, maybe you should at least find out his name. We can't keep calling him Emilio just because he looks like your favorite tejano singer.

"So, what's your name, loverboy?" He cuts the rope off of my legs.

"Martha."

What? Martha Serrano. Off with the blindfold. If I weren't such a macho, maybe I'd cry. But all I can do is laugh like an idiot. My dream man is sitting in front of me Indian-style, her hot pink strap-on dildo pointing to the gods. Jesus.

Pam Ward
A Clean Comfortable Room

Sally had been driving long and hard for eleven hours already. When she saw the blue glow of the deadbeat motel she decided to pull in. She'd seen the Blue Star Motor Inn's giant sign from the highway. CLEAN COMFORTABLE ROOMS FOR $16.99. Sally turned off the exit and drove to the squat stucco building. It had about ten units connected under one slim roof. Nothing but road dirt and concrete. A loud Coke machine sat out front.

She got out and walked quickly to the office. As soon as she stepped in she was hit with the harsh scent of canned meat cooking. The office looked more like a living room. There were two TV sets, a small black-and-white and one color stacked together. There was a small stove and a giant, brown refrigerator with a big dent in it. There was an ironing board and a rotary phone hooked to the wall. A hefty man in loose-fitting overalls sat in a La-Z-Boy covered with duct tape. He looked about sixty-five. His bald head gleamed from the neon. His numb eyes were glued to the set. The man broke into a wide smile as Sally walked in.

"I'm comin'," he said, walking laboriously to the front desk. He had one of those beer guts that hung like a sack of rice. His breath was heavy. When he got close, Sally noticed a gray possum wrapped around his neck. Its wet eyes were watching her.

"What can I get you?" He grinned, revealing a gummy row of gapped teeth.

"How much for a room?" Sally had left in the middle of the night and only had twenty-eight dollars in cash on her. She needed a room before she could hit the ATM in the morning.

"We got some go for thirty-five and some that go for seventeen. Depends. You by yourself?"

"For now."

The man chuckled to himself when she said that. His double chin jiggled. "Well, I guess I can let you take the cheaper one." He sighed deeply. He seemed disappointed he wasn't getting a bigger sale.

"Can I see it first?" she asked.

"Sure, sure. Wait a hot minute. Let me get the keys." The man ducked behind a torn curtain.

Sally leaned across the front desk while she waited. She tapped her long fingernails across the wood. *I hope he doesn't take too long,* she thought. She wanted to hurry up and get to her room so she could lie down. She opened her purse and took out her lipstick. She smeared the deep red on. Sally looked toward the blue glow of the television. *Rosemary's Baby* was on. Rosemary was struggling down the street with a heavy suitcase. She looked pale and worried.

Suddenly there was a horrible racking cough, coming from the dark corner of the room. Sally leaped. It sounded like a hyena. She squinted to see. There, next to the stove, was a wide-shouldered man in an undershirt. Sally hadn't noticed the man before. He blended into the dim corner of the room. He couldn't have been more than twenty. Was probably the older man's son. Sally watched him bring a bottle of whiskey to his lips and drink a messy swig. He licked around his mouth and watched her. He was staring at Sally's large breasts. His gaze never rose above her neck.

Sally was wearing a jean jacket over a thin black slip. She'd just shoved the flap inside her pants. Her bare feet were in pink thongs. To avoid the man's gaze, Sally walked outside toward the Coke machine. She wasn't going to stay in there with some wild-looking fool drooling at her.

She slipped in three quarters and the red can came rumbling out.

"Oh—there you are, darlin'," the older man said, walking outside. "I'm fixin' to get that room ready."

Sally leaned against the hood of her car. It was a warm Arizona night. You could see every star from here. Sally heard a rattling sound behind her. She jumped. It was just a corn chip bag stuck in some weeds. Sally was dead tired and her nerves were shot. She hoped he wouldn't take too long.

The man was back in less than ten minutes. He was carrying an old bucket.

"Well, its all spic-and-span. Got it real nice for you."

Sally hoisted her large purse over her shoulder. She followed the man to the room.

"Here we are, little lady." The man stood firmly in the doorway. Sally had to brush past him to get in. He smelled like hard liquor and farm animals. As soon as she stepped in the room the fumes hit her. It had that rank smoke smell. A scent so thick it was embedded in all the walls, rugs, and drapes. Smelled like it would never go away. Like somebody smoked in there year after year and never once opened a window. The wallpaper was peeling off, the bedspread was a hideous floral orange and the corners had cigarette burns. "I'll take it," Sally said.

The man had her fill out a tiny white slip asking her name and license plate number. Sally fumbled around with her purse and finally counted out seventeen dollars. She handed it to him.

"Now, my name is Edmond. Let me know if there's anything you need, sugar." He leaned over to hand her the room key and his huge body trapped her against the doorjamb. Sally fell back and dropped her purse. The man bent down slowly and handed it back to her. "Watch yourself now. Looks like you need some shut-eye."

Edmond walked outside to the lot. He looked hard at Sally's car. It had about five layers of dirt on it. "I can wash that car there for you, if you'd like. Have it looking real nice. Real sweet. I know how to suds a car down. It's all in the motion you know. Got to go in a circular rhythm, keep your hands rubbing round and round and round. Don't have to press too hard to get a shine." His bald head looked hideous in the lamplight.

"Sleep tight," he said walking off. Sally watched his lumbering stride go back through the office door. He looked back at her before going in.

Sally shut the door. *Banjo-playin' motherfuckers,* she said to herself. She slid the extra lock across the frame. She took off her jacket and laid it on the bed. Sally was beat down. She'd been driving for half a day already. She pulled the blanket all the way back and examined the sheets. They seemed clean. She took off her shoes and pants, then peeked through the drapes.

The road was real quiet now. It was 11:45 P.M. There was only one other car in the lot. She walked to the small bathroom. Some of the tiles were missing. A shower curtain hung limp on a metal rod. The toilet paper roll was half gone. Sally took a hot shower and wrapped herself in the thin, frayed towel. She sat on the edge of the bed. She wished she had one cigarette. Something to take the edge off. She clicked on the TV. *Rosemary's Baby* was still on. She watched the set while sipping the rest of her Coke. She looked around the room. There was a small refrigerator in the corner. She pulled it open. There were four beers strung together on a pale vein of plastic. The last person in there must have left it and the owner hadn't noticed it.

Sally didn't drink. She didn't even want to be tempted. Not now. Not after everything that had happened. Sally hadn't tasted liquor for three years straight. Not since that rainy night long ago. She dialed the front desk.

"Hello, ma'am. Room all right?"

"Yes, it's fine, but I found a six-pack in the fridge. I really don't want it."

"That's all right, ma'am. I'll send Leon down to pick it up."

Sally put the receiver down and put her pants back on. *Leon must be the fool who didn't have the decency to look me in the face,* she thought.

She was buttoning the front of her jacket when she heard a soft knock on the door.

Sally peeked out the small hole drilled over the doorknob.

It was Edmond again. "I'll just take that beer off your hands myself. Leon's busy right now." *Busy?* Sally thought. *That man wasn't doing nothing but jackin' off to* Rosemary's Baby. Edmond crossed the room, looking around it quickly. He walked over to the refrigerator and jerked the handle. He snatched the cans away as if Sally might change her mind. They clanked against his wad of keys. He stood next to her for a moment. She could smell the sour seeping out from his pores. She had emptied a few things from her purse, and a pair of black four-inch pumps was standing erect next to the TV set. He stared at them, too. Sally put one hand on her hips.

"Well, I guess you have everything," she said, using that fake sweet tone she reserved for work. She sure didn't miss Sizzler. Only thing she got from that job was a handful of bad steak knives.

"Yes, ma'am, I reckon I do. I'll just take this on back to the front. Let me know if you need anything else, hear. You be safe now, pretty little thing like you got to watch herself. Lord knows what's out on that road."

Sally started closing the door slowly. He could see her red lips and giant cleavage through the crack. The man took two steps but didn't leave. He reeked of cheap booze. Sally saw a dirty ring around his neck where the possum had been. She inched the door further in and accidentally touched his hand. It was hairy and rough. He looked down at her. His forehead was sweaty and large. Slowly, the corner of his lips curled up into a crooked smile. "I'll take this on, now," he said stepping out. "Call again." Once his feet cleared the door, Sally closed it shut and locked it tight. *Country fools,* she thought to herself.

She waited a moment before taking her jacket off. She went into the bathroom and washed out her slip and hung it on the shower rod. If she left the window open it ought to be dry by morning. Sally lay on the bed naked. Damn, she wanted a cigarette. She searched the room. Nothing. She thought about the last smoke she'd had with William. It was right after they'd made love. Damn, that man was good. He sure knew how to serve it up. She remembered how he cupped her breasts and sucked both nipples at the same time. How he begged her to climb on top of him, plunging himself deeper and deeper. How he tugged her hair just enough, just until her body was one huge arch. Until she felt like pure steel. Like one hot metal rod. Like she might just snap. Sally loved the way he screamed her name when she violently came. Yeah, she'd sure miss her some William.

Sally began playing with her breasts. She slid her hand down to her things. Damn, it was hot. Buck-ass naked and she was still sweating. Sally thought if she got off she could get to sleep. All that road coffee had her fried. She tried and tried but only ended up in a frustrated knot under the sheet. Her long hair was glued to the back of her neck.

She yanked the sheet back and thought about Leon sitting in that office in the dark. There was something peculiar about him. Something backwoods mixed with wild. *Too much inbreeding, I bet.* But there was something else, too. Something simmering like a pot of hot greens on the stove. Sally thought about the cigarette pack rolled up in his sleeve. His thick muscular arms and that tight six-pack stomach. The way his eyes ate her breasts. The way he leaned in his chair with his legs cocked out wide. The worn look to his jeans. The hard tips of his boots. The boy looked pure country. A bona fide hick. All wild-eyed and wooly-haired, too.

But it wasn't like she was in the backwoods. Flagstaff was just five miles away. Sally remembered what the gas station attendant had told her. "Be careful on them roads honey," she'd said. "Some of these small towns are more common than the Deep South. Watch out."

Sally took a bag of pretzels from her purse. She was hungry. Besides the Coke, it was the only thing she'd had in hours. She opened her wallet. She only had eleven dollars left. Her tank was already close to the red line. She had to get some cash fast.

* * *

Edmond walked back inside the office door and opened the cash register. "Sure is a pretty gal up in thirteen." He counted the money and put it back inside. Leon didn't even look up. His eyes were fastened to the set. He watched Rosemary's naked body being shoved against the long table. She was struggling frantically. The men were holding her legs down.

Edmond slumped his large body back in the La-Z-Boy. It was stuffed with old copies of the *Phoenix Gazette*. The newspapers filled the deep hole in the seat. "Yes sirree. A real live citified gal. Should have seen them patent leather hoofers she had up in there. Um, um, um." Edmond wrapped the possum around his neck, but it squirmed so much he let it loose on the ground. It ran to a dark corner of the room. He pulled a handkerchief out and patted his sweaty brow.

"I don't know what a lady like that is doing out here in the middle of the night. Did you see her clothes? Look like she just shoved her nightie in her jeans and took off. Must be another one of them women had a fight with their boyfriends. You see she wasn't carryin' nothing but the clothes on her back. Man oh man. If it wasn't for boyfriend fights and city folks cheatin', we'd be out of business."

Leon didn't say anything.

* * *

Sally laid across the bed. *Rosemary's Baby* was still on. She watched as Rosemary's slender body moved crazily against the hard table. The men pounded her down, took turns thrashing away, while naked old ladies chanted and held both her legs. Sally clicked the TV off. "Demonic shit," she said out loud to herself. She slid under the sheet and got a whiff of the dank smoke lodged in the bedspread. "Damn," she said. "I wish I had just one cigarette. Something to take the edge off." Sally dug around in her purse even though she knew there was nothing.

She wished she hadn't dumped her ashtray out at the gas station. Probably was one butt she could have gotten a good toke from.

Sally scanned the tacky room. It reminded her of all the lonely nights in that hard apartment with William. All those dinners alone. All that waiting and waiting. Looking through windows for hours. All the cars going by, her ears straining hard. Waiting for his rumbling engine. Staying up half the night, smoking pack after pack, wondering when he'd pull in. She thought about all the crazy fights they had in that room. All the broken-up dishes, her clothes ripped in half, the big plates of food that got tossed at the wall. She played back the scene of their last blowout.

It was right after she let him move back in. She'd come home early and found him in the apartment with her coworker. They'd looked like two little kids, stuck in a crosswalk, right before a bus mowed them down.

"Shit," Sally said out loud. "I could sure use a cigarette now."

Suddenly there was a sharp rap at the door.

"Excuse me miss, but I just wanted to see if you needed anything before me and Leon closed the office down for the night. I'm fixin' to go get some fish up at Rusty's. Wanted to see if you wanted some. You was looking kinda hongry when you checked in."

Sally peeked from the hole. Edmond was right there. She could see the hard hairs poking from under his dingy shirt. She could hear Leon's thick, angry cough.

"No thanks," she said through the door. "I need to get some rest. I'm really tired. Thanks for asking." She checked the knob to make sure it was locked. She could see them both step back.

"Well a little shut-eye never hurt nobody. But you sho' don't need no beauty rest." Edmond laughed real loud at that. Leon stepped forward. Sally noticed a pack of Marlboros bulging out from his sleeve.

"Cigarettes," she said under her breath. The nicotine pull yanked her beyond the point of caution. Sally cracked the door. "Mind if I have one to puff on?"

"You can puff on two." It was the first thing Leon said. He

said it really slow. It sounded so sexy. His body was young. Strong and well built, but his face looked like twenty miles of bad road. He snapped the box open and shook the pack until one slid toward her. Sally pulled it out slowly as Leon brought a flame up to her face. His whole hand was a spider web of black tattoos. He had a fresh scar across his brow.

Sally didn't want these two men inside her room, so she stood in the doorjamb and eased the door closed behind her. "I don't like the smell of smoke while I'm trying to sleep," she said, stepping further out. She leaned against the door, facing her car. Her huge breasts gleamed under the moon.

"Where you from?" Edmond asked, taking out an old pipe and pushing some tobacco in it.

"Los Angeles," she said, blowing her smoke out rapidly.

"I knew it! You can always tell city folks. Spot y'all a mile away. Y'all stay in a hurry. Where you headed?"

"The Grand Canyon," she lied. She figured they'd make her out to be a tourist passing through.

"Yeah, I reckon we get a lot of folks wantin' to see that. Been out here nineteen years and ain't laid eyes on it yet. Ain't nothin' but a big hole, I hear. Lots of red rock. Folks line up for it all day. Standing there in the hot sun. Taking pictures and whatnot. Yesterday they said a lady fell the whole two hundred feet to the bottom. Got knocked straight off the trail by one of them loose rocks. Said her scream ricocheted for miles."

Leon almost smiled at that.

"So where are you from?" she asked, bored. Her eyes were on Leon.

"Why we from right here," Edmond said. "Never been nowhere else. Never wanted to go." Edmond adjusted the straps on his overalls and looked over at Leon. "He don't talk much."

Sally tossed her butt toward her tires. Leon flipped the pack open again.

"You might want one for later," Edmond said slyly.

Sally pulled two cigarettes out. She put one in her front

pocket. Both men stared at her heavy chest. She tried to close her jacket but she was so top-heavy, it flapped open again.

Leon jerked one of the beers from the six-pack. He handed it to her.

"No thanks, I don't drink," Sally said, waving the can away.

"Why not? Nothing wrong with a cool drink every now and then," Edmond told her.

Sally was trying to finish her cigarette. She wanted to get back inside. "I don't touch it now. Did though, had a little problem with it."

"Yeah," Edmond said. "If you keep messing with the stuff, nine times out of ten some kind a problem will come up."

Sally remembered her last episode. All the horrible crashing of glass. She watched Edmond drink huge swigs and follow it up with Wild Turkey shots.

"Never learned how to keep away from it myself," he said. "You married?"

"Kinda."

Edmond laughed heartily at that and even Leon, who looked like he never smiled in his life, looked at least less mean.

"I guess I'm kinda married, too," Edmond said laughing, stealing a quick glance at Sally's wide ass when she bent down to pick up some matches lying in the street.

"You can have my lighter," he said. "I got a bunch of 'em at home." Sally glanced up at him. She could see he was torn up now. There was a hint of delirium to his eyes.

"Listen, it was nice meeting you both," she said, stepping back.

"Wait now . . . you want some of this?" Edmond took a small package of crumpled foil from his back pocket. "Best weed around. Y'all can't get this in the city." He handed the package to Leon, who carefully rolled three fat joints.

It was really getting late now. Sally didn't want to spend one more minute with these two. And she wasn't about to blaze up in a parking lot in the middle of the night with some hicks. But

Leon took the large joint and lit the shit up, right there over the hood of her car.

"Well, I'm goin' on to Rusty's," Edmond said. "Whatchu want boy?"

Leon held up two fingers and said, "Kaafish."

"Catfish sandwich and fries?" Edmond looked at Leon a long time.

"Umm hum," Leon said.

"You be careful boy out here, boy. Don't want nothing like what happened last time, you hear?" Edmond walked toward a gray pickup. He hoisted his large body inside.

Sally got up from the curb, taking her last cigarette with her. She'd only planned to talk a few minutes to be nice. Her feet were getting cold now. She was ready to go back inside.

"Well, good night," Sally said to Leon, getting to her door quickly and slipping the lock shut. She watched him from the peephole. Leon was blowing the smoke out real slow.

Sally finally breathed out easily. She washed her face and hands and got into bed. She tossed and turned but couldn't sleep. She tiptoed to the door again. Leon was still out there. He was stretched across her car. One leg hung over her rims. His hand was rubbing his flat stomach. *Oh hell,* she thought to herself.

Sally cracked the door open. "You want to come in?"

Leon smiled and walked inside. He closed the door behind him. Sally sat back on the edge of the bed. Leon sat right beside her. He handed her the lit joint. She inhaled it deeply. It was some strong weed. Leon leaned over and picked up one of her black heels. He was rubbing his fingers over the shiny smooth leather. "You want me to put these back on?" she said sweetly, touching his wide arm.

"Um hum," Leon said. *Must be the quiet type,* she thought to herself. Sally got up and went into the bathroom. Her black slip was almost dry. She pulled it over her head and wiggled out from her jeans. She slid the pumps back on. When she walked out,

Leon was standing just outside the door, waiting for her. His shirt was on the floor. His slick chest was nothing but muscle. He picked her up and pressed her against the wall. She wrapped her legs around his slender waist, and he kissed her crazily, carrying her to the bed. He gently laid her down, covering her neck and breasts with his mouth. He was so tender and sweet. Sally ran her hands over his huge back and through his thick black hair. She could feel his belt buckle against her navel. He was grinding more rapidly now. With more fever. Sally playfully moved away. She wanted this to last.

Leon pulled her back toward him. He straddled her and started kissing her down her legs. When he got to her shoe, he pulled it off and tossed it across the room. He smiled big and lavishly sucked each toe. Sally moaned inside his bushy hair. She grabbed a handful and bit into his earlobes. Leon was bucking like a wild bull now. He pulled her slip over her neck. He grabbed her panties with his fist and snatched them from her leg.

Leon got out of his jeans fast. "Slow down, cowboy, I'm not going anywhere," Sally grinned at his naked body. He had the ass of a twelve-year-old boy. She squeezed it while he put himself inside her. He rode her a long time. Real slow. Groaning and going strong. He was breathing faster and faster. Suddenly he yanked it out and burrowed his head between her thighs. Sally thought she would die. Her whole body was hot. Her thighs were pure steel. Leon put it in again, slapping her wide hips until she couldn't hold back anymore. Her whole body jerked into a maddening spasm. Leon was making a guttural sound. The next thing she knew she was asleep.

Sally was half awake when she found him thrashing away again. He had entered her from behind. He was breathing real heavy, almost wheezing against her. He had her doggy style and she could smell the hard whiskey from his mouth. She went to grab his head and found he was totally bald.

It was Edmond. He was fucking her like a mad dog. She flipped over and all his weight fell against her chest. His heavy gut made it difficult to breathe. He pinched her breasts until she screamed. Sally tried to squirm from under him. She tried to roll over but she was pinned down. His wide thighs held her legs apart. Edmond bit hard into her flesh. Sally yelled in pain.

"Shut up!" he screamed.

He wadded a washcloth and shoved it in her mouth. She dug her nails into his huge back.

Just then, the front door flew open. Leon came across the room and grabbed Edmond off of her. "Sta . . . Sta . . . Staaaaaaap!" he yelled. But Edmond socked Leon across the face, tearing open his new scab again. "You trying to tell me what to do? After I raised your lil' ass! Your own mama don't want ya." Red blood poured down Leon's brow. He threw a punch at Edmond but missed. Edmond smiled wickedly at Leon and smacked him across the mouth. Leon looked like he might cry. "Sta . . . Sta . . . Staaaaap . . . it," Leon stuttered.

"That's right, start bawlin', you big baby! Ha, ha! What's that you say boy? Huh?" Edmond laughed in his face. "Look at you. Got the body of a man and the mouth of a two-year-old. Stammering and carryin' on. Can't say one sentence to save your natural life." Leon's lips started quivering. He was starting to drool on one side.

Sally looked at Leon. She had figured him for the quiet type. She didn't know he was simple.

Leon ran up and rammed Edmond with his head. Edmond snatched the lamp from the table and bashed Leon's skull with it. He fell to the floor and didn't move. Edmond looked crazier than ever. He came over to Sally and slammed her back against the bed. She squirmed with all her might and they both rolled to the shag carpet. The TV was right there in her face. The news flashed a story about a man found with his throat slashed in Los Angeles. An unidentified woman was shot with him.

". . . killed in his own home. Police are looking for . . ."

Suddenly Edmond's foot caught the TV cord and he ripped the set right from the stand. It crashed down and went black.

Edmond was laughing crazily and licking Sally's face. It was then she turned her head and she saw it, her black purse right next to her forehead. He wasn't holding her hands, so Sally stretched out her right arm and rummaged through the contents. She finally felt the cool steel. She took the gun out and blasted him in the face. She fired four times, until he slumped over.

Suddenly it was dead quiet. Sally held her breath. She could hear her heart beating. Her whole chest heaved up and down. Suddenly there was another sound, a scratching from behind the TV. She looked down and saw the gray possum dart underneath the bed. Sally grabbed her clothes and got out. She took Leon's Marlboros and both men's wallets. Combined, they had seventy-eight bucks. She snatched the large key ring and went to the front office, opened the cash register, and found another hundred and a half. She took all the candy bars and bags of chips. She got back in her car and roared off. Sally clicked the radio on.

"Manhunt for possible female murderer. Sally Jones has been missing for two days now. Her husband was found murdered in their Compton home."

Sally punched the lighter in and headed up toward the interstate. *Damn,* she thought. *In two days, I killed three people already. There has got to be a better place to live.*

Francesca Lia Block
Mer, from *Nymph*

She rises up from the water, the drops slicking her breasts, beading tremulous at her nipples. The curve of her hips sheathed tight in something sheer and silver, glimmering beneath the narrow swoon of her waist. She tosses her head and smiles at him; her mouth is like the shadowy place nestled under the fabric that he knows he can never reach. He lumbers across the grasping sand toward the water, his cock leading him, plunging him into the wet salt swell.

When Tom Mac wakes he can still taste the waves and feel his limbs rocking; there is a silver-green light in his head and he has a massive hard-on. He knows there was more to the dream but he can't remember, and after a few minutes his erection is gone.

Maybe I'll go out today, he thinks but he knows he won't. It has been too long already. It will only remind him of how it had been before.

He gets out of bed to take a piss and sees his reflection in the mirror—sandy-blond longish hair and tan bristly skin, the lines around his blue-green eyes. His body has grown thick and slow, the once taut bulging muscles losing their tone. What would Tawny say if she saw him now? That she was right. Right for leaving. That she could have predicted this—the ex-pro living in the house now overgrown with wisteria vines, drinking too much, hanging out on the boardwalk, never touching his board.

Instead of going back to bed he tugs on the shirt that smells the least—a hooded woven one from Mexico, a pair of shorts and *huaraches*. His heart is thumping as if he really is going back to the water—he knows he isn't. But he also knows he has to get to the pier before the sun and the crowds. He has to get out there.

It is still early and gray and damp. A mist hangs in the air, clings to his hair and skin, tasting of the ocean. *Sometimes it is like fucking,* he finds himself thinking for the first time in so long, when you ride the swell, feeling it folding around you glistening and wet and briney. And he can hardly remember either of them.

The boardwalk is almost empty. Later the vendors will arrive with their crystals and T-shirts and cheap sunglasses; the fortune-tellers and clowns and acrobats will come, the body-builders and Rollerbladers and tourists. But now it is just Sage and Whitman and a few of the other homeless whose names no one seems to know, huddled on graffiti-scrawled wooden benches. Even the surfers haven't shown up; the sea looks flat and steely. The cans are brimming with junk food remnants, pigeons are scavenging; there is a slightly toxic smell. Tom thinks, *And this is paradise, this is my paradise.* Remembering Tawny dancing to the drums right here that night with her breasts straining the bikini top and the tie-dyed sarong hanging low under her flat brown stomach. Her hair still crusted with salt and the way she always smelled like summer.

Tom buys five cups of coffee and distributes four to the men on the bench, keeps one, sips it even though it is still scalding, liking the feel of the burn on his tongue. Whitman says, "You up early, Mac," and Tom nods. Had a dream, he wants to say. They would probably understand. They aren't that much different than he is. Dreams, mostly forgotten, that keep you going when otherwise you might decide not to wake up again. And he is the lucky one, isn't he? Has the house to keep away the cold.

The house he'd bought at the height of things when he and Tawny first met, when he wanted a base in Southern California to return to between exotic wave-chasings. It is a small white

Craftsman bungalow with a glassed-in porch, big windows; the wisteria vine with its purple blossoms has grown so thick that not much light got in anymore. Tawny liked the wood floors bare and cool, the rooms mostly empty except for bed and pillows and boards. Now it is cluttered with shit and he keeps promising himself that he is going to do something about that.

Instead of going back he walks down the boardwalk with his cup of coffee. He draws up his hood because the mist is forming drops now, but he doesn't want to go home. The dream is still whirling in the pit of his stomach, making his muscles twitch, scratching at his balls.

The girl in the wheelchair rides toward him out of the grayness. When he sees her Tom MacDougal feels as if he has swallowed a mouthful of salt water and it is caught in his throat. There are beautiful babes all the time, everywhere at the beach, but rarely this. So beautiful that he hardly notices the wheelchair or that her legs and feet are wrapped in tight silvery fabric covered with half-moon shaped spangles.

As she approaches him, she smiles as if she knows him. Her teeth are white and sharp and her lips are stung, wet. He just keeps staring. Her eyes are crystal-green and wide-spaced. Her breasts show through her soaking T-shirt, every curve and swell and the tender dark nipples so he feels as if he is touching them. Then she runs her long slender fingers over her collarbone, the slope of breasts, lingering beneath them and pulls the T-shirt off. Rain spills in rivulets over her perfect brown body. *Perfect,* he thinks, *she is perfect*.

Crazy perfect, like him, alone in the rain, pulling off her shirt for a stranger.

He approaches her slowly, the way you would a startled animal, although she doesn't seem afraid. His voice is hoarse and soft. "You okay?"

She nods, still smiling at him. He tries not to stare at her breasts. They seem too big for her delicate frame, her waist so small and her ribs showing. "You'll get cold, sweetheart."

She shakes her head, swinging the matted blond dreadlocks that hang down to her waist.

"Do you need some help?" he asks her.

She gestures for him to come close. He can feel his cock stirring in his shorts. Smelling her, she is clean, salty. He wants to dive. Her nipples are erect; he wants to feel them against his lips. Everything tingling.

She reaches up and touches the side of his unshaven face with her finger, letting it slide down over his adam's apple. "Take me home with you," she says softly.

The whole impact of the night before is back, his penis throbbing. He takes off the woven shirt and gives it to her. "Put this on. You'll get sick."

She pouts slightly like a little girl but does it, getting caught so that he has to help her, trying to avoid touching her breasts. Her head emerges through the neck hole of the shirt, those eyes and that sly sweet mouth so close to him, that wild hair. "Take me home, Mac."

He figures one of the guys at the beach has told her his name. But still it startles him. And he wants to know.

Tom wheels the girl back up the boardwalk across the street to the house. He leaves the wheelchair at the foot of the porch and takes her in his arms. She is very light but also longer than she looks in the chair. Her lower body feels much more muscular than he would have thought, the tight weight of her ass against his forearms and wrists. Her long slender arms circle his neck the way a child holds on. He feels something like power returning to him, like right before he used to take a wave.

"This is a pretty house," she says, staring at the purple blossoms that have grown over everything. "It's like being underwater."

Sometimes I wish it was, he feels like saying. He puts her down gently on the torn couch, then goes to get her chair.

"Do you want to take a bath? I can give you a pair of pants." She laughs and shakes her head. "What about coffee? Or I think there's a can of soup somewhere."

She makes a little face and laughs again. "You look different," she says.

He squints at her.

"We've met? I think I'd have remembered you, sweetheart."

"It was a long time ago, Mac." She adds matter-of-factly, "You were unconscious."

Tom sits beside her on the sprung sofa. She plays with her hair, pulling the heavy knotty strands up off her face. She has very high cheekbones and a small firm chin, which makes her lips look even fuller. "What's your name?" Tom asks.

"Mer."

He shakes his head.

"Do you want to fill me in here, darling?"

Instead she smiles again and pulls his shirt off of her. She lifts her hands to her hair again so her breasts rise. The areoles are big and dark. He wants to hide his hard cock. She takes his tense hands in hers and presses them against her breasts. An electric shock goes through him at their breadth and smooth fullness. They feel soft and heavy and almost buzzing with sensation. She throws her head back and moans roughly as he fingers her nipples. Her whole body shudders, and she takes his head and gently draws him to her left breast; his tongue circles the nipple and her body is shaking more now. She leans closer to him, pressing her big succulent mouth to his neck. His breath comes in gasps and his heart pounds as if he is drowning. She moves over his rough, bare, sun-darkened chest with her lips. His cock feels huge, full of ocean.

"Who are you?"

She keeps going, looking up at him sometimes, smiling with those sharp white teeth that could tear; he gently touches the back of her head, the tender nape of her neck, stroking her. Her spine looks fluid and fragile. She undoes his shorts slowly, softly, her nimble fingers sliding the zipper down carefully to avoid his erection. Then he's out, big in her hand. Holding him she slithers back up and runs her tongue over his mouth, parting his lips with hers, sliding her tongue into him. The salt taste of his dream. He jolts up feeling her fingers move on his cock. She goes down again, this time her mouth on him, taking him in all in one slide so that he feels the back of her throat.

While she licks and sucks, her lips cupping the tender head of his penis and then swallowing him to the balls, Tom is remembering the dream. That time when he had the accident. What really happened. The waves pulling him down down. No air. Just this endless shining blue that he didn't really want to leave. He could have stayed there. He could have stayed. But then something was holding him; he knew he was safe. Rocking him like a baby. And her strong slender body carrying him back to the light, to the air. Because you belong here, she told him. I can't keep you. Even though you are the most beautiful of all of them. And you know my ocean more than any of them will ever know it. Tom moves with her, his groin spasming, his cock driving farther into her wetness. Suddenly there is that feeling in his balls. He doesn't want it yet but it is too much; he feels his whole body waking from some long sleep, as if he has been underwater this whole time and only now has she rescued him. He gasps for air as he breaks through the surface, his semen spurting out in milky bursts that she swallows, his cock still hard for a long time after, still coming into her lush mouth.

Mer stays with Tom MacDougal in the little beach house with the wisteria vine and the glass porch. No one knows what goes on in there, only that Mac has started surfing again, every day, up at dawn with the kids, taking the big waves, ferocious and fearless as he had been ten years ago. And that his mysterious young girlfriend in the wheelchair sits on the sand and watches him, that when he returns from the sea he plunges to his knees before her and kisses her as if she contains the breath he had lost that time he almost drowned. Maybe she does. People speculate as to how they fuck, what is under the narrow spangled sheath she always wears over her lower body. Some think she is crazy, playing out a fantasy so he can't get inside her. Maybe she'd been molested as a child or raped as a teenager traveling along the coast and that is why she invented the wheelchair thing and the costume. Others think it is real. But Mac and Mer don't care. His mouth on her tender, swollen, glossy breasts making her come when he caresses her nipples; her mouth sliding down the shaft of his thick cock, they rescue each other from land and from the sea again and again.

J. T. LeRoy
Driving Lesson, from *Sarah*

"**W**ell, I would like very much to have my own skirt of leather and my own makeup bag that closes with Velcro," I say to Glad.

"I can get you a big sight more than that," he says and thumps the table.

We start my training right away in the caravans back behind The Doves. I try to tell Glad I know what to do, that I've been with enough of Sarah's boyfriends and husbands that if they had paid me I could buy a gator farm. Glad tells me I have to unlearn bad habits learned by watching drunken whores, no disrespect intended.

"You have to learn to read a man and know when he's just lookin' for fun and when what he really needs is for you to hold him so he can cry his eyes out like a babe," he told me as we drank strawberry Yoo-Hoos and sat on custom satin-covered beanbag chairs. "You have to learn how to listen. There is medicine in that penis bone to help you learn how to love like a real professional."

I take daily lessons from various boys of Glad's, that affectionately refer to each other as baculum, which Glad tells me means "little rod" in Latin.

I practice rolling a condom on a man with my teeth without him knowing. I practice how to take every bit and grain of a man in my mouth. I already knew that one. I'd have contests with Sarah. We'd lay on our backs, side by side on some motel bed, with our heads hanging, tilted back over the side of the bed, till our mouths, esophagus and throat would all line up. Then we'd put in a carrot as deep as we could without gagging. We'd mark the carrot with our top teeth and after we'd see who is the better head giver. Sarah always won.

"You win cause you're older and bigger," I told her once and she slapped my face so hard I saw stars.

"Don't you ever call me old and big," she said and ran out crying.

I acquire tricks, like spraying Binaca on your right hand, so if a date is not on top of his hygiene, you can breathe in the scent of fresh mint from your hand and think of the snowy Alps instead of inhaling his ammonia scent and being reminded of a dirty Porta Potti.

I learn how to trick with men who want to dress in lacy frilly things.

"That's the most difficult one," Pie tells me. Pie was born a woodscolt—a bastard, and half-white on top of that. To his Chinese mother from a traditional Chinese family that ran the only traditional Chinese restaurant in the upper reaches of the Appalachian Mountains, it was a disaster. They tried to keep him hidden by making him tip long beans and slice bitter melon all day and night. All Pie wanted to do was be a Japanese geisha, and as soon as he was old enough he hitchhiked all over ending up in San Francisco. He came back home when his Great Aunt Wet Yah was dying. His Great Aunt Wet Yah was the only one who let him wear her silky undergarments and read to him from a forbidden book on the great geishas she had happened to possess. Wet Yah died and now Pie was working for Glad, saving up to move back to San Francisco and open his own geisha training school for men.

"You have to listen very carefully when you are with a man that wants to dress." Pie uses his hands while he talks, gracefully waving them back and forth as if he were icing a cake in the air. "He might only want to show you how nice he looks in his pink panties and discuss how much he enjoys the feel of the smooth material against his privates. Or he might want to be a lesbian and make love to you as a woman making love to another woman." Pie moves his body in a flowing S, making the silk of his kimono ripple so sinuously as to suggest two women making love. "Or the gentleman might wish to be called a sissy little pantywaist, teased, and otherwise humiliated." Pie shakes his hips and mimics a femmie boy. "You can often make extra by making the gentleman pay to bring in other bacula to laugh at him." I nod and scribble notes in a notebook Glad has given me.

"The gentlemen often do not tell you what kind of cross-dressers they are. You have to listen and take their clues." Pie sits down on a beanbag and looks at me studiously, the slight slant of his eyes accentuated by broad strokes of black liquid liner. "It is your job to figure out, do they want to pretend you are a woman completely, do they want you to be sweet and gentle, do they want you to be forceful and fill their hungry mouth, do they want abuse or gentle guidance? The faster you can figure this out, the more famous you will become."

And Pie is famous. Cross-dressers come from as far away as Antigua to see him. But I don't need to be told which boys are the best. All I have to do is look at the raccoon bone around their neck. The better the whore, the bigger their bone. I heard it said that the bigger bones aren't real, that Glad just melts waxed dental tape onto a small bone until it is bigger. I look at Pie's and it looks authentic. Big and genuine.

"You're ready for your first date," Glad says to me two months after I've started my training. I haven't lived at the motel room in a month. I stay at the caravans. Sarah took off with a rich crooked cargo inspector, and I check the room every day to see if she is back. The plastic attaché case is still gone, but her bubbles are still there in the bathroom so I know she'll come back eventually. I plan to have my own bubbles on the shelf next to hers by the time she gets back. "You think you're ready? You feel okay?" Glad asks as he helps me get dressed in a muted pink leather miniskirt I couldn't wait to show Sarah when she came home. "Ready as snipers at bull ball–cuttin' time," I say, borrowing Sarah's line. I put finishing touches on my makeup the way Sarah taught me. Glad makes me go light on the makeup though. I want to take an iron and straighten out my hair so it flows like floss, but Glad won't hear of it. "You should really oughten not to be wearing any. The natural look will make ya more lettuce then a face palette. Men pay for freckles and curls," Glad says and wipes up my face with his hankie. "Glad, you are a sight worse than a mother dressing her daughter for prom night," Sundae laughs. Sundae is a Texas honey-blonde with a bone bigger than Pie's. Sundae's specialty is cheerleaders. "You'd be surprised by how many football players want a cheerleader with cock," she says adjusting the miniature pom-poms in her hair.

Glad picked out a truck driver everyone knew. "He's a nice man that only wants to diddle you," Sundae says. "Remember to watch the clock on the dash," Pie says and gracefully kisses the air next to either side of my cheeks. "Good luck." Glad just wrings his hands and makes me feel nervous.

* * *

I walk, in the flat white Mary Janes Glad made me wear instead of the spike heels I wanted, out of the caravans with everyone seeing me off, past The Doves, and into the lower lit fluorescent nighttime of the overnight truck lot. The Nice Man's truck is right where Glad said it would be, five rows in and seven across. It is a plain truck, nothing special. No custom anything. The door is a dark blue and I can see my face mirrored on it. I squint my eyes so I can pretend I am seeing Sarah's reflection. I was supposed to tell the Nice Man my name is Cherry Vanilla, but after I knock and he says, "Who is there?" "Sarah" just comes out of my mouth.

At first I'm scared of the Nice Man. He reminds me of a New

Orleans voodoo priest, his eyes rimmed with a thick black tattoo. Then I realize after I sit on his lap a little and he talks to me in his near undecipherable Appalachian twang that he is just a laid-off coal miner. And it's true what they say, the dust settles in every crease of skin like a new layer of pigment.

"Started in the mines when I was ten," he says and places his charcoal-lined hands gently on my waist.

He is from Mingo County, West Virginia. Everyone in West Virginia, no matter how bad off they are, gives thanks that at least they don't live in Mingo County.

"I used to lie in the bed with my brother at night, while my Mama listened to *The Christ Cure* radio show and my Daddy sucked on a piece of coal to help his graveyard cough," he tells me while bouncing me tenderly on his knee. I thought about asking him if he heard my grandfather's sermons too, as his show came on not too long after "The Christ Cure" show and was very popular in Mingo County, but I remember what Glad told me about not getting personal about my life.

"It ruins the fantasy of who they want you to be," Glad had said.

"I do love Jesus," the Nice Man says and begins to run his hands up under my pink skirt and to my peach panties. "And you are such a sweet thing." I hope he will say the name I told him. I want to hear her name while his hands begin to diddle me. I close my eyes and let him rock me and caress me.

"Sarah," he finally whispers into my ear.

"I'm here," I whisper back, "not going nowhere." I let my eyes roll back into my head in pleasure.

Laurie Sirois
Orange Phone

I found a company in the yellow pages, called them up, and went to their downtown office for an interview, which was actually a form-filling session and a rundown of time sheet and log-on procedures. I already had the job, based on my initial phone voice, I guessed. The place was called Orange Phone, and the time sheets were pale orange. I was to work from home, logging on whenever I liked via the telephone keypad and marking the calls I got on the time sheets—but I'm not sure why, as calls were logged by the computer as well. I couldn't lie. I had to record a ten-second intro that would play in a menu of girls' voices for the callers, who would choose their favorite one before punching in credit card information. If it cleared, the call would be forwarded to that woman's house and would begin.

My instructions were to get a guy off in no less than four minutes, and no more than fifteen. For any time amount within that range, I got paid four dollars. That was it: four dollars a call. If the guy wasn't "done" at fifteen minutes, it was my job to cut him off and make him call back if he wanted more. (If I went over fifteen minutes, it didn't matter; I still only got four dollars.) So I would lie and say, "The computer's going to cut us off," at around fourteen and a half minutes and then just hang up in the middle of a sentence. I loved that, cutting off my own moans. It was my favorite part. "Oh, oh baby, you—" I figured if I got four calls an hour, it was double the wage of my day job. But for sex work, it was nothing. And, of course, because I had to be at home and wait for calls, it was hard to do anything else. So I didn't log on very often. The biggest check I ever got was for about eighty dollars: pathetic.

Somehow, I developed interactions with a few regulars who'd find me whenever I was on. I'd had fun recording my message: "Hi, I'm Eve. Tell me your fantasies, and I'd love to indulge you." My voice was deeper than the other girls' and my hope was to stick out from the crowd. There were usually only eight to ten girls logged on at a time. When I'd get a call, I had the choice to accept it or not. But there was this whole list of penalties—if I refused a call when I was logged on, I'd get docked one dollar. Or if a call was less than four minutes, same thing.

I almost always accepted calls, and this was my approach: we'd do introductions, during which I was generally asked what I was wearing and what I looked like. I'd make some shit up, depending on my mood, though usually I was the black-haired girl in nothing but underwear, touching myself. Then I'd say, "What's your fantaseeeee . . ." It was easier to work with whatever idea they already had in their heads than to make something up. A lot of times, the guy would do most of the talking, and I would moan and sigh. Real easy. I was never really naked or touching myself, though occasionally I'd get turned on. (At that point in my life, this disturbed me. Now, it wouldn't.)

I had one guy named John who would call me over and over for up to an hour at a time. He was great: he'd have a porno on his TV and tell me he was a director who traveled the states making them. He'd call me from "Atlanta," "Dallas," "Denver." He was probably just a businessman. But he'd say, "Listen to this scene. Can you hear it?" (I barely could.) "This is my favorite. I directed it; this actress is hot. Can you hear her? Does she sound hot?" and I'd moan and say, "Yeah, she's really hot. I love to listen to her," and wouldn't have to say anything else for a couple minutes while he got it on with himself and his pay-per-view.

But he couldn't get off unless I was on the phone with him. The voyeur needed a voyeur.

I heard from several men who picked my voice because I sounded bisexual. They all then arrived at the conclusion that I was willing to fuck them up the ass with a dildo. This dumbfounded me. Really, several guys made the leap from my voice to the dildo, all in their separate worlds, a synchronicity of thought. It was amazing, and I would fuck them all. A few men would also ask for my home number. A common misconception among johns was that what I really wanted was a boyfriend and not the money. One guy, Steve, would want me to talk him through jerking off, and I would dance with him around his cock, make him travel up the back of it slowly, make him thrust with his hips, then linger at the tip, then jerk up and down, up and down the shaft and he'd say, "You're really good at this. You sound like you have one of your own. Are you sure you don't have one of your own? You really know what you're doing."

One day I accepted a call from a person with a severe stutter. His name—I eventually got—was Jimmy. "I-I-I-I l-live . . . with m-my p-p-p-parents." He said, "I-I'm . . . s-s-slow." We had a little get-to-know-each-other session, and I figured out that he was almost forty and lived in Southern California. He wanted to know what I really did for a living, and by the time he got to that question, I had such a soft spot for him I wanted to tell him. I wanted to tell him I was a kid in San Francisco, trying to create my own life, but struggling with being poor. . . . But it was better to uphold the fantasy, I think, that I was just there for the callers' needs and that I waited for them and loved it.

Jimmy became a regular. It was great because his language challenge drew the calls out, and he'd call back three, four times in a session. He started to tell me more and more about his life. "My . . . b-b-b-broth-th-ther b-b-b-beats me . . . i-in th-th-th-th-the b-back . . . yard. . . . I-I-I-I'm worth . . . less. H-he kn-knows it." I was not able to hide my own concern, but I didn't want to play therapist, either, so I said, more cheerleader-like than parental, "You're not worthless! You're great!" And he'd reply, "N-no. I l-l-l-like it." I was starting to understand. "It t-t-turns me on."

Jimmy wanted me to abuse him, too. After we'd established a certain level of trust, he asked me to tell him to do things. "What kind of things, Jimmy?" "I-I-I w-want to h-hurt m-m-m-m-my-self." I was eighteen. I had a hard time being a creative S/M top, let alone knowing his situation. But he was paying me. "And . . . s-s-s-s-silly th-things. I-I-I-I-I c-c-can do s-s-s-s-silly th-things." "Okay, Jimmy, cluck like a chicken." "Wh-what?" I could hear in his words that he was smiling. "Cluck like a chicken, and jump around the room. You're a chicken." He put the phone down, slowly, and did it. I could hear stuttered clucks approach and recede, and it broke my heart. When he got back, he said, "I-I ha-have a ha-hard-on." "Touch yourself," I said. "I want you to touch yourself and cluck like a chicken. Keep clucking." This was a successful session. He had what sounded like a great orgasm, with these stuttered clucks. I almost cried.

Jimmy kept calling back, week after week, and it got more and more difficult for me. I'd make him tie fabric around his wrist until his hand turned blue, while he was jerking off. Or I'd make him slap himself. Or hold his breath. I was running out of ideas. I'd make him jerk off until he almost came, then make him stop and wait. He loved that one. His stuttering would get excited and almost fluid.

"E-eeeve. I h-h-h—have t-to a-a-ask you s-s-s-s-s-some . . . th-th-thing," Jimmy said one day, as soon as I answered the call. "Go ahead!" I replied. "W-w-w-will you t-t-t-tell m-me how to k-kill my-s-s-self??" He was quiet, waiting for me to respond. "Jimmy, are you serious?" "P-p-p-please . . . p-p-p-lease," he began to beg. Was he serious? Was this a fantasy of autoerotic asphyxiation? More of the self-punishment vibe? "P-p-p-p-please." "Jimmy, I don't want to do that. Let's do something else. Do you have a fantasy?" I asked. "I-I t-told y-you," he replied. That was his fantasy, but where was the line between a story and reality? I tried to soften the wish and told him to place his head under a pillow while he jerked off, knowing that as long as he could talk to me he was getting air. But he was persistent. "I c-c-c-could j-j-jump o-o-o-out th-the win-d-d-dow. I h-h-h-hate m-my f-f-f-f-family. P-p-p-please. T-tell me to j-j-jump."

How long had Jimmy had this fantasy? I tried to talk around it, but he called back several times in succession, and it became clear that he was fixated on wanting to jump. I was getting paid. Was this my job? Would verbalizing the command just give him a huge instant orgasm? Or would he jump out the window? I couldn't take the risk that he would actually do it. I just wanted to get him off at this point, I really did, and I was attached to him. "Jimmy. I'm sorry." "Wh-wh-what!" He said. He knew what was coming. "I'm sorry. I can't do it." I thought about making him call 911, encouraging him to leave his family and live on his own, telling him that he was valuable and that his life was worth having. "I'm sorry, Jimmy," I said again. "B-b-bye," he stammered, sadly, and I hung up. He never called again.

Robert Devereaux
On the Dangers of Simultaneity, Or, Ungh, Mmmm, Oh-Baby-Yeah, Aaah, Oooh . . . UH-OH!

I've related elsewhere the catastrophe that befell when, one Christmas Eve in the late sixties, the archangel Michael, entrusted with the whole ball o' wax while God was vacationing, inadvertently allowed Santa Claus and the Tooth Fairy to cross paths.

By no means was that the archangel's only screw-up. Michael was renowned for screw-ups. But his other major gaffe, which the heavenly host oohed and aahed and tut-tutted over for eternities afterward (though God proved kinder), came when he unleashed, by mischance, the Orgasm Fairy upon the world.

Before the ninth of February 1964, no lovers had ever truly had a simultaneous orgasm, which is to say, one in which amorous jet-fuel propels them at precisely the same moment along precisely the same giddy arc of glee. Michael, you see, had been given the crucial task of assuring unaligned orgasms, since God knew what would happen if two human beings ever experienced such a conjunction. So, around the clock, God's spy into the world's bedrooms tracked copulators (and those who, either through cross-genital stroking, or through mutual masturbation and the visual stimulation it brings, likewise approached synchronous derailments) to ensure that, if only by a hair's breadth, the sexual surge came upon them asynchronously.

For centuries, Michael's sneeze built.

His nostrils tingled as he knocked out of phase the oral bespurtments of Burr and Hamilton weeks before the lovers' quarrel which history—swallowing Hamilton's spin with as much zeal as Burr his sperm—ever after passed off as political in nature.

Michael's right index finger hitched to his upper lip even as its tip flicked toward Toklas and Stein, putting a hair fracture in what would otherwise have been a perfect union. No matter. The pink roses of their twinned mouths and vulvas bloomed with sufficient ooze and pucker that, by any measure, there was plenty of there there.

But the archangel's sneeze peaked just as the Beatles laid their first chord atop the screams of young girls on *The Ed Sullivan Show* and, far more germane to this tale, at the exact moment that Hap and Meg Osborne, de-pajama'd in bed—Hap's pud cuntily beslubbered as it jaunted in and out of his wife—went ballistic. Michael blinked into the sneeze, losing his grip on the groaning pair. In that instant, there came a-borning between them the Orgasm Fairy.

Meg had known her impending climax would be grand. It skittered upward like a megalopolis of skyscrapers rising in time-lapse photography. And when those upswept edifices began jutting and thrusting into the heavens, her detonations pounded out with increasing force. *Ka-boom! Ka-boom!! Oh-my-god-ka-boom!!!*

No perverts they, Hap did his sexual pushups as Meg lay quiescent beneath him, and the bedroom lights they kept of course discreetly off. But an eel-like phosphorescence now coated the air between them. It writhed and wriggled to the bestial gruntings in their throats, to the slippery lock of their loins. The form it took was female. Suddenly Meg and her husband were making love to it as much as to one another.

Worse, Meg found it absolutely delightful!

"Honey," she gasped, "what's—?"

"I don't (umpfh!) know." His words strained up an octave, no longer his deep baritone nor the above-glasses quip-voice of his Sunday-morning funnypapers snap, but rather the scranneled woe-ache that piped from Hap's lips whenever his man-gloop blurted out inside her. "Jeepers, I can't stop myself from . . . you know!"

Nor could she.

The ghostly creature between them grew a new face and soul-kissed both of them, her moon-slick tongue setting Meg's mouth afire with steam and sizzle. Her wanton touch thrilled their bodies in every secret place. Then she vanished, slipping away like sun-glints passing across the hood of a Chevy. But unending orgasm billowed anew even as she vanished, threatening swift terminal overload.

But lo, effulgence unexpected flooded their bedroom with spun gold.

"Be not dismayed," said a distraught angel, for angel he surely had to be. His eyes flitted from Meg to Hap to the wall their ethereal lover had hurtled through. "Pray excuse the intrusion, pardon the liberties, no time, we'll talk on the way."

It was as if the angel embraced them, still coming, and zinged them smack into the bedroom wall. They broke no bones nor did they splat, but arrowed straight through, cradled in the arms of their protector, sweeping past neighborhood homes and out into the night.

Their thighs rocked deliciously. The agony of sensory overload had vanished when the angel enfolded them. In its place, pure pleasure sprang up. "I'm Michael," he said. "We've got to . . . ah, but there she . . . damn!"

Moaning with love for Hap, Meg saw atrocity flash by: another bedroom, bright and tacky. Upon the wall, a sequined matador on midnight velvet thrust an estoque into an enraged bull's back. But what hurt Meg's eyes was the pair of lovers that reached out of a muddle of melted flesh on the bed. The woman was bone-thin, olive-haired, saucer eyed, her head atwitch on a stretched stalk. Her lover's mouth gaped, his shouts dopplering by as he struggled to free himself of their mingled putrescence.

"They're toast, alas. That's how you'd have been," Michael said, blithering on as they brushed treetops and sped through the night. "We've got to stop her before she mucks up the entire world." But what conceivable role, Meg wondered in among a continuing concatenation of body-explosions, could she and Hap play in stopping the Orgasm Fairy? For such was implied in the archangel's statement. He wasn't merely keeping them from turning into orgasmic pudding. She sensed, too, even as they hurtled over forests and graveyards and light-scoured highways, that Michael maintained his task of unsynching lovers all over the globe. Though his face was as calm as wisdom itself, his mind appeared to boast more facets than the eyes of a swarm of fruit flies.

Said Hap in mid-hump, "Isn't that—?"

"It is." They swooped down into an extremely well-known theme park, eerily quiescent by night. Outlines of idled rides evoked TV memories as they slammed down into a brick walk-way and passed along a brightly lit tunnel below.

Meg wasn't sure if her loss of breath came as part of her unending climax or because of what she saw next. Three huge-headed creatures, cartoonish above the waist, humanly naked below, were engaged in white-gloved prick-and-pussy stroking. At the tunnel's far end, an insane phosphorescence corkscrewed up into nothingness. Despite her orgasm, Meg giggled. Then she covered her mouth, at once aghast and aroused. Smoke rose from cotton fingers that caressed squirming thighs. Gloves caught fire. Yet Meg's childhood fantasy friends moaned with pleasure through neck-gauze beneath beak and snout, as below the belt they sizzled and flared.

Again the archangel swept Meg and Hap away, a swift smack upward past hums of fluorescent light, then a zoom into dark-ness. "We're gaining on her," insisted Michael as Hap gasped, "I love you." It was unclear whether he was addressing Meg, or the archangel, or both. Not that it mattered. It was all love. Every shred of life was love. Such was the message of this unending, unifying, edifying climax.

"We'll outfox her," declared Michael as they changed course, trebling their breakneck pace. Meg was blessed with a glimpse inside the archangel's mind. Like skate-scorings on ice, swift tangents etched along the hunted fairy's erratic track, sweeping beyond its obscure end into God-granted certainty.

The Pacific coast, California perhaps. A full somber moon silvered upon a sea of crushed grape. Upon a crag, there loomed a mansion. They burst through it into an opulent bedroom even as the creature they pursued did the same from the opposite wall.

On the bed, a zesty platinum blonde, nipples stopper-hard, rode the stickshift of a grimacing young stud, his hair as tossed and golden on the pillow as waves of wheat in sunlight. "Hang on," said Michael, sweeping her and Hap onto the mattress. Like streamwater sculpting boulders, they slid over the climaxing pair, melding with them, embracing them. The Orgasm Fairy, not yet halted in her mad career, slipped in among them. Meg and Hap kept coming, joining their gasps and groans with the couple on the bed. By God, the warmth and fragrance that rose from them! Meg's mouth tasted the ramping woman's left nipple as the man on whom she performed the buck-and-weave caressed Hap's unstoppable cock where it slipped in and out of Meg.

The archangel issued new directives to the Orgasm Fairy, which she at once obeyed. Meg didn't understand what he said, but the gist—an order to convert mayhem into benevolence—became one with the love the foursome shared.

It was absurd.

All Meg had learned about love in her thirty-three years told her that one needed time to know someone before sex meant anything at all. Not so now. Orgasm, precisely synched and blessed by an angelic presence, opened them up, brought out the best in them, made plain the divinity they shared, the unequivocal love that spilled out of them and into them. At last, their orgasm peaked for real this time, a tower of Everests high. They started an extremely long slow descent, wheeing and wowing like a quartet that Verdi had never quite managed to compose.

Michael gestured at the Orgasm Fairy, who at once vanished in a flurry of sparkles. Her loss devastated them all. "I'm sorry." The archangel was touched by their bereavement. "Sorry as well about—" but he didn't have to conclude the thought, for he had swept her and Hap up in his arms and was already on the move. The young man's pussy-prod slipped out of Meg's fist as her mate's own quim-pleaser de-vulva'd with a pop from the blonde's mouth, like an all-day sucker eased out to renew the joy of its insertion. Anguish warped the young couple's faces, an anguish mirrored, Meg knew, by hers and Hap's.

The archangel sped them backward along their route, soothing, cuddling, assuring them that all would be okay. And Meg felt the sorrow of parting from perfection, even as Hap and Michael embraced and consoled her. Their bedroom bloomed up about them. Aromas of arousal floated in the air, a delight and a torment: her arousal, and Hap's, and that of the unknown pair.

"Happy trails," said Michael.

"But how will we find them again?" Even as the words formed on her lips, he gestured above her nightstand where a paper wafted down like a feather, falling between her clock radio and her crook-necked lamp. Names in gold script, a phone number writ large.

"Wait!" cried Meg.

The angel halted in his swirl.

"Please," she said. "What's heaven like?"

Michael smiled. Just before he vanished, he uttered a soft single word. Meg couldn't parse it but it went straight to her heart. "Oh, Hap," she sighed. "We are blessed indeed."

"Yes, Meg," agreed Hap. "We are."

"Are you thinking what I'm thinking?" In her eye, deviltry glowed.

"You betcha!"

Together they leaped for the phone, laughing as they fumble-punched its buttons. The phone at the other end, in a California mansion by the sea, rang once before it was picked up.

As for Michael, he was ready to fall abject at the feet of The Lord, particularly since even God's toejam gives off an irresistible ambrosial scent akin to that of aroused organs.

But there was no need to grovel.

The Head Cheese beamed. The Orgasm Fairy's hands were busy beneath His robes.

God nodded. "Good work, boy. You wasted no time correcting your mistake. Five deaths is too damn bad, I'll grant you. But hey, it's a small price to pay for the emergence of this delightful creature. That's very nice, little one. Your mouth, please."

She complied.

"Besides, Michael, look over yonder."

Upon a nearby cloud sat the puddled couple, still puddled but blissed out. They were making goo-goo eyes at one another and squirming in the most heavenly of ways. One flesh they had become, united as blissfully as the androgynous creatures Plato had painted in *The Symposium*.

Next cloud over, the trio of lovers from that extremely well-known theme park were whole again, flames undone, their huge cartoon heads alive and integral to them. The sight pleased him. I wish I could describe them for you. But the aforesaid theme park and the exceedingly famous characters these three had once depicted—which now, in some peculiar way, they had become—are the intellectual (yeah, right, make me laugh!) property of a highly litigious and soulless corporation. Still, I think you can guess who they are by the shapes of their ears, the fuzzy grays, the bright yellows, the telltale hat with its telltale hue and ribbon, the eyelashed eyes. I have unshakable faith in the imaginations of my readers.

"Henceforth," said God, "I entrust the Orgasm Fairy with the task of ensuring that simultaneous orgasms don't happen. As she is so very talented, however, she shall be allowed to bring lovers of her choosing extremely close to simultaneity, to join in if she likes, and to give them unforgettable joy. Only the good ones, of course. The nasty, naughty, Godforsaken baddies—by which I mean the bluenoses; the intolerant blithering screwballs on the extremes of an issue; busybody anti-choicers; the so-called Christian right who are misguided miscreants all; soldiers everywhere who allow themselves to be duped by the murderers who appear to be in charge of their lives, but really aren't; dolts, bullies, short-sheeters, tireslashers, blasted numbnuts tailgaters, and others of that nasty little ilk—shall go straight to hell. Ain't no way I'll give those little bastards and bitches any pleasures worth the having."

Michael tried to hide his concern.

"Hey, pardner," said God, chucking him under the chin without moving from His throne, indeed without so much as uncupping His hands from the Orgasm Fairy's sweet pair of luscious, prick-sproinging boobies. "Cheer up. You done good. But I have other plans for you. I'm considering, maybe in five years' time, a sort of vacation. . . ."

And as God filled Michael in on what the archangel's duties would be in his absence and the Orgasm Fairy's head dipped like a feathered cuckoo-bird craning for water, a quartet of TV'd moptops, 'midst twists and shouts as hearty as sex itself, sounded their second chord.

Stacey Richter
When to Use

The most obvious time is after menstruation. But you'll want to use it other times as well—after nervous tension has left you not-so-fresh, to wash away contraceptive jellies or creams, check your contraceptive instructions first, after intercourse of course, this product is only a cleanser, not a means of birth control, to flush away built-up secretions that cause odor, or any time you want to feel clean and refreshed. Remember, this product is to be used for hygiene; it is not recommended as a method of expressing regret for joyless or ill-advised sexual encounters. It is possible, even with repeated use, that some women may not feel clean and fresh. Certain somebodies may look at themselves in the mirror after proper use and notice a halo of taint, an aura of having been "ridden hard and put up wet." If, for example, you've been doing it with a drifter in a parked car behind a bar, with your shoes up against the window, your pantyhose shackling your ankles and your bra pushed up into your armpits (and, furthermore, if you suspect there are a couple of guys standing in the parking lot, smoking cigarettes, drinking beer and watching—and in your drunken state you like this), then this product may be ineffective, despite the light raspberry scent. We recommend you discontinue use entirely if overwhelming sensations of guilt and humiliation ensue when your regular boyfriend finds out. And why would he find out? Because everybody *saw you* either leaving, sucking face or actually doing it with the weird, over-tan guy with the tattooed forehead, and of course all the products in the world will not restore you to "clean" or "fresh." A word about relief: This product does not support the idea of "do-overs," as when playing pool and missing the ball entirely, in which case certain women feel the right to call out "do-over" and shoot again without penalty of any sort. We consider this cheating. Therefore, it doesn't make it better if, on the night in question, your regular boyfriend was off "taking some time to think about things," which means, as we've learned in earlier sets of instruction, that he's off thinking about how badly he wants to dump you and start "seeing" one of your very stacked friends. Who knows? Maybe he would have stayed if you hadn't drunk-enly turned yourself over to the first unwashed mouth-breather who made suggestive comments about the shape of your ass. But it's too late, there shall be no do-overs, and you're destined to remain pathetic, manless and a known slut. You will be largely ignored by your social circle, with the exception of certain guys in shiny shirts who've begun to stare openly at your inadequate breasts. You may start to fantasize while walking or driving around, grief-struck and miserable, about a fresh, clean start where everything is suddenly crisp and blank, like bleached bed sheets, newly washed chalkboards, refinished floors—the ulti-mate do-over. These instructions have this to say about that wish: ha! You should be so lucky. Let's face facts, little lady. It's girls like you who force us to include warnings like Do Not Administer Orally. We're not going to let you out of this one that easy.

Gary Rosen
Champagne Tastes on a Crystal Budget

Derek always said he had champagne tastes on a crystal budget. I never totally understood that—whenever he got some money, he spent it on crystal, and if he got a lot of money, he bought a lot of crystal. But still, every time Derek emptied his pockets at night while he was opening the refrigerator, turning them inside out to show what he got that day, out would pop a square Ziploc bag of crystal, along with other junk—phone numbers of new pals, appointment times for dates scrawled on a matchbook, ink-line drawings of dying bodies with pustules mushrooming out from every piece of flesh, flyers for bands, etc. Everything else was thrown on the floor next to the bed, but the crystal bag was lovingly placed in his purple velvet drawstring drug bag. The little Ziploc bag was so small and elusive that it would attach itself to other things, or stubbornly cling to the bottom of Derek's pocket, or find its way to the inside pocket of his Levi's, etc., and Derek would turn the entire room upside down, figuring that the crystal had slipped out somewhere between the door and the refrigerator, and tear his backpack apart, even though he never put drugs in his backpack cuz he was afraid someone would take 'em while he was walking down the street. "Fuck!" he'd say. "I fucking lost it at New Dawn!" Or "That fucking Eddie—he stole my fucking crystal!" But then he'd calm down when he wrenched the little pack of matte white grains out of his pocket. He'd look at me and turn his bratty-boy face around like he was trying to feign ambivalence, even though he only had three looks on his face he could successfully pull off—a really happy grin, like he'd just been fucked in the ass by an ice cream cone with sprinkles on top; a don't-fuck-with-me look that simultaneously scared off and attracted scads of people; and a puffed-out-lip look in the middle of sex, like this was the most mind-blowing experience he'd ever had. He did the last one too well and too often for it to be real—I think he just created it for tricks, to make them think it was a really good blow job or something, and then his face just naturally made itself up that way during any sex. For a while, though, I thought it was just for me, cuz what we had was so special and all that shit, and it was one of the things that made me fall for him. But anyway, even if his face was kinda unformed and hardwired and could perform only three looks successfully, Derek still tried to show a range of emotions. The look he gave me when he finally found his crystal was one of them—an awkward, apologetic ambivalence, composed by lifting his eyebrows up, pushing his chin down, and extending the right side of his mouth like he had some kinda slow tic. This was his "I did something that was a little fucked up" look, and he got away with murder with it, even though nobody believed he was truly regretful. Derek wasn't sorry about anything he did. That's just the way he was: if he slipped on the ice and tripped his grandma for her last fall, he'd offer up the same look and take the money out of her purse. But nobody cared. That was Derek. "Got some more fucking crystal," he'd say. "What a shitty drug. I got champagne tastes on a crystal budget though," which was really irritating cuz he said it all the time, cuz he probably didn't remember he said it all the time, even though I told him, and cuz he fucked up the meaning of the cliché—if you got champagne tastes on a crystal budget, you buy the champagne, but you run yourself into debt, don't you? I don't know. I never bothered to really figure it out. It just annoyed me.

But that's just cuz I hated Derek for getting away with everything, for being so goddamned self-centered that you couldn't hold anything against him; he would never think of you anyway, so why not just give in. So what if he said the same fucking thing almost every day and he was a crystal addict—we were in San Francisco, what else were we going to do? Besides, I liked that he got crystal, cuz whenever we were pissed off, we could just do a little and I would get an instant hard-on. Derek put his hand on my cock when I first snorted crystal to see how quickly the stuff went to my groin. That's how he got me in the first place—picked me up at a vegetarian burrito place in the Mission and took me home one afternoon, threw me on the bed, took out his bag of speed, and held it out for me. We didn't leave for forty-eight hours. I swear. Two days in his little crappy Tenderloin studio where you could hear the drag queen's stomach upstairs struggle with bad shrimp or death throes—every thirty minutes we heard this explosion of diarrhea and then a toilet flush that shook the bed. We fucked—it was incredible—my body was a million Lite-Brites on at one time, etc. I was high on speed and sex and high on that pale bratty face in front of me that looked like he had just wiped a load of snot on the back of his sleeve, and high on all the mysterious Derek history around me—a picture of Derek on Polk Street, huddled next to a girl, that was taken for one of those trend stories on male hustlers; collages of Derek on a mountain top with angels and syringes hovering about him; matches everywhere, usually with a guy's name on the back of them, comics of grotesque, squat colorful figures fucking each other in the ribs and other exotic places; children's storybooks; teen boys and old ladies ripped from their resting places in magazine spreads and entwined together in languorous perversion; dirty T-shirts, etc. When he left to get more speed, I looked in his journal. Put one of his dirty white briefs next to my nose and took a whiff. Felt like the world had disappeared outside. Feared Derek would never come back. Convinced myself I should leave and get back to waiting for my unemployment check. Began jacking off. When Derek came back with more crystal, he got himself hard, started fucking me, rained a little crystal on my back, snorted it, then told me to switch and do the same. I couldn't get hard so I finger-fucked him and did the crystal from his back anyway. I moved into his place a week later.

Derek got me into hustling. I called it sex work because I went to college and lived in San Francisco, but he just called it hustling. He kept on telling me I'd be really good at it, that guys would like the tough-guy act I was putting on, that I could be a great top, that I could learn S/M and pull in thousands of dollars, that I thought I was better than him, that he was sick and tired of feeling like a slut, that if I hustled it would improve our relation- ship, etc. But my unemployment checks were still coming in, so I told Derek to fuck off; he got that don't-fuck-with-me look when we argued about this, so I knew nothing could stop him, and it was just a matter of time. A few weeks later Derek told me that his major trick, John (a john named John, ha ha), had spot- ted me walking next to Derek and really wanted to have me in bed. He said he'd pay three hundred dollars extra to have me and Derek in bed with him, so I did it. Derek and I did a little crystal, and we ended up at this megahouse in Twin Peaks with white carpeting everywhere, silver and glass tables, bookshelves, expensive coffee table editions of black-and-white male nude photo collections—the whole thing. John was allegedly a doctor who made a fortune selling drugs and prescriptions to users throughout California. Or at least that's what Derek told me. When John opened the door, I hadn't known what to expect, but it wasn't what I saw—an Izod and shorts over a surprisingly buoyant, round body. His hair was straight and thick and almost totally white, and he had that kinda gay face that somehow stays "boyish" until age one hundred or something. He was really friendly, but there was something cold in his eyes. John shook my hand and smiled at me like he had already fucked me a couple weeks ago and I'd loved it or something, like he knew something about me. John ushered us into the bedroom and asked us to get comfortable, got us drinks, and Derek started fooling around in bed. It was the same as when we fooled around at home after I got over the weirdness of it all, except every few minutes Derek would turn around and ask, "Is it okay?" or "Do you want us to do anything else?" or "Can you see everything?" John sat on his faux-fur–upholstered chair, his head propped up on his fist, totally impassive, like he was studying a particularly tough engineering problem. Derek and I were like arms and legs and an extra pair of eyes. When Derek yelled that he was getting close, John yelled out, "Don't come yet!" and got on his knees next to the bed. Derek pulled out of me and came all over John's face. Derek told me to do the same, so I did. John stroked us for a little afterward, his head resting on Derek's inner thigh; John was sitting on the carpet, rambling about getting another designer for his place. He wanted to make it more "California," with lots of redwood. Our come was glazing his face, and it dripped down slowly onto the rug. John went into the shower and Derek told me that we should leave, that John didn't wanna see us after he came out, so we walked out and grabbed six hundred dollars off the kitchen counter. Derek went back in—said he forgot something—then came out five minutes later.

It was my first trick, and I felt like—what—I had gotten over on someone, I guess, and thought Derek would like me more. I felt something—a heat, a high, a rush, but I never really savored the rush, cuz we hooked up with our dealer quick and abandoned the next week in a crystal ice storm. We fucked forever and spent the noncrystal money on Bikini Kill and Huggy Bear discs, matching nipple piercings, and a little silver Victorian coke spoon Derek had been eyeballing for months. I told Derek I loved him while he was fucking me one night, and then he took it as a mantra, spitting the words out in a whisper, over and over again, matching it with his thrusts until he shot in me. I asked him to keep his cock in me as we lapsed into sleep, and he did, but when I woke up, he was on the other side of his bed, and I was empty.

John paged again the next week and wanted both of us there. He told Derek he wanted us to play dress up—he had some kinda cutoff blue jeans fantasy, but we didn't have any, so we stopped off at one of the Mission thrift stores to pick up a couple pairs before we got there. John was a little pissed off that we didn't have the stupid cutoffs on, but his smile never flagged; it just got brittle, and his cold round eyes got a little slittier. Derek and I went into John's marble-and-mirror bathroom and changed into the cutoffs, and when we got into the bedroom, John was on his furry chair again, with no pants, slowly jacking off. He asked Derek if he had got the stuff, and Derek kinda grunted, extra surly, and fished in his pockets forever for the crystal. I didn't know about the deal—Derek musta been holding out on me, but he would have just told me that he forgot about it, so I pretended not to care. John grabbed his little hand mirror, like old Hollywood starlets have—gilded silver with lots of swirls on the back—and laid out a coke-size line. Derek told him that the stuff was strong, but John did the whole line, and then offered us some, which we did. John looked all crystalled out—like he was on the edge of some big discovery but couldn't quite get there. He told us to start making out, to take our shirts off, etc.—and then he told Derek to fuck me. I looked back while I was on my stomach to see John's eyes fixed on a spot in front of his face and his tongue rushing in and out of his mouth like one of those New Year's Eve noisemakers. When Derek and I shot, John snuck up right next to the bed and sprinkled his come on us. He went into the shower. Derek and I both dressed, and were gonna walk out, but John yelled for Derek to stay, so he did. "Dude, I gotta stay. I'll meet you at home," Derek said, with the shrug-smile he had nailed down.

I stopped in Castro Station for a beer cuz no one I knew would be at that shit-ass crystal-troll palace, then walked up Market, figuring Derek was gonna be there, but he wasn't. The crystal was still fucking with my mind, so I cleaned the whole damn place, twice, and even rearranged what furniture we had—which pretty much consisted of swapping the futon with the beanbag and moving the plants that Derek had bought when he decided he needed more nature in his life. Derek still hadn't come home, so I just stayed in, waiting for Derek to get back so we could hang.

Derek didn't come back for two days. I made three mix tapes, looked through my old journals, painted the ceiling of the bathroom silver, organized all of our CDs according to genre (punk, seventies, fucked-up experimental stuff, rap, etc.), and tried to write one poem for each of Derek's piercings—nose, eyebrow, guiche, belly button, nipple. Each time I finished a poem I was pissed off even more that Derek wasn't there, cuz I wanted him to come loping through the door while I was doing this stupid, romantic, literate thing for him. But he didn't come back until three or four A.M. a couple days later. I was drunk. I was pissed. We got into a fight. He said I wasn't his mother. He told me that John and he had spent a couple days fucking around, that he had bought him a couple hundred bucks worth of speed, that John was fucking crazy for him, that John couldn't get it up for the last day so he just spent the whole time jacking off his soft cock while Derek posed for him. Derek showed me the money in his pocket—seven hundred dollars—and said John wanted to take him on a trip to New York next week. I wanted to fuck around, but Derek was worn out—the last thing he wanted to do was deal with his cock. He spent a few hours in the corner drawing in his journal; one drawing was a skeleton fucking an ape. If you can imagine it, there was a lot of love in the drawing—the ape was kinda pouting—but that's where the warmth stopped. Derek wouldn't hug me or touch me or kiss me, and I jacked off in the futon, pissed that John had sucked all the play out of Derek.

Derek didn't sleep with me that night, or the next night, or the next night. I mean sleep in both ways—he didn't spoon me while we were dreaming, and he didn't fuck me in the ass. He was bingeing. I was pissed off at him, so I pretended not to want any crystal cuz it was getting on my nerves, but really I was doing crystal, just not with him. Derek didn't say much when he stopped home to change clothes or grab something to eat—just mumbled something about some trick up in Pacific Heights or hanging out with some bull dyke named Mikee—but I figured he had picked up a couple guys and fucked for days like he did with me that first time. Maybe it was the crystal—I had no evidence—just the acid inside me.

Then Derek's friend Jason overdosed. He was this kid Derek used to hang out with on Polk Street; he turned Derek on to speed, then moved on to smack. He died at his place down at Folsom and Twenty-fifth, just like that, he elapsed. Derek got the call when he was in the shower; he ran out naked, then just stood there with the phone hanging from his hand. We both went to Jason's apartment, just cuz Derek needed to do something, needed to see the body or the place Jason died, or whatever. We took a cab to the Mission, and I held Derek's hand, in between our legs, like we were trying to hide something from the world, or from each other. When we got there, the body was gone. Jason's roommates—John and Boa—were smoking cigarettes in the common room, talking about whether they could get into trouble with the cops, whether the landlord could evict them, etc. Derek wanted to leave—he hated those guys—and when we walked out, he told me that they had killed Jason, that Jason had quit smack a half a year ago, that Boa hated Jason cuz he had slept with John, etc. I thought Derek was crazy, that he just needed to unload, etc., but he kept on it and threatened to call the cops, wanted them put in jail. Then he got all silent. We walked all the way to the Tenderloin. Derek grabbed my hand, and I gave him my sweatshirt, cuz he was really cold. We sat outside our place on the steps, smoking cigarettes, and Derek got all serious, said he didn't want to die alone, said we should go up to Oregon and get out of the city, just live in a little cabin next to a river or something. When we got inside, we did some crystal, and we started messing around, but it wasn't sexual; it was to soothe each other. We just spread ourselves on each other like cream, and we kissed each other a lot. Derek looked into my eyes; his cold blue eyes had darkened a bit, and they seemed on the verge of tears. It was like an ecstasy trip or something—we felt each other's presences or auras ooze out of our bodies and share the bed with us. That night, Derek hung on to me harder than he ever had, closer than he ever had, burying his body in the twists of mine, and I caressed his arm, over and over again, like a piece of beautiful wood.

The next morning, Derek got up, lit some sage, and sat down and meditated. I had seen him do this before—the last time was the first week we were hanging out; he told me he had to clear his mind to see if we could live with each other—the answer was yes. This time he emerged out of a few minutes of Indian-style sitting and told me he wanted to quit hustling. He wanted to get a job, a real job, any job; he could do outreach for street kids— he'd already been offered the gig, he said. He told me I should quit, too, that we should both go straight, that if we really loved each other we'd do that for each other. He had that possessed, bulldog look, scrunching up his nose and furrowing his brow, willing his idea into existence.

He'd take a week, he told me, to finish up with his clients and save up some money, but that was it, and we should both start looking for jobs. I hugged him, and I guess I got this image of both of us helping each other to imagine something different, something beautiful, having the courage to change, etc. Derek had a mind of switches and knobs, while mine was all analog dial—he could just toggle something in there, up or down, and everything would change, in a second, permanently.

The first thing he did was go and get more crystal. He said he needed it to get through the week, that this was the most important week in his life and he had to be up for it, etc. Then he called up a few of his regulars and told them that he was getting out of the business—me and my boyfriend, he kept on saying, we're gonna move to Oregon. I guess he'd changed his mind about getting a job in the city—that's how I learned most of the stuff about Derek's decisions; he would never tell me. I'd just learn it when he told somebody else, like it was something he had figured out a long time ago.

That week went like this: Derek got a book on Oregon, decided he wanted to live in Eugene, gave half of his clothes and CDs away to friends, had a few dates, showed me the pictures he kept in a little shoebox in the closet, put crystal on his cock and fucked me, and bought a pile of crystal to get us through the first few weeks in Oregon. We went partying with his friends almost every night, mostly whores Derek used to hang out with, dykes he trusted, a couple of artist types, etc. Derek was saying goodbyes—one night he did ecstasy and everybody he ran into in the streets was suddenly his best friend; he held everybody's hands and turned eight years old, reciting slowly and precisely where they met and what memory he cherished of them, etc. It looked like he was really gonna do it, that we were really gonna do it— go to Oregon. That night, we stayed out all night, climbed up on top of this little cliff outside of the Castro, and looked at the little cookie-cutter domestic skyline that is San Francisco. It was way cold and windy—we had to smoke the pot.

We were at home watching *Pink Flamingos*—Derek loved John Waters, thought he was the most brilliant guy around—he had his own copy of the movie and knew all the lines. Whenever anybody wanted Derek to do anything political—like sign a petition or go to a medical marijuana protest or whatever—he'd turn them down and say, "Filth is my politics; filth is my life!" I thought it was cool and didn't figure out the reference 'til that night, when Divine makes her manifesto. Anyway, right after that, John paged. He wanted us to get over there. So we cabbed it, and we put those stupid cutoff blue jeans on in the cab, taking our pants off right in the back. Derek didn't wear any underwear—he dared me to suck his cock right there, and I did, cuz I'll do anything on a dare. When we got to John's place, he was waiting for us; he was real twitchy and couldn't stop moving his mouth around, crystal marks. I figured he'd been up for at least a day. John touched me and Derek all creepily, on the chest, moving down to the stomach, and then got all courtly, asking us if the house was too cold or too warm, if we wanted to listen to different music (it was some stupid Steely Dan), if we wanted coffee, if we wanted crystal, whatever. So we did a couple bumps of crystal and then went to sit at the glass table in the kitchen, while John moved back and forth from the cabinet to the countertop, making coffee. He was talking all the time—his medical office was being run by idiots; the nurses were all gossips, except for this one guy who was really cute and maybe raiding the stash of local anesthetics; he met this really sexy guy and did we know him; coffee is really his drug of choice, etc. Derek would say something back to John and roll his eyes to me like, "When do we get the fucking money?"

It seemed like an hour, but we were doing bumps of crystal, so in a very long five minutes, the coffee was done. By that time John didn't want it anymore and neither did we, so we just went into the bedroom and John told us to take our shirts off but leave the cutoffs on. He told us to start, to go on, and so we did. Derek's mouth tasted like it always tasted—tobacco and that bitter pharmaceutical crystal tinge—and we passed our chewing gum to each other during the kiss like a secret message. John jacked off his crystal-crippled cock and kept on saying, "Yeah, that's it," like bad porn. Derek pushed me on the bed and moved me on my stomach, like we usually do it. He started getting the lube out and smearing it in my ass crack, when John said, "Why do you always fuck him? Next time you're gonna get fucked." Derek kept on going but said, "There isn't gonna be a next time." John asked, "What does that mean?" Derek told him, "We're moving to Oregon!" John got up and stood right next to the bed, his soft cock peeking out from below the bottom of his shirt. "What do you mean you're moving to Oregon?" he asked. Derek pulled off of me and told him he was sick of this town and he was leaving. "When?" John asked. "Two days," Derek said, "going to Portland." I reached for a cigarette.

John told Derek that he didn't want him to go, that he needed someone to go to New York with him, and that Derek had already agreed to go. Derek said, "Yeah, well you never brought it up again." John said, "Well, I'm going, next week." I figured John was lying cuz why would he suddenly mention that he was leaving in four days and that he expected Derek to go with him? It was total bullshit. John said, "So, are you gonna come with me?" Derek said, "I can't, dude. I'm moving to Oregon." John sat back down in his faux-fur–covered chair, to get more leverage or something. He stared at Derek like Derek stood between him and 5 million dollars, like an obstacle to be surmounted.

"You can move after we come back."

Derek didn't know what to say to that; he squirmed a little and looked at me for help, so I said, "We've got everything planned," which we didn't. I didn't even know that Derek wanted to move to Portland until now. John was pissed. I'd never seen him like this—he pulled some strange authority out of his ass, like he was back in the doctor's office giving someone a prescription. "You've never been to New York, have you? But you want to go." Derek didn't know where to go now. He changed positions on the bed, sitting up against the headboard. "Yeah, dude, of course," he said. "So come and see it." "I don't know dude." "I'm paying your airfare; we're staying in a great hotel. . . ." Derek asked, "And?" John said, "And I'm giving you a hundred dollars a day spending money."

Derek motioned for my cigarette, so I gave it to him, and he pulled a drag. I still remember looking up at him while his lips were forming around the filter, waiting for his answer. Derek didn't look at me. He just looked straight at John and said, "Okay." John said, "Great," and then started working his cock again. "You guys should go back to work."

So I turned over on my stomach and Derek started fucking me again. I played dead. I left when John went into the shower, said, "See you at home, dude." Derek ran after me, playing dumb. "What?" he asked. "Is it about the New York thing? I've always wanted to go to New York. We can go to Oregon after I get back." But after that, he didn't say another word about Oregon. It was all New York—I'm going to New York, he told everyone he was going to New York; he started playing the Velvet Underground over and over again, etc. Every time I talked to him about Oregon his eyes glazed over and he changed the subject. John picked up Derek in a taxi at our place a few mornings later. Derek kissed me good-bye and told me he'd call, left, then came back and grabbed his baseball cap, then left again.

Derek did leave a message, from the top of the Empire State Building. He claimed to be calling from John's cell phone and said he could see all the way to our place and that I should close the window. When he got back into town, he looked like hell. Told me he hadn't slept in four days, that John and he had done all the crystal that was supposed to keep us in Oregon for a month, that he was sorry, but John had asked him to move in and was willing to pay him lots-o-cash just to live there, so he was gonna live there. I wanted to talk about it, but Derek told me John was waiting outside with the taxi, and he had to run—just wanted to pick up some more clothes. I said, "Wait! We gotta talk about this! What's going on? Are you living there forever? Are you giving up the apartment? What should I do?" He was running around, looking for something, and he said, "We'll deal with it." I turned into the spurned lover. I said, "I thought you wanted to get out of the business. I thought you wanted to live with me in Oregon." Derek was on his way out, but he turned before he reached the door and said what he always says: "Dude, I've got champagne tastes on a crystal budget. It's time for some champagne."

Lucy Taylor
Stiletto

The night was frigid and the coffee so strong you could use it to flush a carburetor. I sat at the counter of the L.A. Diner (That's Last America, not Los Angeles, by the way) and checked out the only other patron, a balding, thick-waisted guy sitting with his back to the wall, going over some books. Tried to calm my nerves by making a game of guessing how big his dick was.

I started with his hands, which were big, thick-wristed, and peppered with dark hair. Full lips and the kind of proboscis people usually buy in a dimestore on Halloween. And when he'd got up to use the restroom earlier, I'd noticed a cowboy jut to his pelvis, like he was either hauling some serious cargo or trying to give that impression.

I figured him for an eight- or nine-incher.

But what the hell, even though I was dressed for the possibility, I didn't plan on fucking Barney McGuire.

Not if I could possibly avoid it.

I glanced at the clock above the door. Ten after one in the morning. Not a lot of time to accomplish what I needed to.

Outside snow drifted past the window, small steady flakes that would add up to a foot or more by daylight. Detroit winters can be brutal. I was thankful to be wearing the full-length fur coat that I'd been nagging Donny to buy me next time he got paid for a smack shipment. He always said no dame needed such an expensive coat, but on a night like this, maybe he would've understood.

The counter girl, Myrna, was coming out of the kitchen with a pot of coffee in one hand and my breakfast in the other. There was a sway to her walk and a droop to her lids that gave her that freshly fucked look. Which, since her boss Barney was here doing his weekly accounting, she might well have been.

Long witchy-looking black hair, a valentine-shaped butt, tits that, from the two inches of cleavage showing at the neckline of her uniform, must be perched on some serious underwire. As usual, she was painted up like a ten-dollar whore—crimson lipstick, kohl eyeliner, gold shadow—and hobbling around in a pair of towering spike heels that gave a succulent jut to her ass.

I'd had the hots for Myrna since we both waited tables at one of Donny's nightclubs and sneaked opportunities to make out in the ladies' room when we could. Then I got a chance at better things with Donny and, not long after that, Myrna went to work for Barney McGuire. Funny, huh? Two nice Detroit gals ending up in the employ of rivals in the numbers, whore, and drug trade.

Myrna slid a plate of grease-drenched eggs and hash browns in front of me. As always, my eyes went to the pattern of raised red scars on the back of her wrists—reminders that Barney, like his buddy the Marlboro Man, had a thing for branding.

"So when do you get off work?"

"When Barney says."

"Which is?"

"Depends on whether or not he's in the mood for any dessert." She seemed to want to change the subject. "So how's Donny? He okay with you bein' here?"

"Donny don't need to know every time I take a piss."

Myrna shrugged. "Your neck."

She reached over and ran her hand over my fur with the mingled lust and timidity of a girl about to give her first blow job. "Mink?"

"Sable."

"Lucky girl. Donny must be a generous guy."

"He can afford to be. Every few weeks, he does a transaction, he takes in fifty or sixty grand."

She picked up my cup of coffee and refilled it. I reached for it just in time to let our fingers brush, nails clinking lightly together. Then I couldn't stop myself from glancing at the clock. Myrna saw me, and her scarlet mouth pouted up like maybe I'd hurt her feelings. Maybe she thought I had a hot date. Night like this, most people aren't in a rush to be anywhere.

I looked around the empty diner. "Weather keeping people home tonight, I guess."

She nodded. "Yeah. Everybody but Barney, I guess, but he's gotta finish the damn books."

It was common knowledge how grumpy Barney got if he had to deviate from any of his comfortable routines. Going over the books at the Diner Saturday night was one of them. Arty Cohen, Donny's right-hand man, used to say Barney would wait to take a shit if it weren't written down on his schedule.

"He's been checkin' you out since you got here," said Myrna. "You don't want him to hit on you, you better leave."

I sipped my coffee. I didn't care what Barney did, as long as he stayed where he was a little longer.

When I set the coffee cup back down, I let my hand stray across the counter and brush hers. She jerked her hand away and glanced over at Barney to make sure he hadn't seen.

"You know what, these eggs just ain't doing it for me this morning. What I really want is something hotter, sweeter."

Underneath the makeup, her cheeks actually darkened to a deeper shade of pink. "Jeez, Viv, this ain't the time. He'll kill us both."

"Nobody lives forever. Don't you have a storage room or a basement? And stop lookin' over at Barney, he'll think somethin's goin' on."

She giggled, scowled, and glanced at Barney all in the space of an eyeblink. "No shit, Viv. We can't. Barney, he don't like games if he ain't winnin'."

I was ready to risk scribbling something on a napkin or whispering in her ear when Barney yelled, "Hey, Myrna, what the hell's going on over there. Do I pay you to make out with my customers?"

Myrna jumped back like he'd jabbed her with a cigarette.

"Fuckin' broads."

He pushed back his chair and strode over to the counter. He was dressed like a banker who had a thing for Liberace. Nice suit, silk tie. Gold cigarette holder and a diamond big as a Chiclet on his right hand. Smile rehearsed and phony as a Fuller Brush salesman about to fuck the farmer's daughter.

Shit. It was almost one-twenty. I didn't have time for this crap.

"Ain't you one of Donny Marshak's girls?"

I nodded.

"He know you're here in my establishment?"

"Me and Donny, we had what you call a partin' of the ways. We're not so close no more, you know."

"He let you go? The man's a bigger dickhead than I figured him for."

"He got a short attention span, Donny does."

"So you're a free woman?"

"You could say."

Barney's expression went cool as a corpse. Like if he let anything show, his skin would crack. But I saw the tiniest, secret smile. Nothing you could even swear for sure was there. Like the smile of a man who's just seen his mistress across the room when he's got his wife on his arm.

He whisked out a card for Jules' Liquor Store and scrawled a number on the back. "Look, hon, I'm takin' off now before I get snowed in. You call me, though. Beautiful woman like you never has to worry where her next meal's comin' from as long as Barney McGuire's around."

I stroked the collar of my fur. "You don't gotta go right now, do you?"

He shrugged, looked almost embarrassed. "My daughter's gettin' baptized tomorrow morning. Don't wanna run the chance of missin' it, you know. Disappointin' her and her mama."

A kid? Funny, but I never thought of guys like Barney havin' kids. Not legit ones, anyways. Or going to baptisms, for God's sake.

"Hey, don't worry, though. I'm a man of my word. You want a job, doll, you got a place with me."

I imagined I could hear the clock over the door ticking. Like it was daring me to do something.

I put a hand on his lapel. "Before you go promising to buy the merchandise, ain't you gonna ask for a sample?"

"Hey, do I look like a guy who'd ask a woman to elope if I didn't plan to marry her?"

"I don't know. What does a guy like that look like?"

The bags below his eyes puckered with irritation. "Look, honey, Donny may go for pushy broads, but—"

I opened the fur coat and let it slither onto the countertop behind me. All I had on underneath was a garter belt and black stockings. I heard the sharp intake of Myrna's breath. Barney's eyes got big as my nipples. His gaze went to my tits, then did a quick up-down of my silk-clad legs and platinum snatch.

He glared at Myrna. "What you starin' at? This is between me and her. Go clean out the freezer. Scrub the john. You *work* here, don't you?"

I couldn't tell if Myrna's eyes were green with jealousy or if she was just pissed because he might get cum on the floor. If it was jealousy, that came as a shock. Barney was as sadistic a bastard as Donny. I hadn't known she cared.

Barney unzipped his fly, grabbed my hair, and shoved me to my knees. His cock sprang out like a party favor, not as outstanding as I'd guessed in the length department, but thick as a rolling pin. When I took him in my mouth, it was like trying to suck down a rolled-up copy of the *Detroit Times*. I risked a look at his face and saw his eyes. They were mean and greedy, like his cock. Full of venom and guile.

You don't work the streets, then become the girlfriend of a mobster, without developing a throat like a vacuum pump and a gag reflex so numbed-out you could swallow swords.

I knew I was doing a great job on Barney. His cock was swollen and stiff and he was ramming himself past my teeth the way men do when they're ready to come. But nothing was happening.

I came up for air. "What do you like, baby? Tell me what you want."

"Hey, take your time. Now that you got my interest, I ain't in that big a rush."

He pushed me down onto the grimy floor, my legs up over his shoulders, bending me back so far that I thought his cock would ram into my tonsils.

A door slammed and I got a glimpse of Myrna disappearing into the kitchen. *Good,* I thought. *Just stay there.*

Meanwhile Barney was fucking with workmanlike concentration, grunting and sweating and pounding away like a carpenter hammering nails with my feet in their four-inch stilettos up over his shoulders.

I thought how I'd been thinking about Barney when I'd gone into my closet to find that pair of silver fuck-me pumps last night. Shoes, everybody knew Barney loved shoes.

I leaned back and arched my pelvis so his cock popped out of me with a sound like a cork leaving a wine bottle.

Before he could reinsert himself, I pulled off one of my pumps, held it to my mouth and ran my tongue, long and strummingly, up the heel. Put the heel in my mouth, sucked on it.

Barney sat back on his ankles. Bug-eyed and unblinking.

I slid the saliva-slick heel up my pussy and twisted it around. Pulled the shoe out so he could see that the leather was shined with my juices, and popped it back inside. He licked his lips and squeezed his dick so hard that the veins on the back of his hand showed.

I bucked my hips and fucked myself faster. I wanted to look at the clock, I wanted to see if Myrna was still in the back, but to know either of these things would distract me, break my rhythm.

Barney groaned and clenched his jaw. He was one of those men who would split a gut before he made a sound during orgasm. Then his cum spurted forward, not onto my pussy or tits as I was expecting, but onto the bar stool where I'd been sitting.

He grabbed me by the hair and jerked my head up, positioned my face over the chair.

"Lick it up, doll. Get every drop or next time I'll cum on the floor."

Not exactly my idea of dessert, but I did what he wanted, lapping the pearlescent ooze while faking little noises of enjoyment.

"You wait here, baby," I told Barney.

"Where you think you're goin'? You don't go nowhere until I tell you to."

"I want to go find Myrna. Make it a three-way."

"Oh." He looked surprised that such an idea could originate from a woman. "Okay, then. Tell that slut she don't act nice, then I won't act nice, either. And believe me, she don't want that."

"Sure, baby." I paused just long enough to pick up my fur from the countertop and put it on. "Cold night, huh?"

"Make it quick. I still gotta get home."

I searched the back room, but didn't find Myrna, so I followed some rickety stairs to the basement. She was slumped on the floor next to a shelf full of canned goods. Tears tracked her face and smudged mascara blackened her eyes.

When she saw me, she grabbed a can of baked beans off the shelf and threw it at me. "You bitch, it's bad enough seeing you again after all these months without having to watch you fuck that scumbag."

I dodged another can. "Stop it! What's wrong with you? I thought you hated Barney."

"I do."

"Then—"

"What is this, your revenge because I didn't trot after you the minute you winked? What are you doing down here, anyway? Why aren't you with him? He needs cream for his coffee, tell him to jerk off in it."

"I told him I was gonna bring you back for a three-way."

"Are you fuckin' crazy?"

"I wanted an excuse to come talk to you."

"We got nothin' to say."

I reached over and tried to wipe away the tear stains. She pulled away.

"Fuck you, now what kind of game are you playing?"

"It's not a game. It's serious."

"Fuck you. I'm going back upstairs."

"No, wait." I grabbed Myrna and forced my mouth against her darkly painted lips. She tasted of mint and just the faintest aftertaste of Marlboro.

"Leave me alone."

I started unbuttoning the black plastic buttons on her uniform. Yanked her bra up and buried my face in her cleavage while I ran my other hand up underneath her skirt. She wasn't wearing panties—probably a concession to Barney's need for instant gratification. I found her clit and rubbed it with my thumb while I slid my fingers up inside her pussy.

"Don't you know why I came here tonight? I came to get you."

"What d'you mean?"

"Didn't we always talk about gettin' out of here? Going someplace warm? Maybe Mexico. Tahiti."

Upstairs I heard the front door open. Footsteps.

"Don't kid yourself. We'll be stuck here till the day we die."

More noise above us. A chair scraped back across the floor. Then shattering, as though a glass had fallen.

"What the hell is that?"

She started to get up.

"No! Stay here!"

I bit down on her nipple. She stiffened, gasped, and then relaxed. I hurt her just a little bit, then moved up to her ear, tonguing the lobe, exploring the folds and whorls inside while I moved my fingers up inside her cunt.

She started to lean back and thrust her hips against me. "Oh, God, Viv!" My first thought was that this was a comment on my pussy-eating skills, but then I saw her eyes.

I twisted around and saw the blood trickling down from the ceiling. First a single stream, then two more. The streams split as they slithered toward the floor, candystriping the grimy, pock-marked wall.

Myrna began to cross herself. "Holy Mary Mother of God . . ."

I put my hand across her mouth and we held on to each other, watching the crimson rivulets come down the wall.

When the front door shut, we waited a few minutes before we went upstairs.

They'd used silencers, Donny's boys, and they'd been right on time. One forty-five, just like Mac Cohen had said they'd do it when I told him how I'd walked into Donny's place last night and found him dead with one of Barney McGuire's calling cards up his ass.

"We can't let that fucker get away with this," Mac had said, and thank God he had meant it.

Barney's body was laid out across the table where he'd eaten his last meal. His face and chest looked like they'd been run over by a streetcar and then snacked on by vultures.

And then that little touch of humor—the heel of a silver fuck-me pump plunged into Barney's eye. Maybe even the same one I stuck up Donny's ass right after I shot him.

Everyone knew that Barney's trademark was a high-heeled shoe—in the eye, up the ass, puncturing a ballsack. Nobody in Detroit finds Donny Marshak with a shoe heel up his ass got any doubts that it was Barney McGuire done it.

"Come on," I said to Myrna. "My car's up the street. We gotta *go.*"

"How? Where'll we go? We don't have any money."

I squeezed her hand. "Hey, would I ask you to elope if I didn't think I could support you?"

I drove. Even wearing a fur coat, with nothing else on underneath, I was starting to get cold. Detroit winters can be brutal, but then, so can Detroit dykes.

Donny hadn't understood why I needed a full length fur, but on a cold January night, holding Myrna's hand and knowing the coat was lined with fifty grand of Donny's money, it went a long way toward warming my heart.

Anne Tourney
Ropeburn

This place is still raw, the channel between my thigh and pussy. Pink, moist, and rickracked by the hairs of a ghost rope. When I touch the tender strip, the skin stings. The pain calls up a vision of a woman spinning naked on a long cord, her legs spread in a ballerina's arc, fingers grasping the highest knots. I can't reconcile that vision with what I've learned about Mary June. I don't imagine her as a suicidal woman, but a sexual one, with a fascination for the promises of rope.

A fascination like mine.

I went to Mary June's house to work through a dry spell in my Master's thesis. I told myself that I needed silence and distance, but what I really wanted was for time to stop. Two years of graduate school had taught me that I knew almost nothing about my thesis topic, the coiled intertwinings of rural American family life. Most of the roots in my own past had been torn, either by spite or circumstance. When I thought about the frayed strings that bound me to other people, I wondered where I had found the nerve to write about strangers' bonds.

I chose a town within driving distance of the university, a town known for its orchards of crooked apple trees. The house sat uneasily at the outskirts of the little community, leaning on its foundations as if it expected to be forced into flight. A long, scrabbly field separated the house and barn from the main road.

As I drove down the rutted path, I could see my landlady standing in the open doorway, her arms crossed over her chest. That stern silhouette sent a current of guilt rushing through me. It was a guilt I couldn't identify, hot and absurd, almost like a backwash of someone else's shame. She frowned at my tank top and shorts as I hauled in the books that would keep me company that summer.

"Didn't expect you to bring a whole library," my landlady said. She lead me through a spartan parlor—I had an impression of yellowed lace and sepia shadows—and down a narrow hallway to the bedroom that would be mine. I set my box of books down on the floor. Dust rose in a soft exhalation, as if I were being welcomed by a restless spirit.

"Maybe I could store some of my books in the barn."

She shook her mule-gray head. "The barn is full of rusted machinery. You'd get tetanus just looking at that mess."

But when I glanced out the window, I saw light spearing through the cracks in the barn's wall boards, suggesting that there was open space inside.

"Has this always been a guest room?" I asked.

The room's former occupant had left no imprint; all sensual memory had been stripped from the room. The paint on the windowsills had flaked away, and the wallpaper seemed to have been torn off the walls by hand, leaving only a few shreds of yellow fluttering against the plaster.

It's only twenty-five dollars a week, I reminded myself. For twenty-five dollars I could tolerate bleak decor.

"My girl used to stay here. My boy stayed in the one opposite." With a jerk of her head the woman indicated the closed door across the hall.

The words "girl" and "boy" threw me. Was my landlady referring to farm help, or to a daughter and son? I tried to imagine her spare, hard body carrying children. I felt like I had some kind of responsibility, as a would-be sociologist, to ask about her life, her family, but her severe words invited no curiosity.

"No visitors after dark," she said. "And no drinking." Then she left me.

I had the dream on the very first night, the one that would wake me almost every night I spent in that house. The dream was always a step ahead of my consciousness, jumping out of my grasp whenever I tried to remember it. But I know it recurred, because I always woke up in the same state: paralyzed, bound. Feeling absolutely alone, yet strangely safe because of my enforced stillness. Once the fog of sleep cleared, I wondered what was holding me here in this room, which offered no sensory comfort, no release from its emptiness. I wondered why I didn't just leave.

On many nights I heard the woman of the house turning fitfully in her own bed, as if she shared my doubts. The floorboards would creak as she padded down the hall to the bathroom, then the heavy porcelain toilet seat would clink as she sat down to relieve herself. I could hear the sounds her body made, hear her sigh, hear her splashing water on her hands. Sometimes I wondered what would happen if I walked out into the hallway to meet her. If I opened my arms to her, would her stony flesh soften against my body?

Days in my room were dim and airless, like abandoned mine shafts. I spent hours watching the stretch of blowzy weeds that lay between my window and the battered, naked barn. The structure was broad and tall, with secretive windows set high on its peeling face. One afternoon, when I was exhausted from not working, I sneaked out to have a look. The landlady watched me from the kitchen window, probably thinking what a nosy fool I was. The gravel bit into my bare knees as I crouched down and peered through a crack in the door of the barn, but when I saw the interior, I forgot that small discomfort. I almost forgot to breathe.

The barn was as empty and as numb with light as a church without pews, except for a woman who hung, naked, from a rope on the ceiling. She drifted like a trapeze artist, her thighs curved around the shaft of the rope, her head thrown back. Her vulva was opened coarsely by the rope's weave, her damp lips sucking the thick strand. With one graceful surge she lifted her body, cunt clinging as she rose, and whirled slowly in the pillar of a sunbeam. The tips of her long, barley-blond hair tickled the cleft of her buttocks, and my own skin tingled in sympathy. As I watched, she played games with the rope, made love to it, licking and caressing the cords. Embracing a knot at the base of the rope with the soles of her nude feet, she bent and straightened her knees in a sensual plié.

The sight of that slow-motion, self-loving dance was agonizing. I wanted to feel that rough, prolonged friction, too, all along the velvet canal that started between my breasts and ended between my ankles. I wanted to arch backward like her, arms fully extended to hold my weight, head flung back, eyelids flickering under the dust that trickled down from the eaves.

Who was the woman? On my few trips into town, I had never seen her. Even if I had, she might have been disguised as a shy country wife, or an overpainted cocktail waitress. I watched her face flush, her muscles tighten. As she reached the orgasm she thought was private, her body quivered all along its length like a bow after the arrow leaves. Ashamed as I was for watching, I could hardly stand the excitement of it. I wanted rope between my thighs—anything between my thighs but my own fingers, which were no substitute for the shock of strange contact. I closed my eyes, wondering if the rope dancer were a sign of pure craziness, but the vision was still as tangible as my own flesh when I looked again.

The woman's shoulders sank, her entire body trembling from her come. My trance ended. I scrambled to my feet and raced back to the house. In the kitchen I collided with my landlady, who had been lingering over a sink full of dishes while I watched the spectacle.

"There's someone outside," I panted. "Someone in the barn." My face went hot, as if I'd participated in that intimate dance.

The landlady stared. In her eyes I saw myself being measured. "No one has been in that barn for nine years."

"But I saw a woman. A woman about my age, with long blond hair. She was hanging on a rope—"

The landlady's face crumpled. A moan leaked from her mouth. The glass mixing bowl she had been drying fell to the floor, bounced once, and cracked.

"Leave my house," she hissed.

Mumbling apologies, I fled.

* * *

Still flushed from the erotic dance I'd seen, I was too full of heat and longing to realize how deeply I had shocked the woman. I didn't know what to do with my desire. I wanted to find someone to pound it out of me, a crazy man, to fuck me till my pulse finally slowed. I had come to that house, to that slumbering town, to finish something that I had to do in order to become someone better. In four weeks I had written almost nothing. I'd given up ambition as easily as a healthy habit.

I wandered up and down the town's main drag all afternoon, stopping at a pool hall near dusk. There was only one other female in the bar, a mountainous woman whose bosom spilled across the table where she sat. A shot glass rested, thimblelike, between her breasts. A lean man, maybe thirty-five, sat beside her. His face was unexceptional until he smiled at me. I saw in his eyes the light I was looking for, a glint of dementia, the shimmer of stopped time. I imagined that face rising up from between my spread thighs, saw that mouth devouring me like a jackal. He beckoned to me, and I sank into a seat at their table.

"You from around here?" The man leaned closer as he spoke. His skin smelled of wind-dried sweat. His eyes were as pale as new nickels against his brown skin.

"I'm just here for the summer. I'm renting a room at the farmhouse on Mullen Road."

"That was Mary June's place," the woman said. "Did you hear that, John?"

Instead of responding, the man got up and went to the bar. He returned with a glass of amber elixir, which he offered to me.

"Who is Mary June?" I sipped the whiskey. Heavy and smooth, it plunged straight through me, making my cunt tingle from the inside. The man called John had long sun-gashes down his tanned cheeks; I wanted to trace those salty grooves with my tongue. His lean hands caressed his beer bottle as if they were entertaining ideas of their own.

"Who is Mary June?" I repeated. My voice came thick and slow.

"That's the wrong question, honey," said the woman. "The question should be, who *was* Mary June."

"And what's the answer?"

"A pretty girl who died of shame."

"Women don't die of shame. That's crazy."

"It sure is," John agreed. "It's crazy and wrong. Mary June never felt a moment of shame in her life."

"Did she have long hair? Blond?"

"Blond and shiny, like grain piled up in the sun. All the way down to her waist. Sounds like you've seen her."

"I couldn't have seen her if she's dead."

"Why not?" John shrugged, as if the dead had as much right to make themselves seen as anyone else.

"I don't believe in ghosts."

"I didn't say you saw a ghost. Maybe Mary June just left a piece of herself for someone to find."

I made a scoffing noise, a snort that made me sound bolder than I felt. A cold awareness was spreading across my skin. My body knew Mary June's story before I had even heard it. My body had experienced her climax on the rope in the barn. My body did not care if the girl who did that rope dance was a flesh-and-blood mortal, a hallucination, or a phantom.

As I was absorbing what John had said, one of his hard hands came to rest on my thigh. His fingers slipped under the fuzzy hem of my cutoffs and tugged at the edge of my panties, which were still sticky from the memories of that bewildering vision in the barn..

"Come for a ride with me, and I'll tell you who Mary June was." John stood up, his hand gliding along my leg. Mesmerized, I stood up, too.

The woman swayed in drunken clairvoyance. "Careful, honey," she cooed. "You don't even know who he is."

"Who are you?" I asked, my caution blurred by desire.

John grabbed my waist with both hands and pressed the length of his body against mine. The interweaving of his muscles reminded me of the strands of a leather whip. He bent his head to whisper in my ear, and his smooth lips grazed the lobe.

"I'm the local expert on Mary June," he said, with a softness I found both startling and sweet. "You might even say I was her brother."

* * *

Mary June used to sneak out of her bedroom while her mother was watching Johnny Carson and take long rides in men's cars through night country, headlights off. Mary June wore short chiffon skirts that flew up around her waist in the spring and stuck to her thighs in the summer. Her panties she either left in her laundry basket back home, or balled up under the seats of her lovers' cars. Cars were her favorite place to fuck, her legs spread in a reckless V while her lover bucked inside her.

She always laughed while she was making love, even when she was coming, as if she were trying to make up for the silence she kept inside her mother's house. Eventually that laughter drove the men away, and her lovers spread the rumor that Mary June screwed like a mad hyena bitch. Only her brother knew how to make the laughter stop.

Mary and John arrived at the farm on Mullen Road on a summer day, just before harvest time. Two weeds plucked from a foster home, the girl and boy held hands as they confronted the woman who would be their guardian. Though they were not related by blood, the children were joined by a rope of coincidence and desperation. The girl was named Mary, the boy John. Both had been assigned the surname of Smith. To escape the anonymity of their names, they had added their birth months and became Mary June and John March.

When the children weren't working on the farm, they invented games that involved one kind of prison or another. Mary June loved these games. Something about the farm made her want to play that way, seeking places in the woods where she could act out her dreams of being bound in coils of rope. She became a prisoner of the Martians, of evil cowboys, or—her most cherished fantasy—of a corrupt county sheriff. The threat of law pleased her, gave her a sense of ritual and weight.

As she and John grew older, familiar games turned strange, and the rope took on a life of its own. John learned how to make Mary June moan, even cry when the pain was especially sweet. But pain became a weak substitute for the contact that Mary June really craved. None of the horny boys in their muscle cars could do for her what John March could do—if only he would let himself enter her. The rope was the only thing that kept her from forcing her foster brother to do what she wanted.

Even though he refused to touch Mary June's berry-ripe nipples, her swollen pussy, John was the only one who could make her cunt dissolve in a shuddering meltdown. All he had to do was watch her peel her flimsy dress off, then wrap her nude body in intricate knots. Tighter, tighter he pulled the rope, until her tender flesh burned. When she lay on her back in the deep woods, her wrists and ankles bound, Mary June never laughed. She was paralyzed by an arousal edged with fear—fear of wild animals, of other men, of the possibility that John might leave her there with her fear and desire and no place to put them.

"There's no blood between us," she pleaded. "We're only brother and sister by accident. Why can't you just get inside me?"

"It's an accident that the whole town believes in," John March said. "If you want me to make love to you, you'll have to leave with me."

But Mary June would not leave the farmhouse. Although Mary June had never called her foster mother "Mama," a bond had grown between the two women that John March would never understand.

* * *

While he talked, John March drove me through the humid night. His hand found my thigh again, dipped down to the silky hot-patch, and rested there, cool and hard. We rode past the orderly shadows of the orchards, past the farms that lay beyond them, to the place where the woods began. He stopped where the road stopped and helped me out of the car. My knees were wobbly, my shorts slippery from the pleasure his voice had been giving me. The darkness swelled with an outcry of frogs, the occasional warning of an owl. John led me through the trees. I couldn't see anything but the white curve of my outstretched arm, but he somehow recognized a trail and knew where it ended.

"Strip," he said hoarsely. "Strip like Mary June did."

I stumbled out of my shorts and giggled as my arms tangled in my T-shirt. John stood behind me, watching me twist out of my panties. I held my hands together behind my back so he could tie the rope around my wrists. He pushed me to my knees and tied my ankles, too, with the rope running upward to encircle my neck. A mosquito landed on my breast and pierced the wrinkly skin of my nipple. I flinched. The rope responded instantly by squeezing my throat.

"Hold still, prisoner," John whispered. His chapped palms cupped my breasts, gently squeezed. I moaned, but I was afraid. If I moved, the rope would strangle me. I thought I could hear Mary June's ghost-breath in the darkness, and I understood why she hadn't laughed. The hands massaging my breasts grew rough. I whimpered. The rope was already chafing my wrists. I wasn't aroused anymore, only frightened. When I heard John unzipping his jeans, I panicked; my body jerked, and the rope tightened around my throat. For a moment my breath left me. When it came back, I screamed.

John knelt beside me, gripping me by the shoulders. "Shush, shush," he murmured into my hair. When my muscles were soft again, he untied me, but the sensation of the rope never left my skin.

"How did Mary June die?" I asked.

But John wouldn't tell me. Instead he described the time Mary June revealed that she had learned how to do something extraordinary, something she'd seen herself doing in a dream. John told me how Mary June's body looked, slim and golden, when she performed what she called her "circus act" for him in the barn. He watched her, his cock leaping inside his jeans while she twisted on the rope in a spectacle of aerial freedom, bellowing like Tarzan one minute, soaring like a Balanchine dancer the next. When she came down, they tumbled into a hot rut, all haste and gratitude. After they had dozed awhile in the August light, he turned her over on her back. If he could make her come over and over again, he thought, until she couldn't speak enough to protest, he could carry her off the farm. But just when he had teased her with his tongue until she was as weak as a new lamb, so limp that he could have lifted her with one hand, their foster mother found them.

John March was driven out of the house. Mary June was allowed to stay, but she was no longer free in any sense. She hid in her room, door locked, while her mother called her vile names through the keyhole. The foster mother knelt down the way Mary June used to when she was sucking a lover's cock, but instead of hot love coming through her lips, there came icy words, words that froze her daughter's blood. Without blood, there was no desire. Without the rope, there was no freedom.

"I'm not going back to that woman's house," I said.

"You don't have to go back," said John. "One thing Mary June never learned was not to stay where she wasn't wanted. She could have left with me. But she wouldn't leave that woman."

"What finally happened?"

John was silent for a moment. "Mary June hanged herself. Our foster mother found her out in the barn."

"Hanged herself," I repeated softly. Now I understood why I had shocked my landlady so deeply. I had seen an enchanted creature dancing on a rope, but my landlady had remembered a suicide. "Was it really because of shame?"

"There's no way Mary June was ashamed. She was proud of the way she was. Proud of her pretty titties, her sweet-tasting pussy. She didn't care what people said."

"Why did she do it, then?"

"How can anyone know? No one knows but Mary June. All I've got to go on is a theory."

"What theory?"

"Mary June hanged herself because she was somehow tied to that old bitch—more tightly than she was ever tied to me."

John's voice trembled. He caught himself before it broke.

* * *

This time John tied me differently. The rope snaked around my wrists, knees, and thighs, but left my vulva exposed, its lips spread like split fruit. I shivered as a night breeze sucked at my inner flesh. John's tongue was hot when it dove into the cleft. *I don't know this mouth,* I thought, but it didn't matter because Mary June had known it. His tongue searched the whorls of my cunt, hunting my clit, and his fingers gripped my thighs until I felt bruises blossoming. As I squirmed, the rope burned my skin. John slid upward. His face gleamed over mine, predatory. I felt his cock drumming against my belly, but when he slid into me, I wasn't ready for its girth. I screamed again—not with fear this time. My instinct was to clutch his back with my arms and legs, but they were bound. I was nothing but open mouth and open cunt, taking the beating of his chest against mine.

"Just lie there," he muttered through clenched teeth. "Nothing else you can do."

Nothing else. Was that what Mary June thought, the last time she felt a rope against her skin? I could see her with that rope, alone in the barn, the weight of the body minimal compared to that of her sadness.

I wasn't anything like Mary June. When I came with that crazy man, I forgot what I was like at all, but there was no sadness in me. Only burning pleasure under fiery skin, and the thunder of all my captive pulse points. The more I struggled to fulfill my come, the longer it was delayed, until the climax turned into a slow, swollen river. My lover bit my nipple, forcing me to peak. I screamed for the third time as his cock hit my core. I couldn't clutch his back, couldn't raise my head to bite his neck—I went crazy that night from not being able to seize him the way he seized me when his body turned iron in one heartbeat, and his shout silenced all the wild things in the forest.

When you're tied like that, your will is taken away, and your accountability. You're roped to your desire. You can't turn away from it any longer. There's nothing else to turn to.

* * *

In the morning I returned to Mary June's house. I didn't have a choice. My books were there, and my notes—all the small things that made up my life. When I saw the house from a distance, standing at the end of a sere stretch of brown land, I thought its frame was leaning even more dramatically. The structure wasn't preparing to flee, as I had first thought: it was ready to collapse. For the first time I noticed all the remnants of farm life that surrounded it: the empty barn, the ramshackle livestock pen, the unidentifiable skeletons of broken tools.

I tried to imagine how two orphaned children would have seen the place when they first arrived. An abundance of space and life, a host of animals to care for, and at the center of all that, a woman who might be won over if the boy and girl could figure out how to open that padlocked heart. I could see how the farm might have thrived for a while. With the children's help, the livestock would have grown fat, the small crop of grain would have flourished. But when Mary June left, taking her heathen sensuality away from the earth, the land hardened itself against the old woman in the house. The livestock sickened. Wherever life had proliferated, it withered.

My books, papers, and clothes lay heaped in open boxes in front of the farmhouse. One of my lacy bras lay on the gravel, embedded in the rocks as if someone had ground it down with a sharp heel. My books had been thrown into the boxes face-down, splayed open so that their spines had cracked. I know the woman in the house was watching as I unpacked my things, brushed away the grit, and repacked them. I saw the flicker of her hand pushing back the curtain in the parlor. I took my time getting my books stacked just right, my clothes neatly folded. I picked up my bra and blew the dust out of the lace eyelets with careful puffs of breath. I hoped she would think of Mary June as she watched me. When I was done, I stood up straight and stared at the parlor window until her shadow finally backed away.

* * *

I'm in the car now, driving back to campus, to my old life at the university. I have all four windows rolled down, my thighs spread so that the breeze blows down the hem of my short cut-offs, licking the secret raw space. In the seat next to me lies the rope John March gave me. It's coiled like a Celtic symbol, its ends disappearing in the endless loop. The patterns of its strands are etched on my skin, as meaningful in their random crosshatching as the intersection of lovers, mothers, siblings.

This is my Mary June rope. I imagine it's the same rope she used for her slow, spinning dance in the barn. Who's to say it's not? The strands keep their dusty secrets wrapped up tight, but I learned some of those secrets from Mary June. How desire can hold its opposite; how captivity can bring you more freedom than you thought was possible.

The sun's angle shifts. The frayed rope turns golden.

Jane Smiley
From *Horse Heaven*

What she could tell when he was taking down her hair, and then unbuttoning her jacket and her blouse, was how many years he had spent with horses. His gestures were smooth and consistent, and once he had his hands on her body, he kept them there. But they weren't eager and hungry; they were quiet and reassuring, warm, dry, and knowledgeable, as if he could find out things about her by touching her, the way he would have to do with horses, the way, perhaps, he would do with Laurita tomorrow, running his hands down her legs looking for heat. His touch, in fact, belied the look on his face, which was disturbed and eager. His touch was almost idle. When he had his hand on her neck, she felt him probe a little knot there, press it and release it, the way her masseuse did, then move down to her shoulder, and do the same there. It was as if no degree of desire could interfere with his habit of taking care. They had been naked for ten minutes when she spoke for the first time. She said, "I bet the horses like you." Eileen, who had been lying curled on the bed, jumped down and went under the bedskirt.

"They seem to, actually."

"You have a nice touch."

"I get along well with dogs, too. Though Eileen hasn't really made up to me."

"And you don't get along with . . .?"

"Owners, maybe."

"Al likes you."

He looked her right in the eye. "Oh, they like me all right. I don't like them."

Rosalind threw back her head and laughed.

"And I don't get along with my wife."

"Is that why you look sad?"

"No doubt. Do I look sad, then?"

"You do to me."

He sighed. "I've been afraid it would get out."

"You looked happy after the race. Well, not happy, but excited. Almost happy."

"I was almost happy. Closest I've been in a pretty long time. She's a bombshell, that filly." Here was where Rosalind fell in love, because Dick had a whole different smile for this filly when he thought of her, a whole separate category of secret delight that crossed his face and pierced Rosalind for some reason she didn't begin to understand. She had been looking for mystery, hadn't she? Well, here it was.

Even so, they could still stop, get dressed, turn back. Their friendly conversation and her laugh showed that. In the atmosphere of the room, there was some levity, some detachment, some pure friendliness that they could build upon to get out of this. Rosalind knew it. But instead she put her fingertips on his lips and ran them gently around, a multitude of her nerve endings tickling a multitude of his. And then she leaned forward, letting her hair fall on his shoulders, and kissed him.

Maybe he wasn't getting along with his wife, but it was obvious that he had gotten along with her fine at some point, or with someone else, because his knowledge about what to do with Rosalind was instinctive and expert. First, he took her face between his hands and very gently and attentively ran his thumbs over her eyebrows, the planes of her cheeks, down the line of her jaw, bringing them to a rest upon her lips, where, after just a moment, he put the tips of them into her mouth. She could feel him touching her tongue and the inside of her lips. Then he smoothed that moisture into her cheeks and chin, over and over, until she was groaning. Then he ran one hand lightly down her throat, reminding her what a long and vulnerable throat it was. Then the other hand. Then he looked at her and kissed her, first just soft kissing, then firmer kissing, then tongue kissing, then gently biting her lips, kissing, biting, kissing, then kissing her neck, then biting, then kissing. Except the bites weren't bites, so careful and considerate were they, as if he were inside her skin and knew exactly what would be exciting and what would be painful. He bit her shoulders, left, then right. Meanwhile, his hands had found her breasts. Al's hands always happened upon her breasts as if he had never felt breasts before, but Dick's hands knew breasts perfectly well, and hers, it seemed, in particular. Pretty soon, but not too soon, his lips found them, too. She closed her eyes, because she didn't want to look at anything but his face now. His face was the only familiar thing in the room, and if she couldn't look at it, then what was happening in her body was too terrifying. Her body was already arching and shaking, but she wasn't orgasming. She was just responding to the lightness of his touch like iron filings to a magnet.

Now his hands moved downward, to her waist. She had not known the waist was an especially erogenous zone, but as he squeezed her waist and ran his thumbs and hands over her belly, she felt her whole lower body turn to fire, and sparks shoot out of her toes. It was as if there were some spot there, near her navel, that was sensitive and he knew it, he knew just where it was and how to activate it. She opened her eyes now and saw that his eyes were closed, and that, furthermore, she was participating unbeknownst to herself. She was rhythmically pinching his nipples, and he liked it. His hands fell away from her waist to her buttocks, and now he wasn't so gentle with her. He squeezed them hard, over and over, pinched them, too, but it didn't hurt. Always there was that quality in his touch of being unable to hurt living flesh. It was alluring, but, more than that, it was fascinating.

While this was going on, she opened her eyes again, and he was looking at her. He looked happy and fond. The look made her moan, because she didn't feel that she deserved fondness from him. Suddenly, and very very lightly, he touched her labia so that she cried out, and as she was crying out, he penetrated her, kindly but firmly, threw back his head, and closed his own eyes, seeming to pull her over himself as easily as a glove.

He penetrated her to the core, didn't he? He knew just how to do that, the way a racehorse knew how to find the finish line: wherever he penetrated her to, that was the core, and she felt it. He eased gently back and forth a time or two, and it wasn't so comfortable just then, but right when she was going to say something, or ask something, she got a wonderful feeling of moisture flooding her, and his penis turning to silk inside of her. She said, "What was that?"

And he said, "Sometimes it takes a moment or two for the foreskin to slide back."

"You have a foreskin?"

"I do, indeed. I was born in Britain when my father was training horses there for some years."

"I'm sorry I didn't notice. I guess I was looking at your face."

He smiled.

But then there was no time for talking, only for probing more and more deeply into this feeling she was having all through her body of melting around him as he went farther inside of her, and just when she orgasmed, he covered her face with his warm hands and made her go where he was inside her and she disappeared.

About two, Rosalind got up and put on a robe, and went over to the window and sat down, looking out over the beach and the dark ocean. There were stars everywhere, even in spite of the lights below. She hunched forward in her chair and looked down, then looked out again, taking her thick hair in her hands, hair that was her lifelong friend. She twisted it into a tail and curled it around her hand, then took a pencil out of a container on the desk and pinned it up. At that moment, she was thinking nothing. You could have asked her to swear, and she would have sworn, under oath, that she was thinking nothing. That she was utterly at peace and blank, well fucked, Al would have said, had said from time to time, referring to himself as well as to her. She put her hand between her legs and smelled her fingers, smelling the both of them together, then wiped her hand on the robe.

What was it that did it? She thought about this long afterward, obsessed about it, even. What was it that switched her so suddenly out of that blank, satisfied state? Perhaps it was the knowledge that the care he had taken of her was impersonal, nothing to do with her, only a quality of his that he brought to everything, something she responded to, but nothing she could claim. And she hadn't intended to claim anything, had she? This wasn't about claiming, it was about investigating. Nevertheless, whatever it was, whether something she thought or something she saw when she turned her head to glance at him on the bed, her blank satisfaction dissolved once and for all into pure longing. All her powers drained out of her then and there, as lost as if they had dissipated into the stars, and tears began to run down her cheeks. Eileen emerged from under the bedskirt and yawned, then stretched, first backward, then forward, with slow relish. Then she espied Rosalind at the window and crawled over to her, low crawl, pushing with her short back legs and swimming with her elbows. Her head was up and her eyes were bright, and she made a funny picture, but she didn't even begin to relieve Rosalind's sadness.

Ernie Conrick
Backhand

Losing in the quarterfinals was the worst part of the U.S. Open. The next worst thing was that it all took place in Flushing Meadows, Queens—no comment necessary there. The next worst thing was that it was painfully hot. The next worst thing was that Oleg, my hockey player boyfriend, ignored me because his babushka was in town and he was ashamed to be seen with his seventeen-year-old blond *devochka*. I think that in English you would say that he has no balls.

But Mariana made up for all of it. I don't need to say a thing about her really, she was a legend in women's tennis before I even picked up a racket. I'm still not sure I like her, even after what happened, but I am sure that I do respect her for not giving a shit about being a six-foot-two-inch Slavic dyke when it was still hard to be anything but a proper lady. And I respect her for what she did for me—although that's fucked up in its own way, as you'll see.

Mariana is an intimidating presence, tall, tow headed, piercing blue eyes that look out from a severe brow and pointed eyebrows. Even at forty-four, her body is rock hard, or at least the muscles are. As for her skin, it's simply spent too much time unprotected under the sun, like all tennis players, and is leathery and tough like a hide, as if it had been skinned from her body, treated by a tanner, and then reattached. Nevertheless, a defiant sensuality shines through those forty-four-year-old wrinkles so that, even as I made a concerted effort to ignore her, I, on occasion, could not help but glance quickly at her from the sidelines and admire the knots of muscles on her calves, or the severe shadow of her jaw.

Of course, she hated me immediately. Rather I should say that she hated me in a very particular way that is unique to women, and possibly unique to Mariana herself. Whenever her eyes would fall on me either during a warm-up or in the locker rooms, I would feel a cold disdain, cold and hard like I imagined her heart to be. She got to where she was by a Nietzschean effort of will, and she could see quite clearly that I was where I was (financially at least) with the generous help of my figure, my long blond hair, my party-girl image, and the pictures of me on the covers of fashion and sports magazines looking kittenish, coquettish, and just plain slutty.

From my own point of view, the only people who complain about it are people who can't do it themselves, but I will admit that I've had more press coverage than the top ten women in the world, and I've never been ranked higher than twelfth. I don't blame her.

She first spoke to me as I walked off the court about two days before the Open. I was having a great day on the court, which bothered me, because I thought I would curse my game if I was too good during the warm-up. I feel better when I am less than my best until the day of the matches. Somewhere in my mind, I believe that you only get so many good games and you need to save them up for the right time.

"Your name is Anna?" she asked as I walked off the court.

I nodded but stayed silent.

"Anna Gramovitch?"

We both smiled weakly at each other. I rubbed a towel up my arm, across the upper half of my chest.

"Do you know who I am?" she asked, gaze following the rag as I slid it across the back of my neck.

"A variant rival to a man," I answered.

There was a pause as she drove her hard blue eyes into mine.

"Let me tell you something . . ." she leaned close. "Think more about your game, less about hockey players."

I rolled my eyes and headed for the locker room, but Mariana fastened an iron grip around my triceps and held me in place. "Gravenfort will eat you alive if your return is not better." She looked me dead center.

"*Spasibo,*" I said. She was old and ugly and retired and irrelevant. I ripped my elbow from her and walked away.

When the Open started I was a victorious tornado. I removed the much-acclaimed but slow and lumpy Gravenfort 6–2, 6–3. Next, I eked out a win over the younger Neptune sister, Valariana, with a perfect shot down the baseline, followed by a perfect backhand and a series of equally perfect serves (even though the press keeps claiming that I cannot serve). She pouted and looked at me like an enraged lemur, but I met her most irate behavior with professional sportswomanship.

The crowd naturally championed their faltering poster girl, but nevertheless, a vocal minority could not resist my golden charm and made their support known.

After my win (4–6, 6–4, 6–4) Valariana's father told reporters I was the product of a Nazi eugenics experiment. Despite these remarks, I noticed he never took his eyes off of the Nike swish on the front of my tennis dress. I suggested that perhaps she would do better next time if she would rid herself of those swinging braids, which surely affect her peripheral vision and make her look ridiculous. I even offered to braid her hair like my stylish coiffure, but this placated neither Valariana nor her rabid sire.

I was looking for Mariana after my victories to remind her that her prediction about Gravenfort had gone horribly wrong, but I did not see her either during or after the matches. I did see her once briefly in the company of Terri Fierce, that amazon with the prominent beak. I wondered what was going on there, but decided that I didn't want to know anyway.

My performance was faultless up to this point. I was in the quarterfinals and faced Christina Hinges, who was, in my opinion, a bit rusty, having been sidelined for six weeks with an ankle injury. Prior to this I had defeated her twice in a row. I fully expected to make cheese out of this little Swiss girl with my obnoxious forearm.

And so, the night before my quarterfinal match, when I should have been at the hotel resting, I was confident enough to accept Oleg's apologetic invitation to dinner. He was very gentlemanly, and obviously wanted to make up to me. Apparently his babushka did not like Ukrainians or some such nonsense. I really didn't give a damn what this old woman thought, but was irritated that he would hide me like that from his family. I was, after all, an international tennis superstar and sex symbol with millions of dollars in paid advertising endorsements. You'd think that the boy would be able to get around some fossilized prejudice in the old bag's head.

Despite his best efforts, our date was a disaster. If he wasn't talking about his mother or his grandmother, he was going on and on about his team's owner, some brain-damaged millionaire named Henry Quillgreen. According to Oleg he had taken most of the money meant for the hockey team and given it to a man who promised to develop barrel rides for tourists over Niagara Falls.

The long and the short of it was that Oleg might be traded to Calgary. When he said this I just looked at him. He must realize that if he moves to Alberta the most he will see of me is the pictures on the Gatorade bottle. I told him he could either make his peace with the Jew or forget about me.

"*Ach,* listen my little fish . . ." he said, leaning in close, ". . . I was just mentioning it to let you know what is going on in my life, that is all."

"Well, now I know."

"Don't be angry, Anna."

"How can I not be? You are such a disappointment."

There was silence for a long time. I drank a Vodka tonic, then two.

"Anna Petrovna," he sighed after a thoughtful puff on his cigar, "You cannot be unhappy with me for long. I have quite a gift for you back at my place, you will—"

"Then I must remain unhappy with you for a while longer, because I am not going to your place tonight," I answered firmly.

"Anna . . ."

While this depressing scene was going on I tried to forget about Oleg by sucking on my drink. I sucked too much and presently felt dizzy. The candles and the glasses and the Caspian beluga swam before my eyes. It was at that moment that I felt a pair of icy blue eyes on me from across the restaurant. It was Mariana.

I almost didn't recognize her at first; she was sitting with two other women at a table across from us wearing a long, sleeveless black dress, flat shoes, and a string of pearls. I chuckled to myself, thinking, "Who has ever seen this woman dressed like this?" At the same time, I must admit that, far from seeming out of place in her clothes, she had a gawky, long-legged elegance to her. The dress made her look even longer than she was, so that she seemed to grow out of the ground like a vine.

Catching her eye, I smiled at her and raised my glass. Her lips tightened around her teeth and her body seemed suddenly rigid, as if she were getting ready to leap right at my throat. I saw her mouth move as she said something to her companions, who looked over their shoulders at me and giggled simultaneously. Then she smiled widely and winked at me.

I took another draught of my Stoli. It all seemed amusing at the moment, to have two famous athletes both flirting with me at the same time; one male, one female. I smiled back at her.

As the evening wore on, Oleg became more unbearable. He wanted to know why I wasn't coming back with him to his apartment. The fact that I was in the quarterfinals of the U.S. Open was apparently not a good enough reason. It occurred to me that he didn't even take my career seriously. Unable to endure him for much longer, and far more buzzed than I should have been the night before a match, I excused myself while he asked the waiter for the humidor.

In the marble ladies' room I looked at myself in the mirror. I looked somewhat tired and sad. Most people do not know that one of my eyes is not straight, it looks off to the side a bit. Maybe this allows me to see the ball coming better, I don't know. But in the mirror it almost seemed as if each eye was connected to a different brain, a different personality, a different person.

I can only look at myself at one eye at a time, strange to say. It is always my straight left eye. This is my strong eye and it seems like the me with which I am familiar. My right eye wanders a bit away from my nose. I have to tip my head to look in this eye and when I do, I am not sure who I see.

My head throbbed. I loosened my braid and combed my locks with my fingers. I flicked some of my hair in front of my right eye so that it no longer looked back at me. That made me feel prettier. Then I played with the straps of my gown and the pendant that hung around my neck. Looking down I could see my cleavage and the slit in my skirt that ran up my thigh.

I once told an interviewer that my skirts were not shorter than the other players, it was just that my legs were longer. Looking at myself in the mirror again, I ran my hands from this slit, up over my pelvis and my tummy, to the spot right below my breasts. The papers were right: I was a gorgeous blond goddess.

I ran some water on my hands, then wet my cheeks and brow. I leaned over the marble sink into the mirror until I was inches from my own face. My thong nipped my pink anus as my haunches extended. "So this is what it looks like to kiss me," I thought. No wonder the boys pay so much attention. My single eye was captivating, luxurious, and intoxicating. My hair was coiled a bit and fell like flames over my chest, while my arms were supple and long, tan from the sun with tiny white hairs standing erect. I pouted my scarlet lips, then licked them with my shy tongue. Without even knowing what I was doing, I closed my eye and kissed myself.

The tip of my nose turned up, as my lips pressed against the cold glass.

"Mmmmmm," I said.

I stayed that way for a moment, my hips swaying back and forth against the marble sink top. Then my eye, my wandering right eye, saw through the falling strands of my hair, into the mirror, and around my shoulder.

Mariana was staring back from the mirror like a wraith in the shadows. She did not move.

I smiled shyly.

"Such a pretty girl," she said in her Czech accent.

"Thank you," I laughed, still leaning over the marble sink.

She slid up behind me, "If only you were not such a brat." And she slapped my ass; she slapped it a shade too hard for it to be a joke, and her hand lingered there without moving.

I straightened up and felt my buttocks tighten and sting against her wide, strong hand. Looking at us in the mirror I said, "I get paid to be a brat," and lowered my eyes.

"Not to me," she said in a low monotone, sliding her hand up to my lower back.

She pulled me toward her—or maybe I lost my balance on my heels—or maybe I just voluntarily settled back into her encircling arms. I really cannot be sure. Her arms were around me and all over me; she was all hands, like some Buddhist bodhi-sattva clawing at the Shakti on his lap. One hand was on my thigh, playing with the slit, another on my waist. A third hand slid up my side to my neck, a fourth cupped my breast, a fifth ran lightly across my nipple, and a sixth pulled at my dress. A seventh hand lifted my hemline several inches; an eighth pulled my hair with a tug so that my chin was forced up to a 45-degree angle. Her lips were rough and cold on my neck, like a hairy bug crawling leg by leg toward my ear.

I heard the door open from the dining room. Startled, I stared open-mouthed into her eyes.

"Please," I whispered.

She wouldn't have stopped unless I'd said something, I am sure of it. And the irony of it was that here I was, the bad girl of tennis, pleading with Mariana to not start a scandal. She had no reason to stop—what did she care, she never hid a thing from anyone. But she did stop for me and smiled almost awkwardly. When the door opened and two Japanese women walked in, she played like she was my older aunt helping me to braid my hair. Wisdom is where confidence meets reality.

The two girls came to the mirror beside and chatted in rapid-fire Japanese. Mariana winked at me in the mirror and squeezed my shoulders with her rough hands.

"Good luck," she said, and turning as if she were leaving a military review, she walked out the door.

When she had gone I looked in the mirror at myself again, this time into both eyes at the same time. I looked different.

* * *

Contrary to my expectations, it was a well-oiled Christina Hinges that showed up to the quarterfinals. To make matters worse, I had a hangover. It was the worst of all possible combinations. I felt as if I was playing in some sort of vacuum without air or noise. It was like an ocean of pain, where the crowd would roar, then hush like waves; and in the interim there would be a hard silence punctuated with my groans and Christina's girlish grunts. My returns were clunky, my backhand weak, and my serves inevitably missed the mark. I tried to salvage my game in the second set, but I could only concentrate for short moments at a time.

It seemed to me that the spectators rose on top of each other like layers of an inverted ziggurat. On top of the highest layer there seemed to be another layer, but this time of opaque entities of oppressive humidity called clouds. They piled on top of each other, up into the air, hanging over the rim of the stadium, looking down on us, pressing in on us like school boys trying to see a schoolyard fight. Lecherous little boys, looking and pointing and whistling and finally spitting—first one drop, then two, then a barrage of thousands, all spitting on me from above. They called a rain delay.

I sat on the bench during the interim, looking at the small squares of space between the strings of my racket. Olga, my coach, asked me repeatedly what was wrong. She told me to wake up and to stop dreaming.

"Are you in love, Anna Petrovna?" she asked.

I shook my head.

Somebody whistled in the crowd. "Come on, Anna!" yelled a deep voice. I turned my face and saw that it was Mariana. She was sitting about three rows behind, between her two companions from the previous night, and wearing the exact same dress. She clapped her hands twice and an almost involuntary smile tugged at the wrinkled corners of her mouth. It seemed to me that she was making fun of me, trying to sabotage whatever concentration I could manage.

In the next set I was so angry that I consistently over-hit the ball and faulted on the serve. Hinges was swinging like the doors of a whorehouse on payday. The coup de grace was delivered by the line judge who obviously hated me and called every shot for my opponent. When I protested, she ignored me, and the crowd cheered, as if it was just more entertainment for them.

They said in the paper that I refused to shake hands with Christina after the match. I don't really remember, but I think that perhaps it was Christina's dirty hands, more than my anger that made me pass her by. She should wash them more often. I have nothing against sportswomanship, but I am not going to get a disease just to be nice, the press be damned.

People would not leave me alone on my way to the locker room. They shoved microphones in my face and leaned in front of me, and Olga would not shut up. I just wanted to be left alone. In my dressing room, I asked Olga to please leave me alone, but she kept talking about my backhand as if I gave a shit. Finally I yelled and threw my racket at the wall. She may claim all she wants that I threw it at her, but she just wants to get on TV. Finally she let me be, and I cried on the carpet between the locker and the massage bench.

I didn't hear Mariana come in. I just heard her voice between sobs and heaves of my chest.

"You were not even trying, Anna Petrovich," she said, "you were thinking of something else . . . or perhaps you have been having too much fun."

I sat up. I hated her.

"You must really decide what you want to be," she said, "A champion or a party girl."

"You were there last night, too."

"Yes, but I am not playing today." She sat down on the bench in front of me, sitting on her hands.

"Is that what this is all about?" I asked. "You want to shame me? Does that make you happy, Mariana?"

"Yes, of course," she answered, with again the hint of smile that came from that borderland between altruism and cruelty.

I cried and lifted my hands to my face. She tried to pull me toward her, to press my head against her lap, but I shoved her away. She tried again.

"Go away," I said in a high and quavering voice, "what do you want?"

"For you to be a good girl," she answered, and crossed her arms in front of her chest.

"And how do I do that?" I cried more, to the point where I could not breathe. I wanted her to pull me to her, but she kept her arms crossed. I reached for her and my slender hands grasped her dress at the knee, then knelt forward onto her lap, between her iron thighs. I wanted her to touch me, "I want to be, Mariana, I want to be." And, sobbing, I wet the cloth between her legs.

I pressed my face to her lap, and she pressed her lap to my

face. My tears soaked her dress through, and then the cloth changed and it wasn't her dress anymore—and it was wet but not with tears.

I looked up at Mariana's face. Her eyes were fierce, severe, and wary. I lowered my eyes to her wet cunt. Her callused hand slapped her thigh sharply, like a ringmaster ordering his bear to dance. Looking up to her to make sure I understood, I pushed aside her underpants and felt her soft brown hair on my lips and nose. I inhaled deeply and took her scent deep inside me. For the moment, I forgot about tennis. To forget about tennis even for one moment feels like those first minutes after my braces were removed, so long ago. It feels strange and easy and finally natural.

As a thirsty pet rodent taking a drink from a water bottle moves the metal ball with its tongue to release the moisture behind it, so I lapped at Mariana's wet cunt. She stood, and lifting her dress with one hand, ground her softness into me from above. I inserted my tongue and, curling it upward, probed her moist, pelvic void. I imagined that every time I licked her, my tongue caught drops of her greatness.

My lips found her hooded clit and I placed it between my teeth like a champagne grape. I sucked her clit, gently flicking my pink tongue in a horseshoe-shaped swish around the hood, then back again; wax on, wax off.

She enveloped my face with her iron thighs so that my next breath must have come from deep inside her. I licked and licked and licked her wet cunt. I closed my eyes and tongue-fucked her with lightning quickness over and over again until my face was awash in her juices. Mariana's hips bucked against my tongue, trying to escape, but I pushed forward and pressed my lips desperately against her swollen labia.

She shoved me from her half-gently. I looked into her eyes and she still had the same fierce expression.

"Lift your arms, Anna," she commanded. When I complied, she removed my tennis dress with a single motion so that I was naked on the floor before her, nipples hard, my pale white haunches that turned to brown thighs, and my downy blond hair between my legs, wet and heavy. While her cold blue eyes appraised me, I unbraided my hair and shook my head so that it fell on my spine and tickled me.

She knelt in front of me so that our knees touched. Her rough hands traveled up my legs to my waist. She kissed me once, lightly on the lips and then . . . crack!

She slapped me, not playfully, hard with the back of her hand. I was not expecting this and was stunned for a moment. Angry, my brows knit and I tried to rise. She pushed me down again.

"Stop it!" I squealed like a kitten, trying to rise again. Her thick arm caught me and I spun around as I was pushed toward the locker. Behind me now, she curled one arm around my waist and hooked my ankle with hers in a grapevine such that I could not rise.

"Stop it!" I repeated, "get off of me!"

"Shhhhhhh," Mariana whispered, "shhhhhhh."

I tried to rise but could not. When I felt her fingers work into my pussy and wiggle inside me I was furious.

I screamed like a girl.

"Shhhhhhh." She added another finger.

I yelled again and tried to rise, my hips inadvertently pushing against her. I bucked.

"Shhhhhhhh, be good," Mariana purred, as she finger-fucked me.

I screamed again, but softer and lower.

"Shhhhhhh." She slapped my ass hard with her free hand.

My screams were no longer really screams.

The door rattled and I could hear Olga's voice on the other side.

"Anna, are you okay?" she asked.

I meant to say, "Help me, I am being attacked!" but all I could manage was, "Olga!"

"Anna, open the door," Olga yelled.

I meant to say, "Help! She is crazy!" But Mariana's hand kept moving in and out of me and she kept whispering, "Shhhhhhhh" into my ear, and I didn't say anything.

"Anna, do you need help?" Olga yelled. Mariana yanked my hair so that my head jerked back. She finger-fucked me hard and fast.

"Anna! I am going to break down the door!"

Her fist entered my hot insides.

"Go away, Olga!" I yelled.

"Anna!"

"Shhhhhhhhhhh."

"I am okay, just go away, Olga, go away!"

Olga went away.

"Shhhhhhhhh, good girl," whispered Mariana, fisting me.

I shuddered and cried; hips and hair flailing. Mariana's fist slammed into me over and over again until I didn't know what was happening. I came so hard that I was almost unconscious. I didn't hear Mariana leave and she didn't say good-bye.

* * *

After this experience I decided that it was, perhaps, time to end my affair with Oleg. He was heading to his babushka's place near Brighton Beach, so I invited myself along, telling him that I had to talk to him seriously. I could have ended it all over the phone, but I didn't. It was more authentic to speak to him face to face.

When I arrived, his grandmother's apartment was in turmoil. His grandmother, hearing that I was arriving for dinner, decided to display her mastery of American cooking by making us a lobster dinner. After locating a seafood store, she was surprised to find that the creatures were sold while still alive. She bought the poor fellow nevertheless. The old lady had it in her head that all fish, live or not, should be prepared in the same way: covered in bread crumbs and butter, and baked in the oven on a cookie sheet at 350 degrees. And so the creature's eight kicking limbs were doused in melted butter and covered in crushed Ritz crackers after which he was placed, much against his will, on the middle rack of a very hot convection oven.

Shortly before I walked through the door the lobster, subjected to such conditions, began to scream. It is true, they can scream. Not only do they scream, they make the most pitiful, plaintive moaning noises that you have ever heard as the exoskeleton is heated.

The old lady had run out of the kitchen and was pacing up and down in the dining room.

"Shut up! Shut up, you little shit!" she said over and over again.

Oleg was in a state of indecision before the oven, holding a skewer in one hand and a potholder in the other.

"Anna, the thing keeps yelling at us . . . this is not supposed to happen." He had a look on his face that I have never seen before, like a little boy afraid to jump in the swimming pool.

"Ahhhhhhhhhhhhhhoooooooooooooooo!" screamed the lobster.

I opened the oven. A smell came out like burning pitch. The poor little crustacean had crawled off the pan, dragging its charred body into a corner in the back. Its antennae had fallen off and the stubs waved frenetically in the smoky air. Its eyes had burst, leaving him blind, and a whitish blue foam came from its mouth. Inside the thick rubber bands, the creature's claws clicked together, straining to free themselves.

"Ahhhhhhhhhhhhhhoooooooooooooooo!" it cried.

Babushka looked over our shoulder, "Still it is not dead!" she exclaimed.

Now Oleg crouched next to me. "I will kill it," he claimed, and took several tentative stabs at the bug with his skewer. The lobster pulled back instinctively. Oleg tried again, but the angle was impossible.

* * *

In the end, it proved very resilient. Oleg finally removed it with tongs and brought it out to the driveway where I smashed it with a shovel repeatedly until it lay still, heaving a final, tiny groan.

"I do not think it would be good to eat now," his grandmother remarked with a grimace, and disappeared inside.

Oleg and I sat on the steps and stared at the smooshed body of the lobster, still smoking in front of us. There was a long pause.

"I'm sorry," said Oleg at last, "Dinner has not gone as planned . . ." I nodded.

"Anna . . . did you have something to tell me?" he asked.

I shook my head. "No," I answered. I rested on his shoulder and sighed. I felt so heavy and tired.

"No," I said again, "but Oleg dear."

He raised a questioning eyebrow.

"Next time I will cook."

Nell Carberry
Night Train

Well, I'd say we were drunk except that neither of us drinks, but we'd drunk enough lattes to send us into the next galaxy. My skin was tingling, and Joe kept picking up my hand and dropping it, each time dragging a finger across my palm.

He was young and tattooed and shaved and pierced, and I was about ten years older. "Vanilla skin," he called me. But he wouldn't tell me his last name, or what he did, so I told him, no way would I take him home with me. I was that kind of girl, but I wasn't *that* kind of girl.

"So let me ride the train home with you, at least," he said. "Let me make you feel safe."

I didn't feel safe around him. He had pale skin and deep blue eyes, and the slightest hint of a brogue. The tattoos were mostly Celtic designs, and his pale scalp stubble hinted that when it grew, he had dark hair. *Black Irish,* I thought.

It was 2 A.M. on a Sunday night, and we boarded the train at Broadway-Lafayette. Both dressed for city combat: white T-shirts, black jeans, heavy boots.

And we entered an empty car, empty but for the trash blowing around.

And as we approached a seat, he said, "So you won't fuck me at your place, Nell?"

"Not without further particulars," I replied.

At this point we were kissing and sucking each other's fingers, sticky with the coffee we'd downed. We'd both been bad drinkers once, but now coffee and sex were the drugs of choice.

"Not in your house," he said again, and grabbed my shoulders from behind, licked my neck. I would have told him anything right then, but then he quickly slid his hands down my arms and grabbed my wrists. He pulled my arms overhead, and kept both wrists trapped in one meaty hand.

With the other, he pulled out a set of handcuffs. They jangled so loud. Just at that point, the doors flew open. Last stop in Manhattan.

"You can get off now, if you'd like," Joe said, and loosened the pressure on my hands just a bit.

But I shook my head. *Let's see where this goes,* I thought.

"You could take me home to your bed," he hissed, and shook the handcuffs.

"No," I said, and Joe flipped open the cuffs and slammed them on my wrists, carefully suspending me from the overhead pole. I was still facing away from him, but I could see everything he was doing in the smudged subway window. My feet barely touched the floor.

We were underground, in a tunnel beneath the East River.

"I'm not a bad man," Joe explained. "I just don't like to be denied."

Then he yanked my shirt up and exposed my bra, shoving a hand into the soft, sweaty cotton. He came around so he was facing me and pulled my breast to his mouth. The cuffs hurt my wrists, but they seemed to build the sensation in my nipple. I was moaning. Joe was silent. His tongue was long and pink, and I could smell smoke on his skin. He lapped at my breast like a baby. His jeans bulged. I tried to move closer, get more of his mouth on my tit, but he backed away. And again, he moved behind me.

First stop in Brooklyn, York Street, the ghost town stop. Still, I looked over my shoulder to see if anyone was entering. For a moment, I had a flash that Joe would make whoever entered the car join our handcuff party. I felt ashamed. And very hot.

"I get off in six stops," I said, suddenly angry.

"Oh, you do, do you," Joe said, impishly. "Then we'll have to hurry this along."

Joe unbuttoned my jeans and yanked them to the floor, where they lay in a heap around my feet. I felt doubly trapped, a cloth bond around my legs, a metal one around my wrists. I was still wearing underwear, stupid white cotton briefs, because while I always wanted sex, I never believed I'd get it on the first date.

"Practical panties," Joe said, and ground himself into my back. I could feel his erection looking for a place to rest, and as he slid around my ass, it fit perfectly in my ass crack. I could hear Joe unzip and in the window I saw his cock rise in the air, bobbing. Sweat dripped off his face and onto my back. I heard him reach in a back pocket, and that familiar metallic sound, ripping, stretching.

"Next time," he growled, as he rolled it over his cock, "you'll put it on with your mouth."

"What makes you think there'll be a next time?" I snapped. Then he spanked me once, and I moaned.

"Don't pretend with me, Nell."

And then he stuck his hand in my panties and ripped them off. They fell in a heap, too. And before I could object, he had one hand dithering my clit, the other stroking my ass crack.

"You really have to get home?" he murmured into my hair.

"No!" I moaned. "I mean, yes."

"All right," he sighed. Then he grabbed my breasts and plunged his cock deep into me.

Suddenly we were one with the train's rhythm, just as it rose above the ground, into the sparkling Brooklyn sky. His cock was the right size for me, and he kept hitting my G spot like he had a map. When I tried to back into *him,* he would hold me still.

"You are my little fuckdoll tonight, Nell," he said, and then two stops from my destination, he pounded at me in earnest, fingering my clit all the way. The only sounds: the train, moans, the unmistakable sound of precome mixing with latex. And because of the way we were positioned, we could see ourselves fucking in the window.

As could anyone who was in the station. A few sleepy partiers gaped at the next stop, but they didn't get in. One man actually did a double take: a rarity in New York.

And all the while, the heat was rising in me, and Joe's cock was pulsing. His hands pinched my nipples, as if trying to pull the orgasm out of me.

"I feel so embarrassed," I said.

"No . . . you . . . don't," said Joe, pumping with each word for emphasis. "No. You. Don't."

Now Joe was groaning, and he was very close. His hand drifted to my face, and I nipped his fingers with my mouth, drawing them in, sucking them, and he came closer. One and a half stops to my destination.

"You're my fuckdoll, and you'll do anything I tell you," said Joe. "Tell me what you are."

"I'm your fuckdoll and I'll do anything you say."

"No, I said, 'anything I tell you.'"

I was quiet.

"Say the words right, or I'll pull out and leave you in the train."

Words were just words, I thought. And I needed that orgasm. Still . . .

Then he said it.

"Nell, please."

So he needed it, too.

"I'm your fuckdoll," I said slowly, and Joe pumped me with every word, and I was seconds from going over the edge.

". . . and I'll do anything you tell me."

And then we came together, bent, standing, convulsing, seeing ourselves in the glass, panting, coming some more. As soon as we stopped quivering, Joe moved quickly to unchain me and zip himself up. My arms ached, my mouth was dry, and I could have done it the rest of the night.

Joe yanked my pants up and picked up my ripped panties from the floor.

"Joe needs Fuckdoll's number," he said in a sweet pleading voice, and so I wrote it, quickly, on the soiled and sweaty cotton. It didn't occur to me to do otherwise.

The doors of the subway train parted, and we kissed, Joe nipping my mouth, just a little.

He grabbed me by the shoulders and propelled me out of the train.

"You gave me what I wanted, now I'll give you what you really want," Joe said. I turned to face him.

"My last name's O'Riley," he smirked. Then the doors closed again. And he was gone.

Nalo Hopkinson
Ganger (Ball Lightning)

"Issy?"

"What."

"Suppose we switch suits?" Cleve asked.

Is what now? From where she knelt over him on their bed, Issy slid her tongue from Cleve's navel, blew on the wetness she'd made there. Cleve sucked in a breath, making the cheerful pudge of his tummy shudder. She stroked its fuzzy pelt.

"What," she said, looking up at him, "you want me wear your suit and you wear mine?" This had to be the weirdest yet.

He ran a finger over her lips, the heat of his touch making her mouth tingle. "Yeah," he replied. "Something so."

Issy got up to her knees, both her plump thighs on each side of his massive left one. She looked appraisingly at him. She was still mad from the fight they'd just had. But a good mad. She and Cleve, fighting always got them hot to make up. Had to be something good about that, didn't there? If they could keep finding their way back to each other like this? Her business if she'd wanted to make candy, even if the heat of the August night made the kitchen a hell. She wondered what the rass he was up to now.

They'd been fucking in the Senstim Co-operation's "wetsuits" for about a week. The toys had been fun for the first little while—they'd had more sex this week than in the last month—but even with the increased sensitivity, she was beginning to miss the feel of his skin directly against hers. "It not going work," Issy declared. But she was curious.

"You sure?" Cleve asked teasingly. He smiled, stroked her naked nipple softly with the ball of his thumb. She loved the contrast between his shovel-wide hands and the delicate movements he performed with them. Her nipple poked erect, sensitive as a tongue tip. She arched her back, pushed the heavy swing of her breast into fuller contact with the ringed ridges of thumb.

"Mmm."

"C'mon, Issy, it could be fun, you know."

"Cleve, they just going key themselves to our bodies. The innie become an outie, the outie become an innie. . . ."

"Yeah, but . . ."

"But what?"

"They take a few minutes to conform to our body shapes, right? Maybe in that few minutes . . ."

He'd gone silent, embarrassment shutting his open countenance closed; too shy to describe the sensation he was seeking. Issy sighed in irritation. What was the big deal? Fuck, cunt, cock, come: simple words to say. "In that few minutes, you'd find out what it feels like to have a poonani, right?"

A snatch. He looked shy and aroused at the same time. "Yeah, and you'd, well, you know."

He liked it when she talked "dirty." But just try to get him to repay the favor. Try to get him to buzzingly whisper hot-syrup words against the sensitive pinna of her ear until she shivered with the sensation of his mouth on her skin, and the things he was saying, the nerve impulses he was firing, spilled from his warm lips at her earhole and oozed down her spine, cupped the bowl of her belly, filled her crotch with heat. That only ever happened in her imagination.

Cleve ran one finger down her body, tracing the faint line of hair from navel past the smiling crease below her tummy to pussy fur. Issy spread her knees a little, willing him to explore further. His fingertip tunneled through her pubic hair, tapped at her clit, making nerves sing. *Ah, ah.* She rocked against his thigh. What would it be like to have the feeling of entering someone's clasping flesh? "Okay," she said. "Let's try it."

She picked up Cleve's stim. So diaphanous you could barely see it, but supple as skin and thrice as responsive. Cocked up onto one elbow, Cleve watched her with a slight smile on his face. Issy loved the chubby chocolate-brown beauty of him, his fat-cat grin.

Chortling, she wriggled into the suit, careful to ease it over the bandage on her heel. The company boasted that you couldn't tell the difference between the microthin layer of the wetsuits and bare skin. Bullshit. Like taking a shower with your clothes on. The suits made you feel more, but it was a one-way sensation. They dampened the sense of touch. It was like being trapped inside your own skin, able to sense your response to stimuli but not to feel when you had connected with the outside world.

Over the week of use, Cleve's suit had shaped itself to his body. The hips were tight on Issy, the flat chest part pressed her breasts against her rib cage. The shoulders were too broad, the middle too baggy. It sagged at knees, elbows, and toes. She giggled again.

"Never mind the peripherals," Cleve said, lumbering to his feet. "No time." He picked up her suit. "Just leave them hanging."

Just as well. Issy hated the way that the roll-on headpiece trapped her hair against her neck, covered her ears, slid sensory tendrils into her ear-holes. It amplified the sounds when her body touched Cleve's. It grossed her out. What would Cleve want to do next to jazz the skins up?

As the suit hyped the pleasure zones on her skin surface, Issy could feel herself getting wet, the mixture of arousal and vague distaste a wetsuit gave her. The marketing lie was that the suits were "consensual aids to full body aura alignment," not sex toys. Yeah, right. Psychobabble. She was being diddled by an over-sized condom possessed of fuzzy logic. She pulled it up to her neck. The stim started to writhe, conforming itself to her shape. Galvanic peristalsis, they called its ability to move. Yuck.

"Quick," Cleve muttered. He was jamming his lubed cock at a tube in the suit, the innie part of it that would normally have slid itself into her vagina, the part that had been smooth the first time she'd taken it out of its case, but was now shaped the way she was shaped inside. Cleve pushed and pushed until the everted pocket slid over his cock. He lay back on the bed, his erection a jutting rudeness. "Oh. Wow. That's different. Is so it feels for you?"

Oh, sweet. Issy quickly followed Cleve's lead, spreading her knees to push the outie part of his wetsuit inside her. It was easy. She was slippery, every inch of her skin stimmed with desire. She palmed some lube from the bottle into the suit's pouched vagina. They had to hurry. She straddled him, slid onto his cock, making the tube of one wetsuit slither smoothly into the tunnel of the other. Cleve closed his eyes, blew a small breath through pursed lips.

So, so hot. "God, it's good," Issy muttered. Like being fucked, only she had an organ to push back with. Cleve just panted heavily, silently. As always. But what a rush! She swore she could feel Cleve's tight hot cunt closing around her dick. She grabbed his shoulders for traction. The massy, padded flesh of them filled her hands; steel encased in velvet.

The ganger looked down at its ghostly hands. Curled them into fists. Lightning sparked between the translucent fingers as they closed. It reached a crackling hand toward Cleve's shuddering body on the bathroom floor.

"Hey!" Issy yelled at it. She could hear the quaver in her own voice. The ganger turned its head toward the sound. The suits' sense-memory gave it some analog of hearing.

She tried to lift her head, banged it against the underside of the toilet. "Ow." The ganger's head elongated widthways, as though someone were pulling on its ears. Her muscles were too weakened from the aftershocks. Issy put her head back down. Now what? Think fast, Iss. "Y . . . you like um, um . . . chocolate fudge?" she asked the thing. Now, why was she still going on about the fucking candy?

The ganger straightened. Took a floating step away from Cleve, closer to Issy. Cleve was safe for the moment. Colored auras crackled in the ganger with each step. Issy laid her cheek against cool porcelain; stammered, "Well, I was making some last night, some fudge, yeah, only it didn't set, sometimes that happens, y'know? Too much humidity in the air, or something." The ganger seemed to wilt a little, floppy as the unhardened fudge. Was it fading? Issy's pulse leapt in hope. But then the thing plumped up again, drew closer to where she lay helpless on the floor. Rainbow lightning did a lava-lamp dance in its incorporeal body. Issy whimpered.

Cleve writhed under her. His lips formed quiet words. His own nubbin nipples hardened. Pleasure transformed his face. Issy loved seeing him this way. She rode and rode his body, "Yes, ah, sweet, God, sweet," groaning her way to the stim-charged orgasm that would fire all her pleasure synapses, give her some sugar, make her speak in tongues.

Suddenly Cleve pushed her shoulder. "Stop! Jesus, get off! Off!"

Startled, Issy shoved herself off him. Achy suction at her crotch as they disconnected. "What's wrong?"

Cleve sat up, panting hard. He clutched at his dick. He was shaking. Shuddering, he stripped off the wetsuit, flung it to the foot of the bed. To her utter amazement, he was sobbing. She'd never seen Cleve cry.

"Jeez. Can't have been that bad. Come." She opened her thick, strong arms to him. He curled as much of his big body as he could into her embrace, hid his face from her. She rocked him, puzzled. "Cleve?"

After a while, he mumbled, "It was nice, you know, so different, then it started to feel like, I dunno, like my dick had been *peeled* and it was inside out, and you, Jesus, you were fucking my inside-out dick."

Issy said nothing, held him tighter. The hyped rasp of Cleve's body against her stimmed skin was as much a turn-on as a comfort. She rocked him, rocked him. She couldn't think what to say, so she just hummed a children's song: *We're stirring cocoa beneath a tree / sikola o la vani / one, two, three, vanilla / chocolate and vanilla.*

Just before he fell asleep, Cleve said, "God, I don't want to ever feel anything like that again. I had breasts, Issy. They swung when I moved."

The wetsuit Issy was wearing soon molded itself into an innie, and the hermaphroditic feeling disappeared. She kind of missed it. And all the time she was swaying Cleve to sleep she couldn't help thinking: For a few seconds, she'd felt something of what he felt when they had sex. For a few seconds, she'd felt the things he'd never dared to tell her in words. Issy slid a hand between herself and Cleve, insinuating it into the warm space between her stomach and thigh till she could work her fingers between her legs. She could feel her own wetness sliding under the microthin fiber. She pressed her clit, gently, ah, gently, tilting her hips toward her hand. Cleve stirred, scratched his nose; flopped his hand to the bed, snoring.

And he'd felt what she was always trying to describe to him, the sensations that always defied speech. He'd felt what this was like. The thought made her cunt clench. She panted out, briefly, once. She was so slick. Willing her body still, she started the rubbing motion that she knew would bring her off.

Nowadays any words between her and Cleve seemed to fall into dead air between them, each not reaching the other. But this had reached him, gotten her inside him; this, this, this, and the image of fucking Cleve pushed her over the edge and the pulse-burst of her orgasm pumped again, again, again as her moans trickled through her lips, and she fought not to thrash, not to wake the slumbering mountain that was Cleve.

Oh. "Yeah, man," Issy breathed. Cleve had missed the best part. She eased him off her, got his head onto a pillow. Sated, sex-heavy, and drowsy, she peeled off the wetsuit—smiled at the pouches it had molded from her calabash breasts and behind—and kicked it onto the floor beside the bed. She lay down, rolled toward Cleve, hugged his body to her. "Mm," she murmured.

Cleve muttered sleepily and snuggled into the curves of her body. Issy wriggled to the sweet spot where the lobes of his buttocks fit against her pubes. She wrapped her arm around the bole of his chest, kissed the back of his neck where his hair curled tightest. She felt herself beginning to sink into a feather-down sleep.

"I mean the boiled sugar kind of fudge," Issy told the ganger. It hovered over her, her own personal aurora. She had to keep talking, draw out the verbiage, distract the thing. "Not that gluey shit they sell at the Ex and stuff. We were supposed to have a date, but Cleve was late coming home and I was pissed at him and horny and I wanted a taste of sweetness in my mouth. And hot, too, maybe. I saw a recipe once where you put a few flakes of red pepper into the syrup. Intensified the taste, they said. I wonder. Dunno what I was thinking, boiling fudge in this heat." Lightning-quick, the ganger tapped her mouth. The electric shock crashed her teeth together. She saw stars. "Huh, huh," she heard her body protesting as air puffed out of its contracting lungs.

Issy uncurled into one last, languorous stretch before sleep. Her foot connected in the dark with a warm, rubbery mass that writhed at her touch, then started to slither up her leg.

"Oh, God! Shit! Cleve!" Issy kicked convulsively at the thing clambering up her thigh. She clutched Cleve's shoulder.

He sprang awake, tapped the wall to activate the light. "What, Issy? What's wrong?"

It was the still-charged wetsuit that Cleve had thrown to the foot of the bed, now an outie. "Christ, Cleve!" Idiot.

The suit had only been reacting to the electricity generated by Issy's body. It was just trying to do its job. "S'all right," Cleve comforted her. "It can't hurt you."

Shuddering, Issy peeled the wetsuit from her leg and dropped it to the ground. Deprived of her warmth, it squirmed its way over to her suit. Innie and outie writhed rudely around each other; empty sacks of skin. Jesus, with the peripherals still attached, the damned things looked like they had floppy heads.

Cleve smiled sleepily. "I's like lizard tails, y'know, when they drop off and wiggle?"

Issy thought she'd gag. "Get them out of my sight, Cleve. Discharge them and put them away."

"Tomorrow," he murmured.

They were supposed to be stored in separate cases, but Cleve just scooped them up and tossed them together, wriggling, into the closet.

"Gah," Issy choked.

Cleve looked at her face and said, "Come on, Iss; have a heart; think of them lying side by side in their little boxes, separated from each other." He was trying to joke about it.

"No," Issy said. "We get to do that instead. Wrap ourselves in fake flesh that's supposed to make us feel more. Ninety-six degrees in the shade, and we're wearing rubber body bags."

His face lost its teasing smile. Just the effect she'd wanted, but it didn't feel so good now. And it wasn't true, really. The wetsuit material did some weird shit so that it didn't trap heat in. And they were sexy, once you got used to them. No sillier than strap-ons or cuffs padded with fake fur. Issy grimaced an apology at Cleve. He screwed up his face and looked away. God, if he would only speak up for himself sometimes! Issy turned her back to him and found her wadded-up panties in the bedclothes. She wrestled them on and lay back down, facing the wall. The light went off. Cleve climbed back into bed. Their bodies didn't touch.

* * *

The sun cranked Issy's eyes open. Its August heat washed over her like slops from a bucket. Her sheet was twisted around her, warm, damp, and funky. Her mouth was sour and she could smell her own stink. "Oh, God, I want it to be winter," she groaned.

She fought her way out of the clinging cloth to sit up in bed. The effort made her pant. She twisted the heavy mass of her braids up off the nape of her neck and sat for a while, feeling the sweat trickle down her scalp. She grimaced at the memory of last night.

Cleve wasn't there. Out for a jog, likely. "Yeah, that's how you sulk," she muttered. "In silence." Issy longed to know that he cared strongly about something, to hear him speak with any kind of force, the passion of his anger, the passion of his love. But Cleve kept it all so cool, so mild. Wrap it all in fake skin, hide it inside.

The morning sun had thrown a violent, hot bar of light across her bed. Heat. Tangible, almost. Crushed against every surface of her skin, like drowning in feathers. Issy shifted into a patch of shade. It made no difference. Fuck. A drop of sweat trickled down her neck, beaded a track down her left breast to drip off her nipple and splat onto her thigh. The trail of moisture it had left behind felt cool on her skin. Issy watched her areola crinkle and the nipple stiffen in response. She shivered.

A twinkle of light caught her eye. The closet sliding door was open. The wetsuits, thin as shed snakeskin, were still humping each other beside their storage boxes. "Nasty!" Issy exclaimed. She jumped up from the bed, pushed the closet door shut with a bang. She left the room, ignoring the rhythmic thumping noise from inside the closet. Cleve was supposed to have discharged them; it could just wait until he deigned to come home again.

Overloading, crackling violently, the ganger stepped back. Issy nearly wept with release from its jolt. Her knees felt watery. Was Cleve still breathing? She thought she could see his chest moving in little gasps. She hoped. She had to keep the ganger distracted from him, he might not survive another shock. Teeth chattering, she said to the ganger, "You melt the sugar and butter—the salty butter's the best—in milk, then you add cocoa powder and boil it all to hard crack stage. . . ." Issy wet her lips with her tongue. The day's heat was enveloping her again. "Whip in some more butter," she continued. "You always get it on your fingers, that melted, salty butter. It will slide down the side of your hand, and you lick it off—so you whip in some more butter, and real vanilla, the kind that smells like mother's breath and cookies, not the artificial shit, and you dump it onto a plate, and it sets, and you have it sweet like that: chocolate fudge."

The sensuality in her voice seemed to mesmerize the ganger. It held still, rapt. Its inner lightnings cooled to electric blue. Its mouth hole yawned, wide as two of her fists.

As she headed to the kitchen, Issy made a face at the salty dampness beneath her swaying breasts and the curve of her belly. Her thighs were sticky where they moved against each other. She stopped in the living room and stood, feet slightly apart, arms away from her sides, so no surface of her body would touch any other. No relief. The heat still clung. She shoved her panties down around her ankles. The movement briefly brought her nose to her crotch, a whiff of sweaty muskiness. She straightened up, stepped out of the sodden pretzel of cloth, kicked it away. The quick movement had made her dizzy. She swayed slightly, staggered into the kitchen.

Cleve had mopped up the broken glass and gluey candy from yesterday evening, left the pot to soak. The kitchen still smelled of chocolate. The rich scent tingled along the roof of Issy's mouth.

The fridge hummed in its own aura, heat outside making cold inside. She needed water. Cold, cold. She yanked the fridge door open, reached for the water jug, and drank straight from it. The shock of chilly liquid made her teeth ache. She sucked water in, tilting the jug high so that more spilled past her gulping mouth, ran down her jaw, her breasts, her belly. With her free hand, she spread the coolness over the pillow of her stomach, dipping down into the crinkly pubic hair, then up to heft each breast one at a time, sliding cool fingers underneath, thumb almost automatically grazing each nipple to feel them harden slightly at her touch. Better. Issy put the jug back, half full now.

At her back, hot air was a wall. Seconds after she closed the fridge door, she'd be overheated and miserable again. She stood balanced between ice and heat, considering.

She pulled open the door to the icebox. It creaked and protested, jammed with frost congealed on its hinges. The fridge was ancient. Cleve had joked with the landlady that he might sell it to a museum and use the money to pay the rent on the apartment for a year. He'd only gotten a scowl in return

The fridge had needed defrosting for weeks now. Her job. Cleve did the laundry and bathroom and kept them spotlessly clean. The kitchen and the bedroom were hers. Last time she'd changed the sheets was about the last time she'd done the fridge. Cleve hadn't complained. She was waiting him out.

Issy peered into the freezer. Buried in the canned hoarfrost were three ice-cube trays. She had to pull at them to work them free of hard-packed freezer snow. One was empty. The other two contained a few ice cubes between them.

The ganger took a step toward her. It paddled its hand in the black hole of its mouth. Issy shuddered, kept talking: "Break off chunks of fudge, and is sweet and dark and crunchy; a little bit hot if you put the pepper flakes in, I never tried that kind, and is softer in the middle, and the butter taste rise to the roof of your mouth, and the chocolate melt all over your tongue; man, you could almost come, just from a bite."

Issy flung the empty tray into the sink at the other end of the kitchen. Jangle-crash, displacing a fork that leapt from the sink, clattered onto the floor. The thumping from inside the bedroom closet became more frenetic. "Stop that," Issy yelled in the direction of the bedroom. The sound became a rapid drubbing. Then silence.

Issy kicked the fridge door closed, took the two ice-cube trays into the bathroom. Even with that short walk, the heat was pressing in on her again. The bathroom was usually cool, but today the tiles were warm against her bare feet. The humidity of the room felt like wading through spit.

Issy plugged the bathtub drain, dumped the sorry handful of ice in. Not enough. She grabbed up the mop bucket, went back to the kitchen, fished a spatula out of the sink, rinsed it. She used the spatula to dig out the treasures buried in the freezer. Frozen cassava, some unidentifiable meat, a cardboard cylinder of grape punch. She put them on a shelf in the fridge. Those excavated, she set about shoveling the snow out of the freezer, dumping it into her bucket. In no time she had a bucketful, and she'd found another ice-cube tray, this one full of fat, rounded lumps of ice. She was a little cooler now.

Back in the bathroom, she dumped the bucket of freezer snow on top of the puddle that had been the ice cubes. Then she ran cold water, filled the bathtub calf-deep, and stepped into it.

"Sssss . . ." The shock of cold feet zapped straight through Issy's body to her brain. She bent—smell of musk again—picked up a handful of the melting snow and packed it into her hair. Blessed, blessed cold. The snow became water almost instantly and dribbled down her face. Issy licked at a trickle of it. She picked up another handful of snow, stuffed it into her mouth. Crunchy-cold freon ice, melting on her tongue. She remembered the canned taste from childhood, how her dad would scold her for eating freezer snow. Her mother would say nothing, just wipe Issy's mouth dry with a silent, long-suffering smile.

Issy squatted in the bathtub. The cold water lapped against her butt. Goose bumps pimpled the skin of her thighs. She sat down, hips pressing against either side of the tub. An ice cube lapped against the small of her back, making her first arch to escape the cold, then lean back against the tub with a happy shudder. Snow crunched between her back and the ceramic surface. Issy spread her knees. There was more snow floating in the diamond her legs made. In both hands, she picked up another handful, mashed it into the V of her crotch. She shivered at the sensation and relaxed into the cool water.

The fridge made a zapping, farting noise, then resumed its juddering hum. Damned bucket of bolts. Issy concentrated on the deliciously shivery feel of the ice melting in her pubic hair.

"Only this time," Issy murmured, "the fudge ain't set. Just sat there on the cookie tin, gluey and brown. Not hard, not quite liquid, you get me? Glossy-shiny dark brown where it pooled, and rising from it, that chocolate-butter-vanilla smell. But wasted, 'cause it wasn't going to set."

The television clicked on loudly with an inane laugh track. Issy sat up. "Cleve?" She hadn't heard him come in. With a popping noise, the TV snapped off again. "Cleve, is you?"

Issy listened. Nope, nothing but the humming of the fridge. She was alone. These humid August days made all their appliances schizo with static. She relaxed back against the tub.

"I got mad," Issy told the ganger. "It was hot in the kitchen and there was cocoa powder everywhere and lumps of melting better, and I do all that work 'cause I just wanted the taste of something sweet in my mouth and the fucker wouldn't set! I backhanded the cookie tin. Fuck, it hurt like I crack a finger bone. The tin skidded across the kitchen counter, splanged off the side of the stove, and went flying."

Issy's skin bristled with goose bumps at the sight of the thing that walked in through the open bathroom door and stood, arms hanging. It was a human-shaped glow, translucent. Its edges were fuzzy. She could see the hallway closet through it. Eyes, nose, mouth were empty circles. A low crackling noise came from it, like a crushed Cheezies bag. Issy could feel her breath coming in short, terrified pants. She made to stand up, and the apparition moved closer to her. She whimpered and sat back down in the chilly water.

The ghost-thing stood still. A pattern of colored lights flickered in it, limning where spine, heart, and brain would have been, if it had had those. It did have breasts, she saw now, and a dick.

She moved her hand. Water dripped from her fingertips into the tub. The thing turned its head toward the sound. It took a step. She froze. The apparition stopped moving, too, just stood there, humming like the fridge. It plucked at its own nipples, pulled its breasts into cones of ectoplasm. It ran hands over its body, then over the sink; bent down to thrust its arms right through the closed cupboard doors. It dipped a hand into the toilet bowl. Sparks flew, and it jumped back. Issy's scalp prickled. Damn, the thing was electrical, and she was sitting in water! She tried to reach the plug with her toes to let the water out. Swallowing whimpers, she stretched a leg out: Slow, God, go slow, Issy. The movement sent a chunk of melting ice sliding along her thigh. She shivered. She couldn't quite reach the plug and if she moved closer to it, the movement would draw the apparition's attention. Issy breathed in short, shallow bursts. She could feel her eyes beginning to brim. Terror and the chilly water were sending tremors in waves through her.

What the fuck was it? The thing turned toward her. In its quest for sensation, it hefted its cock in its hand. Inserted a finger into what seemed to be a vagina underneath. Let its hands drop again. Faintly, Issy could make out a mark on its hip, a circular shape. It reminded her of something. . . .

Logo, it was the logo of the Senstim people who'd invented the wetsuits!

But this wasn't a wetsuit, it was like some kind of, fuck, ball lightning. She and Cleve hadn't discharged their wetsuits. She remembered some of the nonsense words that were in the warning on the wetsuit storage boxes: "Energizing electrostatic charge," and "Kirlian phenomenon." Well, they hadn't paid attention, and now some kind of weird gel of both suits was rubbing itself off in their bathroom. Damn, damn, damn Cleve and his toys. Sobbing, shivering, Issy tried to toe at the plug again. Her knee banged against the tub. The suit-ghost twitched toward the noise. It leaned over the water and dabbed at her clutching toes. Pop-crackle sound. The jolt sent her leg flailing like a dying fish. Pleasure crackled along her leg, painfully intense. Her knee throbbed and tingled, ached sweetly. Her thigh muscles shuddered as though they would tear free. The jolt slammed into her crotch and Issy's body bucked. She could hear her own grunts. She was straddling a live wire. She was coming to death. Her nipples jutted long as thumbs, stung like they'd been dipped in ice. Her head was banging against the wall with each deadly set of contractions. Issy shouted in pain, in glory, in fear. The suit-ghost leapt back. Issy's butt hit the floor of the tub, hard. Her muscles were twitching spasmodically. She'd bitten the inside of her mouth. She sucked in air like sobs; swallowed tinny blood.

The suit-ghost was swollen, bloated, jittering. Its inner lightning bolts were going mad. If it touched her again, it might overload completely. If it touched her again, her heart might stop.

Issy heard the sound of the key turning in the front door.

"Iss? You home?"

"No. Cleve." Issy hissed under her breath. He mustn't come in. But if she shouted to warn him, the suit-ghost would touch her again.

Cleve's footsteps approached the bathroom. "Iss? Listen, did you drain the wet . . ."

Like filings to a magnet, the suit-ghost inclined toward the sound of his voice.

"Don't come in, Cleve; go get help!"

Too late. He'd stuck his head in, grinning his open, friendly grin. The suit-ghost rushed him, plastered itself along his body. It got paler, its aura-lightnings mere flickers. Cleve made a choking noise and crashed to the floor, jerking. Issy levered herself out of the bath, but her jelly muscles wouldn't let her stand. She flopped to the tiles. Cleve's body was convulsing, horrible noises coming from his mouth. Riding him like a duppy, a malevolent spirit, the stim-ghost grew paler with each thrash of his flailing body. Its color patterns started to run into each other, to bleach themselves pale. Cleve's energy was draining it, but it was killing him. Sucking on her whimpers, Issy reached a hand into the stim-ghost's field. Her heart went off like a Gatling gun. Her breathing wouldn't work. The orgasm was unspeakable. Wailing, Issy rolled away from Cleve, taking the ghost-thing with her. It swelled at her touch, its colors flaring neon-bright, out of control. It flailed off her, floated back toward Cleve's more cooling energy. Heart pounding, too weak to move, Issy muttered desperately to distract it the first thing that came to her mind: "Y . . . you like, um, chocolate fudge?"

The ghost turned toward her. Issy cried and kept talking, kept talking. The ghost wavered between Issy's hot description of bubbling chocolate and Cleve's cool silence, caught in the middle. Could it even understand words? Wetsuits located pleasurable sensation to augment it. Maybe it was just drawn to the sensuousness of her tone. Issy talked, urgently, carefully releasing the words from her mouth like caresses:

"So," she said to the suit-duppy, "I watching this cookie tin twist through the air like a Frisbee, and is like slow motion, 'cause I seeing gobs of chocolate goo spiraling from it as it flies, and they spreading out wider and wider. I swear I hear separate splats as chocolate hits the walls like slung shit and one line of it strafes the fridge door, and a gob somehow slimes the naked bulb hanging low from the kitchen ceiling. I hear it sizzle. The cookie tin lands on the floor, fudge side down, of course. I haven't cleaned the fucking floor in ages. There're spots everywhere on that floor that used to be gummy, but now they're layered in dust and maybe flour and desiccated bodies of cockroaches that got trapped, reaching for sweetness. I know how they feel. I take a step toward the cookie tin, then I start to smell burning chocolate. I look up. I see a curl of black smoke rising from the glob of chocolate on the light bulb."

Cleve raised his head. There were tears in his eyes and the front of his jogging pants was damp and milky. "Issy," he interrupted in a whisper.

"Shut up, Cleve!"

"That thing," he said in a low, urgent voice. "People call it a ganger; doppel . . ."

The ganger was suddenly at his side. It leaned a loving head on his chest, like Issy would do. "No!" she yelled. Cleve's body shook. The ganger frayed and tossed like a sheet in the wind. Cleve shrieked. He groaned like he was coming, but with an edge of terror and pain that Issy couldn't bear to hear. Pissed, terrified, Issy swiped an arm through its field, then rolled her bucking body on the bathroom tiles, praying that she could absorb the ganger's energy without it frying her synapses with sweet sensation.

Through spasms, she barely heard Cleve say to it, "Come to me, not her. Come. Listen, you know that song? '*I got a weakness for sweetness* . . .' That's my Issy."

The ganger dragged itself away from Issy. Released, her muscles melted. She was a gooey, warm puddle spreading on the floor. The ganger reached an ectoplasmic hand toward Cleve, fingers stretching long as arms. Cleve gasped and froze.

Issy croaked, "Is that you think it is, Cleve? Weakness?"

The ganger turned its head her way, ran a long, slow arm down its body to the floor, back up to its crotch. It stroked itself.

Cleve spoke to it in a voice that cracked whispery on the notes: "Yeah, sweetness. That's what my Issy wants most of all." The ganger moved toward him, rubbing its crotch. He continued, "If I'm not there, there's always sugar, or food, or booze. I'm just one of her chosen stimulants."

Outraged tears filled Issy's mouth, salty as butter, as flesh. She'd show him, she'd rescue him. She countered:

"The glob of burned sugar on the light? From the ruined fudge? Well, it goes black and starts to bubble."

The ganger extruded a tongue the length of an arm from its mouth. The tongue wriggled toward Issy. She rolled back, saying, "The light bulb explodes. I feel some shards land in my hair. I don't try to brush them away. Is completely dark now; I only had the kitchen light on. I take another step to where I know the cookie tin is on the floor. A third step, and pain crazes my heel. Must have stepped on a piece of light bulb glass. Can't do nothing about it now. I rise onto the toes of the hurting foot. I think I feel blood running down from heel to instep."

The ganger jittered toward her.

"You were always better than me at drama, Iss," Cleve said.

The sadness in his voice tore at her heart. But she said, "What that thing is?"

Cleve replied softly, "Is kinda beautiful, ain't?"

"It going to kill us."

"Beautiful. Just a lump of static charge, coated in the Kirlian energy thrown off from the suits."

"Why it show up now?"

"Is what happens when you leave the suits together too long."

The ganger drifted back and forth, pulled by one voice, then the other. A longish silence between them freed it to move. It floated closer to Cleve. Issy wouldn't let it, she wouldn't. She quavered:

"I take another step on the good foot, carefully. I bend down, sweep my hands around."

The ganger dropped to the floor, ran its long tongue over the tiles. A drop of water made it crackle and shrink in slightly on itself.

"There," Issy continued. "The cookie tin. I brush around me, getting a few more splinters in my hands. I get down to my knees, curl down as low to the ground as I can. I pry up the cookie tin, won't have any glass splinters underneath it. A dark sweet wet chocolate smell rising from under there."

"Issy, Jesus," Cleve whispered. He started to bellow the words of the song he'd taunted her with. The ganger touched him with a fingertip. A crackling noise. He gasped, jumped, kept singing.

Issy ignored him. Hissing under his booming voice, she snarled at the ganger, "I run a finger through the fudge. I lick it off. Most of it on the ground, not on the tin. I bend over and run my tongue through it, reaching for sweetness. Butter and vanilla and oh, oh, the chocolate. And crunchy, gritty things I don't think about. Cockroach parts, maybe. I swallow."

Cleve interrupted his song to wail, "That's gross, Iss. Why you had to go and do that?"

"So Cleve come in, he see me there sitting on the floor surrounded by broken glass and limp chocolate, and you know what he say?" The ganger was reaching for her.

"Issy, stop talking, you only drawing it to you."

"Nothing." The ganger jerked. "Zip." The ganger twitched. "Dick." The ganger spasmed, once. It touched her hair. Issy breathed. That was safe. "The bastard just started cleaning up; not a word for me." The ganger hugged her. Issy felt her eyes roll back in her head. She thrashed in the energy of its embrace until Cleve yelled:

"And what you said! Ee? Tell me!"

The ganger pulled away. Issy lay still, waiting for her breathing to return to normal. Cleve said, "Started carrying on with some shit about how light bulbs are such poor quality nowadays.

Sat in the filth and broken glass, pouting and watching me clean up your mess. Talking about anything but what really on your mind. I barely get all the glass out of your heel before you start pulling my pants down."

Issy ignored him. She kept talking to the ganger. "Cool, cool Cleve. No 'What's up?'; no 'What the fuck is this crap on the floor?'; no heat, no passion."

"What was the point? I did the only thing that will sweet you every time."

"Encased us both in fake skin and let it do the fucking for us."

The ganger jittered in uncertain circles between the two of them.

"Issy, what you want from me?"

The ganger's head swelled obscenely toward Cleve.

"Some heat. Some feeling. Like I show you. Like I feel. Like I feel for you." The ganger's lower lip stretched, stretched, a filament of it reaching for Issy's own mouth. The black cavity of its maw was a tunnel, longing to swallow her up. She shuddered and rolled back farther. Her back came up against the bathtub.

Softly: "What do you feel for me, Issy?"

"Fuck you."

"I do. We do. It's good. But what do you feel for me, Issy?"

"Don't ridicule me. You know."

"I don't know shit, Issy! You talk, talk, talk! And it's all about what racist slur you heard yesterday, and who tried to cheat you at the store, and how high the phone bill is. You talk around stuff, not about it!"

"Shut up!"

The ganger flailed like a hook-caught fish between them.

Quietly, Cleve said, "The only time we seem to reach each other now is through our skins. So I bought something to make our skins feel more, and it's still not enough."

An involuntary sound came from Issy's mouth, a hooked, wordless query.

"Cleve, is that why . . ." She looked at him, at the intense brown eyes in the expressive brown face. When had he started to look so sad all the time? She reached a hand out to him. The ganger grabbed it. Issy saw fireworks behind her eyes. She screamed. She felt Cleve's hand on her waist, felt the hand clutch painfully as he tried to shove her away to safety with his other hand. Blindly she reached out, tried to bat the ganger away. Her hand met Cleve's in the middle of the fog that was the ganger. All the pleasure centers in her body exploded.

A popping sound. A strong, seminal smell of bleach. The ganger was gone. Issy and Cleve sagged to the floor.

"Rass," she sighed. Her calves were knots the size of potatoes. And she'd be sitting tenderly for a while.

"I feel like I've been dragged five miles behind a runaway horse," Cleve told her. "You all right?"

"Yeah, where'd that thing go, the ganger?"

"Shit, Issy, I'm so sorry. Should have drained the suits like you said."

"*Chuh.* Don't dig nothing. I could have done it, too."

"I think we neutralized it. Touched each other, touched it: we canceled it out. I think."

"Touched each other. That simple." Issy gave a little rueful laugh. "Cleve, I . . . you're my honey, you know? You sweet me for days. I won't forget any more to tell you," she said, "and keep telling you."

His smile brimmed over with joy. He replied, "You, you're my live wire. You keep us both juiced up, make my heart sing in my chest." He hesitated, spoke bashfully, "And my dick leap in my pants when I see you."

A warmth flooded Issy at his sweet, hot talk. She felt her eyelashes dampen. She smiled. "See, the dirty words not so hard to say. And the anger not so hard to show."

Tailor-sat on the floor, beautiful Buddha-body, he frowned at her. "I 'fraid to use harsh words, Issy, you know that. Look at the size of me, the blackness of me. You know what it is to see people cringe for fear when you shout?"

She was dropping down with fatigue. She leaned and softly touched his face. "I don't know what that is like. But I know you. I know you would never hurt me. You must say what on your mind, Cleve. To me, at least." She closed her eyes, dragged herself exhaustedly into his embrace.

He said, "You know, I dream of the way you full up my arms."

"You're sticky," she murmured. "Like candy." And fell asleep, touching him.

Poppy Z. Brite
Homewrecker

My Uncle Edna killed hogs. He came home from the slaughterhouse every day smelling of shit and pig blood, and if I didn't have his bath drawn with plenty of perfume and bubble stuff, he'd whup my ass until I felt his hard-on poking me in the leg.

Like I said, he killed hogs. At night, though, you'd never have known it to see him in his satin gown. He swished around the old farmhouse like some kind of fairy godmother, swigging from a bottle of J.D. and cussing the bitch who stole his man.

"Homewrecker!" he'd shriek, pounding his fist on the table and rattling the stack of rhinestone bracelets he wore on his skinny arm. "How could he want her when he had me? How could he do it, boy?"

And you had to wonder, because even with his lipstick smeared and his chest hair poking out of his gown, there was a certain tired glamour to Uncle Edna. Thing was, the bitch hadn't even wanted his man. Uncle Jude, who'd been with Uncle Edna since he was just plain old Ed Slopes, had all of a sudden turned het and gone slobbering off after a henna-headed barfly who called herself Tina. What Tina considered a night's amusement, Uncle Jude decided was the grand passion of his life. And that was the last we saw of him. We never could understand it.

Uncle Edna was thirty-six when Uncle Jude left. The years

and the whiskey rode him hard after that, but the man knew how to do his makeup, and I thought Uncle Jude would fall back in love with him if they could just see each other again.

I couldn't do anything about it, though, and back then I was more interested in catching frogs and snakes than in the affairs of grown-ups' hearts. But a few years later, I heard Tina was back in town.

I knew I couldn't let Uncle Edna find out. He'd want to get out his shotgun and go after her, and then he'd get cornholed to death in jail and who'd take care of me? So I talked to a certain kid at school. He made me suck his dick out behind the cafeteria, but I came home with four Xanax. I ground them up and put them in Uncle Edna's bottle of J.D. that same night. Pretty soon he was snoring like a chainsaw and drooling on his party dress. I went out to look for Tina. I didn't especially want to see her, but I thought maybe I could find out where she'd last seen Uncle Jude.

I parked my bike across the street from the only bar in town, the Silky Q. Inside, the men stood or danced in pairs. A few wore drag, but most were in jeans and flannels; this was a working man's town.

Then I saw her. She'd slid her meaty ass into a booth and was cuddled up to one of the men in it. The other man sat glaring at her, nearly in tears. I recognized them as Bob and Jim Frenchette, a couple who'd been married as long as I could remember. Tina's red-nailed hand was on Bob's thigh, stroking the worn denim.

I walked up to the table.

Jim and Bob were too far gone to pay me any mind. Tina didn't seem to recognize me. I'd been a little kid when she saw me last, and she'd hardly noticed me then, bent as she was on sucking Uncle Jude's neck. I stared into her light blue eyes. Her lashes were clumped with black mascara, her lids frosted with turquoise shadow. Her mouth was a lipstick wound. Her lips twitched in a scornful smile, then parted.

"What you want, boy?"

I couldn't think of anything to say. I didn't know what I had meant to do. I stumbled away from the table. My hands were trembling and my cheeks flaming. I was outside, unchaining my bike from the lamppost, when Tina came out of the bar.

She crossed the deserted street, pinning me where I stood with those wolf-pale eyes. I wanted to jump on my bike and speed away, or just run, but I couldn't. I wanted to look away from those slippery red lips that glistened like hog grease. But I couldn't.

"Your uncle . . . ," she whispered. "Jules, wasn't it?"

I shook my head, but Tina kept smiling and bending closer until her lips were right against my ear.

"He was a lousy fuck," she said.

Her sharp red nails bit into my shoulder. She pushed me back against the lamppost and sank to her knees in front of me. I felt hot bile rising in my throat, but I couldn't move, even when her other hand undid my pants.

I tried to keep my dick from getting hard, I truly did. But it was like her mouth sucked the blood into it, right to the surface of the skin. I thought she might tear it out by the roots. Her tongue slithered over my balls, into my peehole. There came a sharp stinging at the base of my dick, unlike anything I'd felt when other boys sucked it. Then I was shooting my jizz into her mouth, much as I didn't want to, and she was swallowing it like she'd been starved.

Tina wiped her mouth and laughed. Then she stood, turned, and walked back to the bar like I wasn't even there. The door closed behind her, and I fell to my knees and puked until my throat was raw. But even as the rancid taste of half-digested food filled my mouth and nose, I could feel my dick getting hard again.

I had to whack off before I could get on my bike. As I came on the sidewalk, I imagined those fat shiny lips closing around me again, and I started to cry. I couldn't get the nasty thoughts out of my head, things I'd never thought about before: the smell of dank sea coves and fish markets, the soft squish of a body encased in a layer of fat, with big floppy globes of it stuck on the chest and rear like cancers. And the thoughts were like a cancer in me.

As fast as my feet could pedal, I rode home to Uncle Edna. But I had a feeling I could never really go home again.

Paula Bomer
Two Years

He was the one to give her head when she was on the rag. He liked it, the saltiness, the nastiness of it. He grabbed her legs so hard it left bruises, because she claimed she didn't want him to go down on her when she was bleeding. Yeah, right. Her pussy was so clean anyway, even when she bled. The shock of it. He tongued her asshole, too. Fresh as a daisy, this girl. Broad daylight, on the lumpy futon on the floor of his room in an apartment in Allston, Massachusetts. Totally naked, their skin pale and visibly human—veins, pimples—lit by the sun streaming in, the bright, midday sunlight. Some torn sheets hanging in the windows, not providing much protection from the fierce light. As they move, dust rises in the streams of light, surrounding their glowing bodies. It was noon, maybe 2 P.M. They'd been having sex all morning. Hungover sex, "hangover helper" he called it. She propped her head up on a pillow so she could watch his face in her cunt, the top of his forehead, his receding hairline, the dark, almost black strands of hair, his long, long hair, falling past his shoulders. Rock drummer hair. He'd look up at her. Pull his mouth away from her and she could see it, his mouth, dark where her blood streaked him. I fucking love your pussy, he says quietly, a finger inside of her.

They didn't have much in common. He didn't read, and she wasn't from the Boston area, but he changed her life the day he ate her out for an hour straight, moving the vibrator around inside of her, outside of her and finally sticking a finger up her ass and—she came. For the first time. A huge, huge blood-curdling, screaming, flying-across-the-room orgasm, that ended with her smacking her head against the wall. Did he levitate her? How'd she get so far off the ground, so high in the air? After that, he owned her. Not that he necessarily wanted to, but he did, and so that was that. And then she was terminally in his bedroom, naked, begging for it. Please, Curt, please. Don't leave me. Don't, don't. Taking her clothes off, wanting him so badly, falling to her knees. Her hands gently petting his head, God, Curt, oh, oh, moving his head ever so slightly, as he eats her out for the ten-millionth time.

Actually, it wasn't always that way. At first he had to coax her. Come on, let me kiss you down there. She was barely nineteen and she'd blush. Oh don't do that. That's gross. Oh no it's not. And she'd let him do it and she'd get so excited and yell stop, stop and pull him up and into her. Which was fine. He'd fuck her and he liked doing that. She was ten years younger than him and skinny and—ten years younger than him. Pale nipples on her pointy little tits and a long perfect stomach with the tiniest little bulge resting in her narrow hips. Her pink, little girl cunt, with youth fluffing it up and dripping out of it. You're made for sex. You're built for this. Your pussy should be in magazines. And he'd roll onto his back and sit her on top of him and lean her back, with her knees stretched as far apart as they could go, and instinctively (or maybe someone had told her, but he doubted it, because every other guy she'd fucked before him was some young, dumb college jock who'd fuck her doggy style with the lights off), gently, saying, yeah, yeah, with her left forefinger and middle finger, she'd pull herself wide open for him. Wide open in the middle of the day. He liked it. Liked seeing all that.

Later, they'd go shoot pool down the street. Or he'd be playing and the bass player would pick them up and drive them to the club. She'd watch him play drums. Standing directly in front of the stage with her friend Katie. The two in nearly matching Betsey Johnson skintight minidresses. Her mouth slightly open, shiny pale lip gloss, moving awkwardly to the music. She was a horrible dancer. And afterward, she would come right up to him. Stand next to him, step on his foot. Sorry, she says sheepishly, her brow anxiously furrowed. He just wanted to talk to his friends. And sometimes he had schmoozing to do—label people, a guitar player who may want to use him. His mother might be there. No matter, there'd Sonia be, right next to him. Her breath stinking of beer and cigarettes. She'd drink four beers during his set and smoke half a pack. Her arms folded nervously over her tiny chest. Her hair limp against her moonish face. Her mascara smeared. Okay, okay, sometimes he'd be talking to a cute girl. He played in a band for God's sake! Most of the time, the girl would be a friend's girlfriend. No matter, Sonia would freak out. Her face stuck in this weird nervous position. He noticed then her double chin, from the way she held her head smooshed back into her neck. She wasn't fat, she was skinny, but she'd tense up and her chin would fold into itself. It was ugly. Her insecurity made her ugly. He hated her then. Wanted her far away from him.

But then he'd drink four beers, and eventually Katie would drag Sonia away somehow, so Katie could talk to some guy, and he'd have fun talking to his friends. Smoke some weed. And then the bar would be closing—this was Boston, the bars closing at 2 A.M.—and he actually would want to bring her to Nat's house, some of the times. Sometimes, he didn't want to bring her. Sometimes, he just didn't want to deal with her, her being nervous and jealous. Other times, he wanted her warm body around, her cute, young, young body, her skinny legs sticking out of her tight minidress, wanted all that nervousness even, that he would pound out of her later. Pound pound pound her late at night, early in the morning, in the dark of his room, on the futon, sometimes as the sun came up. She was loud when he did it. And so it would start all over again. And as the sun trickled through the sheets in the windows, then he could see her. Another day wasted in the lemon freshness of her youthful pussy, another day of playing with her young body and she bent over and under him with such desperation and abandon. Later, at four or so in the afternoon, he'd get her to buy him breakfast at the diner down the street. Then she'd go home to shower and change into another one of her slutty outfits—he didn't let her keep clothes at his house anymore. That he put an end to. He'd be listening to Neil Pert drum solos, playing air drums, and he'd hear the answering machine pick up, "Curt, Curt, are you there?"

Sonia, Sonia, go away! Why was it so hard to make her leave him? He treated her like shit—well, except for the fucking. He fucked her right. He couldn't help himself. A woman's body in his face and he had to do his job. It was enough for her, or so she claimed, but she was miserable. She'd given up all her self-respect, and for what? For his face between her legs. She was crazy. Sometimes, he blamed it all on her ass, but you can't base a relationship on an ass. Her flat, white, smooth as silk ass. Skin like a baby's. It killed him. A shapeless ass, small as a boy's. He loved her ass and loved opening her legs up underneath her ass. He didn't love her anymore—maybe he never did—but when she showed up at three in the morning, letting herself in with the keys he needed to take away from her, not turning on the lights, saying, I need you, I need you, slithering in bed with him, crying, breathing unevenly, uninvited, what could he do? Her mouth on his cock and he'd be hard in seconds and then it was too late. He had to get those keys from her. And tell her it was over.

He asked for the keys outside of the diner on Harvard Avenue one warm spring afternoon. She'd just bought him French toast with bacon, orange juice, and a cup of coffee. He asked her for the keys, saying, this is not working, I need my space right now, it's not you it's me, like that, on the street, so that she couldn't start taking her clothes off. Or throw too much of a hysterical fit, although she wasn't much into self-control. During that last breakfast in the diner, she'd been weepy and whiny, we only see each other twice a week, I mean, I guess it's okay, but why don't you want to see me more? What's wrong with me? What don't you like about me, sniffle, sniffle? I can change, I can, I really can.

No you can't. No one can. I can't either. He tries to tell her that *that* is what he doesn't like about her, the what don't you like about me, I can change. The sheer lack of pride. He can barely look at her when she starts in with that pathetic shit. How could he have let it go on for two years? Two years . . .

So what happens next? He already started fucking that girl in Portland, the one with the nice Volvo. She stunk of money. And she lived far away. Although he could see a future with her, her money, her scowl, her no-bullshit attitude. The opposite of Sonia's wimpiness. He needs a hard-headed woman, just like Cat Stevens says. Meanwhile, lots of hang-ups on the machine. Then a message from her. I need to talk to you. He doesn't call back. More hang-ups. Then a week later, another message. And then, a week after that, he picks up for some reason and it's her. Just let me see you one more time. I need to talk to you. OK, he says, I'll drive over in the cab, I'm driving tonight.

He drives over. It's dark, around 9 P.M. He honks. He's not parking. He's not going in there. The cab idles in front of the yellow house where she lives. He sees her come out the door and he steps out of his cab, leans against it. It makes him feel secure. She's lost weight, she's even skinnier than before. Her hair seems longer, stringier. She's wearing a tight miniskirt, like always. Those skinny legs look like he could break them with two fingers. She walks down the steps and onto the sidewalk. He folds his arms. He's not gonna let her make him feel guilty. He doesn't owe her anything, except seven hundred bucks. He doesn't owe her himself though, he doesn't owe her. He's afraid she's gonna fall down, she seems so weak, so pale, so helpless. Did he do this? It's her life, it's not his responsibility. Give me one more chance she whispers, and he can barely hear her, the motor of the cab hums loudly. Did he read her lips? Please, give me one more chance, I can change, she croaks. One more, one more. But his arms remain folded, and he shakes his head, no. He gets in the cab and he sees out of the corner of his eye that she's walking back to the yellow house, and he's so relieved, he was afraid that she'd do something crazy, jump on the cab, throw herself at him, and he drives away, wishing he could go all the way to Portland tonight.

Ah, Sarah in Portland. Lays there like a board, but her pussy's as slick as a seal. When she comes, she makes the tiniest of noises, moves her hips one centimeter. Blip. And it's over. It's as if all that money keeps her mind off of her body. It's a relief. It's . . . low pressure. It feels like fucking a wife would. No more screaming and thrashing about. No more hysteria. No more Sonia! No more.

Curt drives, his breath a little uneven, to a parking lot behind a convenience store. There, he rolls down his window and smokes half of a joint. It costs fifty bucks to lease a cab for the night. He needs to make at least fifty bucks. Christ, he wants to do more than break even. The pot starts numbing his mind. He feels better. He feels relieved. A tiny bit of sadness creeps into him, but he shrugs it off.

He pulls over to the cab stand on Harvard Avenue. A gaggle of BU girls walks down the street, swinging their glistening hair around in the clear New England night. They get in the cab in front of him and he pulls up to take its place, then turns on the radio and a Rush song is playing and he thinks, this is good, this is a good sign, and he takes his hands off the wheel, and with the utmost precision, air drums all of the fills. Tonight he'll try his luck with the rest of the college students in Boston, those girls out on the town who, drunk and terrifyingly young, hopefully will need a ride somewhere, and pay him to give it to them.

Michael Stamp
Trolls

Marcus took the stairs slowly, putting his grocery bags down while he stopped to rest on the second-floor landing. The fifth-floor climb to his apartment got worse every day. If he'd had any sense he would have changed apartments years ago after Don died, gotten something on the first floor, or at least found a building with an elevator. But somehow he couldn't bring himself to leave the place they had shared. There were too many wonderful memories. And now it was too late. His building was rent-controlled, and if he gave up his apartment he'd never be able to afford another one.

He'd only walked a block from the small Asian grocery store, but his emphysema made him feel twenty years older. That's what three packs a day for thirty-four years could do to you. How many years had Don bugged him to quit, telling him he should take better care of himself? Funny how things had turned out. Here he was, still plugging along, and Don was dead. The tightness in his chest had subsided after the short rest. Marcus picked up the bags and started up the stairs again.

"Need some help with those, Mr. Tyler?"

Marcus looked up to see Kelly, the boytoy from 5C, standing on the third-floor staircase. Marcus smiled. He might be too old to attract boytoys, but he wasn't too old to enjoy the view. Kelly was bare-chested and wearing cutoffs so short Marcus thought he saw the tip of the kid's cock peek out from the frayed denim of his left pant leg. He couldn't help staring at the sturdy legs covered with reddish down, a sharp contrast to the broad chest, which was completely hairless. Of course he might have had chest hair. The kids today got rid of hair in places they didn't want it.

Kelly didn't wait for Marcus to answer. He took the bags and bounded up the stairs, taking them two at a time. Marcus craned his neck so he could get a good look at Kelly's bubble butt as he ran. Moments later Kelly was back downstairs, patting Marcus on the arm. "I left the bags outside your door, Mr. Tyler," he said.

"Thanks, Kelly." Marcus looked the twenty-something up and down appreciatively. "You're looking good tonight, boy. Got a hot date?"

"Sure do," Kelly replied. "I'm going to The Roundup."

"Well have a good time," Marcus told him. "And play safe."

"Always, Mr. Tyler," Kelly answered with a big smile, showing off perfect, straight, white teeth. Then he was down the stairs and out the front door.

Marcus shook his head as he watched him go. Getting old sure sucked.

He put a frozen entrée into the microwave. Marcus couldn't remember the last time he had actually cooked. He used to love it, but there wasn't much enjoyment in cooking for one, and even less in sitting down to a nice dinner by yourself.

When he still had Don to cook for, he'd spend hours in the kitchen trying out all kinds of new recipes. Don would eat whatever Marcus put in front of him and pretend to like it. His lover had always been a basic, meat-and-potatoes kind of guy, although the meat he liked best you couldn't buy at the neighborhood grocery store.

He swallowed his last bite and finished the second of two beers he allowed himself each night. A smile crossed his lips as he recalled Kelly standing on the stairs tonight, looking like a proud, young stallion. He envisioned the young stud at The

Roundup, moving through the horde of other hard young bodies, their sweaty chests rubbing against each other in a male mating dance. Marcus stood up to clear the table and was surprised to find his pants bunched at his crotch. Jesus, he had a boner! That sure didn't happen much anymore. He took out his hard-on and stroked it. He was a respectable six inches, certainly no stud, but he'd always been enough for Don.

Don himself had owned eight inches, but for reasons Marcus could never fathom, his lover had always loved getting fucked more than fucking. Once in a while Marcus would ask to have Don's rod up his ass, and Don would oblige, but he never seemed to enjoy himself as much as when Marcus was inside him.

Too bad they didn't have Senior Night at The Roundup. Maybe he should go down there anyway, Marcus thought. He could picture the faces of the young men when they saw him, potbellied and bald, with desperation written all over him. He probably couldn't even pay one of them to have sex with him. They'd take off so fast it would be as if someone had yelled "Fire!"

What was it Don used to call old men like him when they were young? Gnomes? No—trolls, that was it. Trolls. When he and Don were Kelly's age, Marcus couldn't imagine himself ever turning into one of those ugly old men, yet it happened to everyone. But if you were lucky, you had someone to grow old with, someone who wouldn't be disgusted by your sagging tits and shrunken ass. He thought he'd have Don, but Don had been gone for almost twenty years, a victim of the plague that had somehow managed to pass Marcus by.

Marcus sighed. You can't live in the past, he told himself.

He went into the living room, opened the cabinet under the television, and looked through his porn collection, settling on *Crotch Rocket* starring Johnny King. Maybe he couldn't go to The Roundup tonight, but he was going to be there in spirit.

He slid the cassette into the VCR and sat down, holding his cock in one hand and the remote control in the other. He fast-forwarded through the credits and pushed play just as Johnny King came on screen. The movie had always been one of his favorites. It was amateurish and technically poor, but he and Don both loved it. Maybe because it held such fond memories.

They had seen it for the first time at the MalePlex. It was over thirty years, but Marcus could still remember sitting in the last row of the balcony, with Don kneeling between his legs, deep-throating Marcus's cock. Watching the flickering television screen, he could almost feel Don's breath on his skin, feel Don's black curls between his fingers as he held his lover's head against his crotch. When he closed his eyes he could almost hear the thump thump of Don's hand hitting the bottom of Marcus's seat as he jerked himself off while he pleasured Marcus.

Even now he could still picture the dreamy look on Don's face. He loved sucking cock, especially Marcus's. They'd come together that night, Don's body jerking so violently he'd fallen back against the seat in front of him. Marcus had ended up shooting all over Don's chest while Don's come had sprayed the empty seats around him.

As black-haired Johnny King started going down on a blond Adonis, Marcus spit in his hand and began to stroke himself. He smiled as he remembered doing this with Don. They'd sit together on the couch, reciting the insipid dialogue along with the video while they worked their cocks. They'd always tried to hold off as long as they could so they could come with the porn star, but they'd never lasted. Don would always end up with his head in Marcus's lap, swallowing his lover's cock, then before long Marcus would be on top of Don, sliding that cock into Don's waiting hole. Marcus looked down at his cock, resting limply in his wet hand. Shit! He'd come without realizing it. And he hadn't needed Johnny King. Just the memory of Don.

"Johnny King always did do his best acting with a mouthful of cock, didn't he, Marcus?"

Marcus turned in the direction of the voice. "He sure did—" he began. He sat frozen, then turned slowly to see the figure sitting beside him on the sofa. "Don?" he asked, barely able to generate enough saliva to speak.

"That's right, Marcus, it's me, in the flesh . . . so to speak."

Marcus stared at him, unbelieving. It was Don, all right; there was no denying it. His black curls were as unruly as ever, his smile just as welcoming. But his body was young and strong, the way it had been before the disease had eaten away everything that he was and made him almost unrecognizable.

It was impossible, yet there he sat, broad-shoulders, incredibly pumped-up pecs, his thick eight-incher standing at attention. Marcus had so many questions, yet the first one out of his mouth was, "Why are you naked?"

Don grinned. "You don't need clothes where I came from."

"Where did you come from?"

"You know the answer to that, Marcus."

Marcus did know, but was afraid to say it out loud.

"I've really missed you," Don told him.

"I've missed you, too. There hasn't been anyone since you."

Don looked skeptical. "A hot man like you alone all these years? I don't believe it."

"I was never a stud, Don, even though you always made me feel like one, but at least I was young. Look at me. Now I'm old *and* ugly."

"Not to me." Don slid over and put his arms around Marcus, kissing him deeply while his hands worked quickly to get Marcus out of his clothes.

Marcus felt the old stirrings immediately. He returned the kiss, clinging to his lover like a drowning man. It had been so long. He lay back, reveling in each sensation as Don's long, talented fingers explored every inch of him. His body had always come alive at Don's touch, but this time he felt different. He couldn't be drunk, not on two beers, but he felt that way. And in his drunken state each part of his body Don touched seemed to physically change.

When Don stroked his shoulders, Marcus felt them broaden.

After Don's hands passed over his chest, Marcus felt his nipples grow hard and his sagging tits tighten into muscular pecs. Don licked Marcus's belly, and suddenly the rounded flesh became flat and hard.

Don's mouth slid down Marcus's body, covering it with kisses. He stopped to rest between his legs, sliding his hands under Marcus and cupping his ass, using the hold to pull Marcus toward him, guiding his lover's cock into his waiting mouth. Don squeezed his ass cheeks and Marcus could feel his shrunken ass bunch up firm and high. Marcus lost himself in the feel of Don's wet warmth surrounding his hard flesh. His cock was lengthening as Don's talented mouth sucked him deeper and deeper into his throat. Don's nose was buried in his graying bush, but still his cock grew. He'd been ready to pop the moment Don touched him, but he forced himself to hold back, wanting the moment to last.

"Let go, Marcus," Don told him, his voice vibrating through Marcus's skin. And to help him, Don slid a finger deep inside Marcus's hole and massaged his prostate.

Marcus gave a strangled cry and gripped Don's hair as he came, shooting again and again. Never in his life had an orgasm lasted so long. Don kept Marcus in his mouth, swallowing it all, refusing to let even a drop escape his throat. When Don finally released his cock, Marcus felt his long, thick pole slap his thigh. His body felt so totally different he could almost believe it had actually changed, but he knew that wasn't possible.

"You make me feel young again, Don," he murmured, ruffling Don's dark hair.

"You are young again, Marcus. Go look at yourself."

Going along with the joke, Marcus got up and went into the bedroom. When he saw his reflection in the wall mirror he stopped, stunned at his transformation. He looked thirty, but he'd never looked as good the first time around as he did now. The broad shoulders, the flat stomach, the powerful chest, and bubble butt he thought he had imagined belonged to him. They were actually real.

So was his cock. And it didn't only equal Don's. It surpassed it. Marcus hefted it in his hand. The fucking thing had to be at least ten inches, and so thick he could barely get his thumb and forefinger around its girth. "I don't understand," he said in bewilderment. "How could this happen?" he asked.

"It was always in you, Marcus," Don said from the doorway. "It was what I saw whenever I looked at you."

Marcus couldn't stop staring at himself. Needing to confirm his eyes weren't deceiving him, he pinched his nipples. He ran his hands down the hard flatness that was now his stomach, still expecting it all to disappear the moment he touched it. His eyes kept coming back to his cock, the most incredible change of all. And even more unbelievable than its size was the fact that it was hard again. After all Don had taken from him only moments ago, his erection was again straining against his belly. He glanced at his bed, then at Don. "I want to fuck you," he said.

Don laughed. "I thought you'd never ask."

"Can I?" Marcus asked.

"You never asked permission before."

Marcus said, "No, I mean—will I be able to fuck you, the way you are now?"

Don grinned sheepishly. "Sure. You didn't think I'd come all this way without making sure you could fuck my ass when I got here."

"Then come to bed."

His voice had barely formed the words and Don was there with him, the two of them jockeying for position like wrestlers. Marcus pinned Don down under him, then flipped him over onto his stomach. Don surrendered without a fight, resting his head on his arms and raising his ass high in the air.

Marcus licked his lips at the sight of the perfectly rounded buttocks yielding before him. He pulled apart the cheeks and buried his face in Don's ass, inhaling deeply. The smell of Don's ass had always been an aphrodisiac for him. His tongue sought the small pink hole, bathing it in spit. He worked his tongue inside the ring and heard Don moan. Hadn't it been just as long for Don as it had for him?

Marcus pulled back, pleased to see Don's pucker had increased in size from a dime to quarter. He dove back in, laving the tunnel, spurred on by the sounds of pleasure coming from his lover. He would have been happy to just keep rimming Don's hole, to continue savoring the taste of the man he loved, but Don was squirming and shifting his ass, impatient for the main course.

"Your tongue feels a foot long," he moaned, "but you know what I want you to put up there. Fuck me, Marcus! Fuck me now!"

Marcus placed the tip of his cock at the opening of his lover's magnificent body. Finally, after all these years, he felt worthy of entering it. He grasped Don's hips and slid his cock into the spit-lubed hole.

Don's body shuddered at the contact. "It feels like a two-by-four," he whimpered.

Marcus thrust tentatively at first, but then overcome with desire, he rammed himself inside Don's ass and began to fuck more furiously. Again and again he pulled out a little, only to plunge his cock in deeper with the next thrust. Don quickly found his rhythm, and they began to move as one.

Soon Marcus felt the familiar tightness in his chest that came from any kind of exertion. He was frightened, but he didn't stop. He would pay any price for this chance to be with Don again. He increased his speed, fucking more like machine than man, slamming his groin against Don's ass with such force his lover was now lying flat on his stomach. The pain in his chest was spreading, and his heart was beating so fast he thought it would burst. Each beat echoed in his ears. He felt light-headed, but still he continued.

He was so close. Another minute, he begged. Please let me come in Don just one more time—

Marcus cried out, and all at once the pain in his chest was

gone. His hips bucked wildly as his cock pumped wave after wave of come into the man who lay beneath him. Even in the throes of orgasm, he was aware of Don's hips moving against the mattress. When his body was finally spent, Marcus let his full weight come down to rest on Don's back.

Only when he felt Don moving under him did Marcus muster the energy to lift himself off the other man. He rolled off his lover's body and lay back beside him. When Don turned over, he could see the evidence of Don's own orgasm glistening on his sweat-coated skin.

Marcus raised himself up on one elbow. "I wish this night could last forever."

"It can," Don told him. "If you come with me."

Marcus dipped his head and lapped lazily at a glob of come on Don's belly. "Come with you?" he asked.

"It's why I came back, Marcus. To get you. You're ready to go, aren't you? There's nothing here to keep you, is there?"

Marcus glanced around. The place had ceased to be a home the moment Don wasn't there to share it. "No, nothing," he said. "My home will always be wherever you are."

"Then let's go."

When they reached the doorway, Marcus glanced back to where the figure lay unmoving on the bed. He was going to ask Don if the old man would be coming with them, then thought better of it. Even without asking, Marcus knew the place where Don was taking him was no different than The Roundup. No trolls allowed.

Tsaurah Litzky
Reading *Lolita* on the 9:25

I elbow a fat old lady with white hair out of the way in order to get a window seat on the Amtrak 9:25 Silver Eagle, nonreserved, to Washington, D.C. As I push past her, my shoulder bag rams into her side. Her mouth opens wide in a surprised "O" but she says nothing, probably pegging me as violent, confrontational and deranged. She shakes her head, closes her mouth and moves down the aisle.

A long scream is rising inside my throat but I force myself to push it back down into my belly as I put my bag under the seat and get out my book. I am traveling down to Maryland to spend Thanksgiving with my family but am not feeling at all thankful; I am reading *Lolita* as I have to lecture on it for my erotic lit class next week. I find this to be an excellent manifestation of the Jungian law of synchronicity, for certainly I am as obsessed, as craven, as whacked out by love as Humbert Humbert. My lover is no longer in love with me. He is planning to move to Alaska, near the Arctic Circle, to study Eskimo creation myths. Perhaps he was never more than a myth of my own creation, because when I phone him he says, *who are you, why are you calling me, I don't know you,* and slams the receiver down.

I open *Lolita* and begin to read. I am at the place where Humbert has spent his first night of bliss at the Enchanted Hunters Hotel with his Lolita. He does not share the mechanics of this coupling, instead he waxes romantic. He says the vision he saw when he orgasmed within her was of a fire opal dissolving within a ripple-ringed pool.

A woman with her bleach blond hair in two girlish pigtails, which would be far more suitable on Lolita, pauses in the aisle and asks, "Hi, anyone sitting here?" "Yes," I grunt, but she does not hear or pretends not to hear me. "Goody-goody," she says, "I have to take a load off my feet." She parks her substantial bottom in the seat next to mine. I wonder how much of my anger and rage toward other people has to do with my failures in love? Is it sexual frustration that makes me want to push this woman out of the seat, grind her under my shoe? I think there is no help for me and I immerse myself in *Lolita* again, though I fear I will find scant comfort there.

When the conductor comes to punch our tickets he tells us that a magician will be coming through the train to do tricks as part of a promotion for the new Amtrak advertising campaign: Amtrak—the magic railroad of your life.

My seatmate bats her overly mascaraed eyelashes at the conductor. She is wearing a big, cheese-colored diamond engagement ring and matching diamond wedding band. She giggles, "Tee-hee, tee-hee, maybe he will pull a rabbit out of his hat and I can bring it home for the kids, but my husband would just kill me, tee-hee, tee-hee." I try to imagine the husband; is he a good old boy or a would-be serial killer who wears black nylon panties under his golf suit? The conductor smiles blandly at the silly woman and moves on down the car.

I return to my book. *Lolita reclines on the bed next to Humbert Humbert. Her soft lips part, she whispers in his ear.* I wish for an exotic new obsession to replace the would-be Arctic anthropologist; maybe a twelve-year-old boy à la Mary Kaye Le Tourneau or a sweet ten-year-old lass with the tiniest swell of budding breast, her pink nipples the size of a dime. I have a modest reputation as an erotic writer but for the past few years my love life has been so meager, puerile, and psychotic, I have to do all my research in my head, the pages of the tabloids, or the amorous confidences of my friends. I am beginning to feel like a fraud and am desperate for real flesh and blood inspiration, but right now all I have is *Lolita*.

My neighbor pulls a book from her shopping bag, *Five Days in Paris* by Danielle Steel. We read as the train stops at Newark, at Metro Park, at Princeton Junction. Then my neighbor gets restless; she squirms in her seat like she has a diaper full of ants. She pushes her elbow into me, breathes her tuna fish breath into my face, "What are you reading?" she trills in her squeaky voice, and leans over even further, almost poking her nose into my chest. When she sees *Lolita* printed on top of the page, she starts to squawk, "Why, why, . . . that's a dirty book!" I want to do violence to her again, grab her by her twin pig tails, twist her head off her neck, but I control myself and pull back. I force myself to look hard into her small, glassy eyes. "You better believe it," I say, grinning ferociously and I have scared her now. She cranes her head out, looks up and down the aisle. All the seats are taken. She picks up her book, opens it in front of her face, stares at the pages. We move down through the morning past Trenton. At the Philadelphia stop, she gathers up her bag, trying not to look at me, and moves to a just vacated seat down the aisle.

A new set of travelers, bustling with suitcases, shopping bags, back packs, enters the car. A shadow falls over me and a low-pitched male voice says, "Excuse me, Miss, anyone sitting here?" I look up to see a huge, black man. His hands visible at the level at the top of the seat are the size of baseball gloves. Because he is so tall and his head is above the luggage rack, I can see his stout neck, but not his face. The russet corduroy fabric of his trousers is exceeding fine. "No, sir," I say, "this seat is not taken." He shoves his satchel and what looks like a tripod onto the luggage rack.

"Thank you, Miss," he says and he sinks down into the seat next to me. I really want to look at him, to see if the face matches the elegant voice, but I am too shy. I start to read again. *In an effort to amuse and perhaps excite her, Humbert takes Lolita to see the world's largest stalagmite.* I am thrilled the dark stranger called me "Miss" instead of the dreaded "Ma'am," which makes me feel old and spinsterish. Despite my romantic disappointments, I am as eager and curious for the world as I was when I was the same age as Lolita. The stranger did call me Miss; perhaps he finds me blithe, artful, a nymphet. I read on: *Humbert and Lo quarrel because she asks him how long they are going to live in stuffy cabins, doing filthy things together and never behaving like ordinary people!*

I allow myself to look at my neighbor. His heavy-lidded eyes are half shut as if in meditation, his small, slightly beaked nose is a bit too delicate for his broad face. His large, full lips seem puckered for a kiss and there is something about the strong, forward thrust of his jaw that excites me. His skin is a creamy light caramel color, his mouth darker, almost chocolate. I wonder if this is the color of his cock. Perhaps he likes to be pursued, perhaps he would like to be seduced. I wonder what he would say if I leaned over and, making my voice sweet and girlish, softly whispered in his ear, *Please may I rest my head between your manly legs?* Would he let out a slow, surprised sigh, then nod? Would he lift the corner of his long suit jacket up so my head could burrow inside? Would he jump up and yell *This woman is a sex fiend!* and then rush away down the aisle? I am not bold enough to try, so I return to *Lolita.*

It is a bright, fall day and the leaves on the trees outside the train window are turning red, gold, colors of passion and heat. We cross the Delaware River. The sight of water, the slow, undulating waves make me think of the ebb and flow of sex, and I can not help but steal another glance at my fantasy lover. His head is leaning forward, his chin resting on his chest. He is asleep.

His skin is oily and his face shines like new copper. I want to place my cheek against his and let his oils moisten my dry face. His arm, under his brown suede blazer, is as wide as my thigh. In repose, with his massive frame, he has the dignity of an ancient monolith. I close my eyes and on the screen inside my head I see him turning toward me, his arms open. Suddenly I am naked with him on a bed in a dark room lit by a single candle. His vast self is glistening, shining in a corona of light. I am on my back and his huge body covers mine totally, maybe in the way Humbert covered little Lolita. My imaginary lover knows just how to support himself on his elbows and knees so that his weight is off me. The top of his big, meaty sex taps against my pubes, teasing me. We are kissing in a tender, lingering way, his big mouth envelops mine, holds it open. His tongue moves inside, dances a slow and languid rhythm, a samba. He has one giant hand cupped beneath my ass. The middle finger, high inside the deep fissure, is moving to that samba beat. He puts a second finger inside and then a third and I want more. I wonder if I could expand to contain his fist, his arm, his whole being?

Such thoughts are driven from my mind as he swallows my entire mouth in a juicy kiss. Then he moves his great head down; first he kisses my inner lips, then he sucks them; he kisses, he sucks. He moves his tongue high inside my vulva and finds the tiny button there. He tongues it a bit roughly, matching the increased rhythm of his fingers moving in and out of my butthole. I am going to die with pleasure but then, he spares me. Keeping his fingers solidly in place, he raises his head, his whole body over mine. He kisses my eyes, my neck, then very slowly, he pushes his giant flute inside me so I am filled by him both front and back. I have never been so full. His fingers and his sex stitch to and fro as he strings me up on a thread of fire, but I feel no pain. My arms cling to him, my flailing legs fan our heat. We come together, melt, as he explodes into me. Beneath our magic room the earth spins to a stop. He holds me, enfolds me. We sleep.

"Wilmington, Delaware, Wilmington, Delaware," the conductor calls out, "Passengers departing the train at Wilmington, please make sure you take all your personal belongings."

I return to the conscious world, damp, sweating, my legs spread wide so my knee is touching his. He is still sleeping, does not seem to notice. I can smell myself, even through my tights and heavy, velvet leggings. The smell seems so strong it could wake him, wake a pack of wild dogs, wake the world. I clap my knees together trying to contain it. The train pulls out of the station, leaving the city spires, the smokestacks of Wilmington behind.

I look around for my book; it has slipped to the floor between his feet. Do I dare reach between his legs to retrieve it? What if I wake him? I observe his breathing is deep and regular, he seems totally zonked. I decide to go for it. As I bend down, my arm knocks against his calf muscle, which is hard as a boulder. Slowly, I reach out for *Lolita*. My fingers are just closing around the spine of the book, when suddenly he sighs, shifts in his seat, clamps his legs shut. He's got my arm and head in a scissors lock! Directly in front of my eyes, on the grimy, gray carpet beneath the seat, is a white business card with a picture of the top half of a smiling woman whose naked breasts are the size of basketballs. Right beneath the woman's humongous breasts in bright red letters it says *Dial 1-800-Big-Bust*. What I really want to do is dial up a genie to get me out of this mess. I squirm my ass back on my seat and gingerly pull my head out from between his legs. I think that this has got to wake him and it does.

He opens his eyes, which are a surprising blue. "Who are you?" he says, "What the hell do you think you're doing?" I manage to straighten myself up into some semblance of a sitting position. I scramble around in my head for the right words, knowing full well there are none. "I-I-I dropped my book," I stutter, "I didn't mean to wake you." "Nah," he says, "You just like to dive between strange men's legs." He's not annoyed, he's amused, he's even smiling at me. His teeth are big and white as sugar cubes. I like this, I haven't met a man with a sense of humor since 1992.

"That was a lot better then a "Do you come here often?" he says. He's still smiling and I realize he's giving me the old once-over. His eyes rest on my small breasts, made more prominent by my padded bra, then he eyes my crotch. His nostrils swell and he, very faintly, sniffs. I close my legs tight, try to squeeze my sex up high inside me so he won't smell me but it must be already too late because he sniffs again. I introduce myself, tell him I'm a writer. I start to chatter nervously about *Lolita*. I am still clutching the retrieved book in my hand. I wave it about as I talk at him, but what I'm really saying is; please don't find me ridiculous, please don't take my pathetic chatter for desperation, even though it is. "I know *Lolita* is about an old guy and a young girl," he says, "but I never got around to reading it, there's got to be more to it then that; what's is it really about?"

"It's a one-sided love story," I tell him.

"I know how easy that can happen," he says. "When I meet someone I like I want it to work out so much, I try to ignore it if we're not compatible." He adds, "I've been in too many of those one-sided things." "So have I," I respond, thinking of the would-be Eskimo anthropologist and the one before him, the one who would only do me doggy style.

My seatmate looks at me very seriously, "So, you've been around the block too," he says, "It's hard to find someone who sees you how you are and is not trying to make you into their private fantasy." "I'll say," I answer, surprised and delighted at the turn the conversation has taken, "That's part of what *Lolita* is about, that and not knowing that real love is about give and take."

"My last girlfriend was a looker," he says, "she was forty with the body of a twenty-five-year-old, but her eyes, her eyes were old and tired; they said, she'd been everywhere, done everything, there was nothing I could give her." He sighs, "But you," he continues, "You have young eyes, like a girl, you're open to life. That really attracts me."

I know this is a miracle. I put my hand out and tell him my name. He immediately grasps it in his. His palm is sweating, maybe he is as nervous and thrilled as I am. When I ask him his name, he tells me that it is Jimmy Horn and he is a jazz flautist.

He is returning from a concert in Philadelphia to his home in D.C. He collects flutes, and he says, has over eighty of them. "I'd like to see your flutes," I say, smiling up at him, widening my eyes, flirting. He smiles back. "That could be arranged," he says. He pulls a card from his inside jacket pocket and hands it to me.

The card has a picture of a long, silver flute and his name and phone number. I slip it inside the waistband of my tights so I won't loose it and Jimmy leans over, leering, trying to peek inside. He is so cute and sweet I want to kiss him. Before I can, an unhappy-looking man in tails and a top hat comes down the aisle of the train toward us. It is the magician promised by the conductor. When he stops by our seat, he pulls a bunch of red paper roses out of his sleeve. "For you, madam," he says, bowing from the waist, "thanks for traveling Amtrak."

I take the roses from him and then he makes his way down the car. "Can I have those roses," Jimmy says, his face opening into a big grin. "Sure, but why?" I ask. "I'll stick them in my flute to remind me of you." He rolls his eyes at me. I want to tell him that I want to stick him in my flute, but instead I place the bunch of paper roses across his knee. I put the copy of *Lolita,* which has been resting in my lap, away in the pack by my feet. Then I move closer to Jimmy, put my hand lightly on top of the nice, big bulge between his legs and, gently as a nymphet, I squeeze.

Alma Marceau
From *Lofting*

I was fifteen, Sharon a year my senior, both of us "Equestrian Counselors" at a sleep-away camp in the Adirondacks, hired on for the season—trading three months of strenuous, stall-mucking labor for a token salary and the privilege of riding in our spare time. I was tall and timid, with olive complexion and a sun-streaked auburn mane; Sharon small and confident, her face all Irish contrasts, flawless skin creating a pleasing pale distinction to a frame of black hair. Though probably plain to an unbiased eye, to me she was beautiful—everything about her, but especially her shoulders: broadly set for a girl, the angles tanned and rounded like brown eggs, they beckoned to my fingers; never before had I known such a desire to caress.

Deferring to Sharon's superior knowledge, I followed her lead as we worked in the paddock and barn and took campers on the trail. She seemed happy for my company and assistance, and clearly enjoyed as much as I did the opportunity to discuss bits and saddles, to argue schools of equitation, or simply to exchange horse platitudes about Hanoverians and Thoroughbreds, Arabians and Swedish Warmbloods. I was surprised and gladdened when, little by little, as if she were testing a decision to befriend me, she began to share with me more personal thoughts. Before very long, she confided to me a sad story of alcoholic parents and a childhood of neglect and emotional abuse.

I was deeply gratified that Sharon had made me her confidante, a role which was new in my experience. I was sensible of a need to reciprocate, and perhaps because I had no story to offer that was comparable to hers in pathetic depth (and perhaps, too, because I had an unconscious need to unburden myself), I began to detail every experience or thought that had ever caused me emotional pain or mental turmoil. With almost saintly patience, Sharon listened while I described my insecurities, fretted over my chronic asocialness, agonized over my appearance. Through it all she remained tranquil, sympathetic, uncritical—until I mentioned my obsessive escape to self-pleasuring, whereupon she suddenly raised a quizzical eyebrow.

I was mortified. Had I made an awful mistake? Had zealousness clouded my judgment, leading me to attribute a liberality to my confessor she didn't possess? I felt cold perspiration beading on my forehead as waves of humiliation and dread washed over me. My face must have gone ashen, for Sharon noticed my discomfort and asked if I was feeling sick. I hesitated, unsure if I should explain the true cause of my sudden distress. Something benevolent in Sharon's expression—the genuine concern I saw reflected in her gaze, or a sympathetic inclination I read in the curve of her neck—decided my answer, and in that instant it seemed to me that I was making a great wager, risking a friendship that, although only days old and more incipient than fulfilled, had already become profoundly important to me.

I blurted out the truth: that I feared my admission of excessive masturbation had repulsed her—then awaited her reaction with a nearly unbearable sense of impending loss. Her answer was to gather my head to her breast and start giggling. *What was this?* I asked myself. Was she making fun of me? But if so, why the tenderness?

Still smiling, Sharon explained that it wasn't my masturbatory habits that had given her pause, only my description of them as "obsessive." Sexual release, she said—whether by self-stimulation or otherwise—had always been as natural to her as breathing. And no one, she added, would call themselves air-obsessed.

"Oxygen, Claire. You look like the type who needs it all the time. I'm going to tell your friends!"

I laughed and hugged her to me, holding back tears of relief as the tension broke.

* * *

The next few days at camp would have been perfect but for the rapidity with which perfectly enjoyable days pass. I spent as much time as I could with Sharon: we rode and talked, raked out stalls, fed and watered the horses—the dirtier the job, the more fun we had.

I was aware that my attraction to her was more than platonic. My pulse quickened in her presence; her looks and touches made me wet between the legs, and I understood exactly what that meant. Yet at the same time I had no idea what to do with these feelings, nor was I sure whether they were at all mutual. I certainly had neither the skill nor the confidence to initiate any sort of investigative foray.

On the day before camp was to end, Sharon and I were alone in the barn, working—tidying up for the last time, making an inventory of lost and damaged tack. Outside there poured a steady thin rain, and it seemed as though the day's drear were reflecting the unspoken sadness we felt at our impending separation. Sharon lived far from the city and, somehow, despite our mutual promises to visit and write, there was a tacit understanding between us—a stoical acceptance of probabilities—that we were at the beginning of journeys that would soon take us in very different directions. We knew, in a way that usually only adults know but rarely acknowledge, that our good-byes the next morning would likely be final ones.

Our chores finished, we stood side-by-side, reclining in the manner of horsewomen, with our backs and the flats of one boot against the exposed studs of the barn wall. Sharon lit a cigarette, cadged from one of the maintenance crew, which we silently passed between us until it burned down to the filter. Then, as though punctuating a decision, she crushed out the fag end with the twist of a heel and turned to face me.

"I love you, Claire," she said suddenly, and held my eyes with her own as she draped the back of her hand on my bare shoulder.

Surprised and overwhelmed by this sudden fulfillment of a secret wish, I began to tremble with excitement. For I knew somehow that this was no declaration of chaste love: the spark that flashed when Sharon's fingers touched my arm was more than electrical static; it conducted an emotional charge as well.

Still shaking with joyous anticipation (and perhaps a little fear), I closed my eyes and moved my head toward Sharon's in expectation of her gentle kiss. When I leaned forward to meet her lips, however, I encountered only empty space. I looked up to find that instead of offering me her mouth, Sharon had retreated slightly, and now stood watching me with narrowed eyes. Her expression confused me: not because it was malevolent, but because it seemed sly and detached, when every scrap of hearsay relating to love had led me to expect that her face would mirror all the unguarded affection and warmth that I knew was radiating from my own.

Wordlessly, Sharon brought her hands to my waist, then unfastened my belt and tore open the fly of my jeans, popping the buttons from their holes with one sure downward tug. Without a pause she slid my pants and underwear to the floor, inclined her body against me for the first time, then brought a leg up between mine. Pressing her face to my neck, she kissed and then bit sharply into the skin below my ear, a tiny nip crimped off between the edges of incisors, like a cat's hit-and-run love bite, but painful all the same. She sucked avidly at the wounded spot, which assuaged its tenderness but did nothing to reduce my bewilderment.

Suddenly she released her lips from my bruised flesh, and I tensed in reflexive expectation of another attack. But when her mouth bent again to my neck, it was only to whisper in my ear—

though what she said was perhaps more scathing and provocative than any physical torment I might reasonably have feared.

"I want to fuck you like a boy."

I was stunned and abashed; my head reeled and I felt as
though a fist instead of a heart were pounding within my chest.
For several terrible seconds a storm of fear and doubt raged
within me—until at last I recalled a certain *douceur* in Sharon's
intonation, a muted playful note that seemed to mitigate the
crude brutality of her harsh and unexpected words.

I calmed myself and managed to regain some perspective on my
situation. What made Sharon's behavior so disturbing, I knew, was
that it bore no resemblance to what I'd supposed "sex" would be
like; it lay beyond the range of even my imaginative understanding. Yet just as I was reconciling myself to the limits of my com-
prehension, I was suddenly forced to acknowledge that part of me
knew *exactly* what to make of my condition, for I now realized that
without consciously intending it, I had responded to the insistent
pressure of Sharon's leg by parting my thighs.

With her knee wedged firmly against my groin, Sharon raised
a hand to my face, then gently swept my eyelids closed with the tips
of her outstretched thumb and index finger: the same formal gesture, I recognized with a shiver, that one would use on a corpse.

There was a sudden rush of movement, and in a fraction of a
second my hands were seized, slammed together, and immobi-
lized. I opened my eyes to find Sharon spinning loops of leather
rein around my wrists with the practiced motions of a rodeo cowboy hobbling an upended calf. Satisfied that my bindings were secure, she took up the free end of the rein, turned this round a nail
that projected from the wall above me, and then pulled it until my
hands and arms were drawn forcibly up and over my head. All at
once I felt her tongue dart across my teeth and lips; desperate for
physical contact, I tried to suck it into my mouth, only to be
balked at each attempt by its slippery, teasing surface.

Breaking our kiss, Sharon fixed me with the same sly, objecti-
fying squint as before, and I watched as her mouth formed itself

into a slight pout, heavy with lower lip, but louche and self-con-sumed rather than beckoning. She extended her tongue for a moment in order to moisten a middle finger with saliva, and then lowered her hand to my sex. Before I knew what was hap-pening—for there was neither verbal warning nor the least prefatory caress—she thrust a finger deep within me. Strangely, I felt no pain other than a negligible sting; I only knew that my hymen had been torn when a tiny trickle of blood began to cool against the inside of my thigh. With a gloating smile, Sharon raised her stained hand to my face, then put her fingers in her mouth to suck them clean. Her pride at having robbed me of my virginity was obvious, but so far out on my own erotic current had I ridden that I registered her "crime" almost dispassionately, as though it were a bit of third-party gossip, or an event in the life of a fictional character, instead of my own.

After once more kissing my lips—chastely this time—Sharon dropped to her knees before me. Her hands, palms held together like those of a supplicant, slipped between my thighs and then canted from the wrists, coaxing my legs apart. She paused for a moment, staring at my half-exposed genitals as if in contempla-tive devotion, a votary before the oread's shrine. Then I felt the wet heat of her breath suffuse my vulva, an advance signature of the soothing conflagration that immediately followed when her mouth, feverish to the touch, was pressed to my pussy. After a flurry of dispersed kisses, she took my clitoris between her lips, at first merely holding it with her teeth abutting its tip, like a sun-flower seed about to be hulled, then mildly sucking at it, then lolling it about with soft passes of her fluttering tongue. Soon, however, I began to crave bolder attention: for no matter how they were actually intended, Sharon's delicate pressures and gen-tle insinuations were becoming a tease. I wanted satisfaction, and notwithstanding my youth and inexperience, I somehow knew that under the present circumstances tenderness—even pro-longed tenderness—would never suffice.

I wanted to be devoured, but I'd been ratcheted to such a

debilitating pitch of arousal that even had I dared to ask—and such daring was decidedly beyond my power—I would have been unable to articulate my wishes. As if intentionally to compound my frustration, Sharon again pulled away without warning, leaving me to buck my pelvis in a vain attempt to press myself against her mouth, now held just beyond my reach. Then, while looking in my eyes to gauge my reaction, she extended her tongue tip until it barely touched my clitoris, then quickly retracted it away, her face beaming with delight at my travail. I was in an excruciating bind: unable on the one hand to satisfy a white-hot need; precluded, on the other, from releasing any of the crackling tension which gripped my body.

Sharon continued to flick at my clitoris with her tongue. Once or twice when she applied increased pressure, I felt the muscles of my abdomen tense preorgasmically, but she always relented at the very moment when the next touch would have vaulted me into the redeeming abyss. I tried to force the issue by rubbing my thighs together, but this proved ineffectual. A profound despairing shame overtook me: a feeling of humiliation, aggravated by a sense of impending failure at my inability either to satisfy myself or to make Sharon satisfy me.

Apparently sensing the advent of my emotional crisis, she abruptly changed her tack.

"Claire," she asked, "are you okay?"—her voice now filled with loving concern. "What's the matter? I thought you liked what we were doing. I'm so sorry if I made you feel bad . . . we can stop. Do you want me to stop?"

I couldn't answer her. Although I was dying for release, I worried she might use any reply I gave to further her cruel game of denial, which—notwithstanding her gentle words and soothing tone—I was not convinced had ended.

But then Sharon broke the impasse by posing another question, one that for all purposes was rhetorical since I could respond to it in only one way.

"Do you want me to make you come?" she asked. "Is that it?"

"Oh, yes!" I cried, desperation overcoming prudence and fear. "Are you sure?"

"Yes, Sharon, please—I'm sure. Please make me come, please . . ."

I knew by her smile, which was both approving and victorious, that I'd at last hit on an adequate reply.

Sharon circled my waist with her hands, then slipped them under my T-shirt. Her fingers strummed across the corrugations of my ribcage before coming to rest on my bare breasts. Finding my nipples, she forsook preliminary caresses, and instead began directly to roll the points between her thumbs and forefingers, applying vicelike pressure until the sensitive flesh was tender-raw and reddened. Both the roughness of the treatment and my tolerance for it surprised me, for I'd no idea as yet that sexual arousal could elevate the threshold of pain. Sharon increased the torsion on my nipples, triggering a precritical disgorgement: suddenly my pussy was so wet that for a moment I feared I might have peed myself in my excitement. Smiling with satisfaction, she lowered herself to her knees and began to lap at my vulva, painting it slowly with stripes of saliva, barely touching the tip of her tongue to my clitoris at the end of every upstroke.

This was more than I could stand: I pushed myself down upon her mouth, but this time, thankfully, instead of evading my motions she actively met my thrusts. With her hands on my buttocks, mauling their flesh as she pulled me violently onto her tongue, she at last treated me to that severity which in sexual extremis is the only true kindness. Half a minute more of blissful friction and I came—thrashing, moaning, biting my lips—my pussy shuddering against Sharon's ravenously sucking mouth, all my senses—of time and place, of sound and motion—jumbled and confused, running together like colors, until the border between self and the world dissolved, and for one numinous instant my "I" was absorbed into the purest of imaginable pleasures, and I knew, even before it was over, that I'd tasted something I would no longer be able to live without.

Shaun Levin
The Whole Bloody Story of My Life from Beginning to End

Just listen to this. You're not going to believe it. I was on the tube, right, coming home from the studio, right, and there was this guy on the train. We were eyeing each other like fucking animals. And I just knew something was going to happen. I could tell he was really into me. I could tell he really wanted me. I knew exactly what I was wearing, and I could tell it was making him hot. He was so fucking gorgeous, and he just couldn't keep his eyes off me. And I let him, fuck, I let him stare as much as he wanted to, right. And then he got up, and it was like he had some fucking dog collar around my neck. He yanked me out of my seat, and I was off. After him. We were way past King's Cross, past the Angel. But I wasn't going to let this one get away. He was fucking gorgeous, and I was shaking, I was, I was so fucking nervous I thought I'd shit in my pants. In these new fucking cords. I thought I was going to die.

Anyway.

His place wasn't far from the station, but I could tell I'd never be able to trace my way back later. I could tell there was no way I'd find my way back to the station. It's not like I know my way around London after all these years. Take me to a part I've never been before, and every house and street looks the fucking same to me. Identical. But I was being led by him, right, fucking dragged along like a dog. His boots were thudding on the pavement as if they were saying: fuck you all out there. I don't give a fuck what you all think. I live here. This is my fucking street. I've never had that, you see. I've never had that feeling in any place. So it was like I could feel it through him. Fuck, I could have carried on walking behind him forever.

But then we got to his house. Just this regular fucking house. He opened the front gate as if he didn't give a fuck whether I was behind him or not. He unlocked the front door, and we walked up to his flat on the first floor. One of those converted houses with about six fucking flats in one house. He said his brother owned the whole place. He said his brother felt sorry for him. He said he felt sorry for him and let him stay in one of the flats. And then inside. Inside there was no light. The blinds were down, and he kicked the door shut behind him, and there was this dead fucking silence. Like: Shut the fuck up, nobody talks from this point on.

I knew he was going to turn round and lash at my face with a fucking knife. I knew it. I thought, *This guy's going to whip out a fucking chain from his back pocket and fuck my head in.* And I thought, *What the fuck. There's no way I'm going to get out of here so just fucking enjoy yourself.* And did his place stink. Fuck, that place smelt foul. Cigarettes and dirt and smelly clothes, and I just thought, *You English are so fucking grimy. You're all fucking slobs.* And that was when I knew this guy would never hurt me.

He came at me, grinning, grinning like some fucking evil fuck, but I just kept my eyes on his. I let him play his game. His face was this close to me, this close, and he put his mouth on mine. He held the back of my neck and pushed my mouth open with his tongue as if he wanted to dig through me. He was quiet, not a word, and I wasn't going to risk saying anything. I wasn't going to make a fool of myself by saying something really stupid. Then he bit my bottom lip, here, look, look what he did, left his mark on me, and then he stepped back. He stepped back to look at me and started to undress right there in the fucking living room. In that fucking pitch-dark living room that stunk of wet ashes, armpits, and shit-stained underwear. He knew I was watching him. He took his time taking off his jacket, unbuttoning his white cotton shirt, massaging the hair on his chest, pinching his nipples. He stood there in his boots and jeans, and I knew with every pore in my fucking body that this guy was going to fuck me and it was going to be so fucking good.

He was like a fucking animal, I'm telling you, thick and hard and covered in dark red hair. He left his clothes on the floor and walked into his bedroom, sweat glistening on him like fucking dew in a spider's web. You can't imagine what it was like. I just wanted to go down on my knees and lick his whole fucking body. I did. I was ready to lick the fucking floorboards his shoes had stood on. I imagined looking up at the fur on his shoulders and his chest and stomach and him pulling me to my feet and saying: Boy, I'm going to fuck your pussy.

Fuck it, you know how smooth I am. You know how sometimes my body feels as soft as a cunt and I'll do anything to get a man to fuck me. I'll follow him into his bedroom and beg him to stick his cock inside me. I'll call fucking strangers on the phone and leave the door open for them to come in. That's what was going to happen here. But no begging this time, right. He was fucking hot for me. He was going to fuck me like a fucking wolf, and there was nothing I could do about it. I took off my All-Stars and my cords, then my T-shirt. I left them lying there in the hallway and went into his bedroom and lay back on the bed, just watching him take off the rest of his clothes. He stared at me while he undid his trousers and scooped out his cock. He looked at me as if he could kill me and he said, "I want your arse so fucking badly. Show it to me. Lie back like that and let me see. Let me see where I'm going to stick my fucking cock."

And I did just what he said. Fuck. He was so fucking hot for me.

"I'm going to fuck your arse," he said. "I'm going to fuck it so good. I'm going to fuck your arse like it's the only thing in this fucking world."

This guy couldn't get enough. Can you picture it. Can you

picture him there talking to me, saying, "I want to be inside you, man. I want to fuck you so hard and long and sore. I want to fuck that soft smooth cunt of yours. Come on, show me. Spread your arse like that. Yeah. Let's see."

By then I'd propped myself up on his pillows, holding my arse open and watching him pull off his boots, then his trousers and socks. He wasn't wearing any underpants, and his cock stood out like a fucking flagpole, jerking up and down every time he said "fuck" as if his prick was some fucking worm-monster waiting to get stuck into my fucking arsehole.

He came at me with a vengeance. He did. He pushed those cushions off the bed and jerked my legs over my head and buried his tongue up my arse like there was no fucking tomorrow. I wanted his whole fucking face in there. I wanted him slobbering all over me, making noises with his mouth so it'd feel like the sounds were coming from inside me. His tongue pressed against the lips of my arsehole, and I lifted myself up and held on to the back of his shoulders and pulled him into me deeper. And he made those noises, those fucking animal noises, as if he couldn't get enough. Like a mangy fucking mutt caged and starved for days. He whimpered and growled and chewed into my arse as if he didn't care what was going to happen.

And his bed was like ice. Believe me. I'll never forget that. Like ice. Sheets like a fucking ice rink. But smelly. Fuck, did they stink. Damp and creased and smelly. I could feel the fucking cum stains melting under my back. And his hot tongue between my legs.

"Open up," he said. "Open." And I swear I could have screamed or fallen in love between each syllable. "Come on, baby," he said. "Come on. Open up for me."

I could have ripped myself in two for him to be inside me. I pulled my arse cheeks apart and felt his face push further into me. I don't know if you've ever felt this way. I don't know if you've ever trusted someone like that. Have you? Have you ever trusted someone to do to you whatever they wanted, and you knew they'd never hurt you?

And when his tongue wasn't enough, he tucked his shoulders

under my knees and brought his cock to my arsehole. He stared at me without blinking and slowly made his way into me, chiseling his cock inside, jerking it back and forth. He was in. He stopped. He closed his eyes and let out this gush of air that was a scream and a sigh. Then he drew his cock out to the tip and slid it back in and kept whispering, "Open up, open up, open up." And I watched him moving in and out of me, and he looked so fucking tormented. Fucking deranged, believe me.

He was sweating like a pig, right. And grunting. Every time he stuck his cock into me he'd snort like a pig, like a desperate fucking animal that had lost all control. His body became darker as the sweat made his hair a damp mat on his skin. My legs were aching as if I'd been holding them up in the air for fucking ages. I needed to lower them, so I slid them off his shoulders and made them a ring around his back. I put one arm around his neck and clung to him like a baby. I pulled myself up and filled my mouth with his hairy nipple. I sucked on it and drank sweat out of his fur and told him to fuck me.

"Oh, God," he said. That's what he said. He said, "Oh, God, I'll fuck you. I'll fuck you. I'll fuck you so hard. I promise."

With my other hand I wiped the sweat off his back and rubbed it into my chest. My skin was already slippery from the sweat dripping off him. He pushed me onto the bed and stared at me. His face was beautiful. I touched his cheek and stroked his forehead and ran my fingers through his hair and traced them down his spine. His body tensed as if he was about to pounce. I clung to his arse cheeks and drew his cock deeper into me, slowly, reassuring myself. I wanted to say: Look. See? I've got all of you inside me.

Are you listening? Are you listening? Can you imagine this? Can you imagine what this was fucking like? In the middle of fucking nowhere with this stranger inside me, and I knew it was going to be fine. I knew that all he wanted was to fuck me. That he wanted me to lie there and take his big fat red-haired cock up my arse.

Then he said. He said, "You like it, don't you?" He said, "You love me fucking you."

"I do," I said.

"You do what?"

"Love it." I said. "I love it."

"What do you love?" he said.

I said, "I love you fucking me."

And then, just like that, he lifted his hand and slapped me across the fucking face. Hard. The pain shot from my cheek to my arsehole like a dart ripping through me. Then he just grabbed my legs and yanked my body down onto his cock and hugged his arms around my knees and shoved his cock into me and used my body to pound into as if I wasn't there and he pulled my arse toward him over and over. And I just let go. I just closed my eyes and let go as if I was doing some fucking yoga exercise, some kind of meditation, right. Fuck, I don't know, some mind and body split. I was looking down at myself and thinking: Fuck, this is amazing. I'm nothing. I feel nothing, and I'm fucking loving it. And then he fucking snorted up this big wad of gob from the back of his throat and spat into my face.

And I could feel again. I could feel how soft my arse was around his cock. I could feel how tight his arms were around my knees. I could feel the fur on his chest rubbing against my legs. And I wished he'd slap my face again. God, I fucking prayed he'd hit me before he came. Because I knew he was close. I knew by the way he was grunting and roaring and then his cum shot into me and dripped from my arse down to my back and he just dropped my legs and fell on top of me.

My face was under his armpit, drenched with sweat, and fuck knows how long since he last washed. He was gasping like he'd just run some fucking marathon. I put my arms around his back and stroked him. His skin was coarse and slippery. I ran my fingers up and down his back, combing his hair, until he rolled off me, slowed down his breathing, and just stared at the ceiling.

"Okay," he said. He said, "Okay. Okay." He said, "You can fuck off now."

I was lying there and there was nothing inside me and I

thought, *How the fuck am I going to get out of here.* I wanted to ask him if I could stay. I wanted to say to him: Let me be here with you. Let me stay here at least until it gets dark outside. Then I can go. I don't want to be out there where everyone can see me. Please, I'll lie here and be still. And when it's dark, I'll go. I should have said that to him. I should have. All I wanted was to be near him. But I kept quiet, I kept hoping he hadn't meant what he said, or that he'd fall asleep and forget. I should have said to him: You don't have to be afraid. You know that. I don't expect anything from you.

But he got off his bed and moved into the living room. He gathered up my clothes and walked with the bundle to the door. He opened the door and chucked everything onto the landing. I walked past him and was going to ask if he really wanted me to go but he stared at me with such disgust I couldn't bear saying anything to him. I couldn't but I still wanted to and I felt my cock go hard and I just said, "Let me stay with you. Please. Let me stay."

His face wrinkled up as if I was the juice at the bottom of the rubbish bin. I should have said: I can love you more than anyone in this world. I can love you like nobody can. But I didn't. He held the door open with his foot and stood with his arms folded across his chest. I looked up at him, at that red fur covering his chest, at his massive nipples above his hands. Then he grabbed his cock and wiped my arse juices from it and onto the wall outside his place. He stepped back inside and slammed the door. And that was it.

I put on my top, hoping someone would come up and see me naked. Fuck, maybe he was even watching me. I tied my laces, my trousers still round my ankles, my arsehole facing his door. I walked back the way we came, looking straight ahead, making sure I didn't see the street name on the corner wall. I know what happens when you come back for more from these guys. I took a left, I think, I think it was a left, and I kept walking. The sun was still out but the air had turned cooler. I love this kind of weather, the kind of weather we've been having lately, that crisp brisk-walk kind of weather. It reminds me of when I was a kid. Going fishing with my grampa. Sitting in his boat at the mouth of the river before the sun came up.

I wandered around for ten minutes before I saw the café. I was sure I'd been there before. The name looked familiar. Maybe they'd done the place up since I was there last. It was bright. Yellow and orange walls and this bright blue furniture. The guy behind the counter stared at me. He just stared at me, and I thought, *Aren't you open yet? Was there a sign on the door I didn't see?*

"You alright, mate?" he said.

"Could I just have a coffee," I said.

"Anything else?" he said.

Because I remember him asking that. I remember him asking if I wanted anything else. And I remember him calling me "mate." I think he did. I think he said, Anything else, mate? Because when he said that, I knew I had to get out of there. I knew that if he asked me one more question I'd answer him the way mad people do when they latch on to you at a bus stop. I'd end up telling him the whole bloody story of my life from beginning to end.

I said just tell me the way to the tube, and he frowned and said, "Coffee's on the house, mate." He said, "Stay. Drink it before you run off." I said I had to be somewhere. I said I'd forgotten that I had to be somewhere. And I did. I did have to be somewhere. I had to be here with you, didn't I? The ride home's a blur now. Maybe because I kept my eyes shut on the train. Maybe because no one ever looks at you in this city.

I had a quick shower at home and changed into some clean clothes. When I looked at myself in the mirror everything seemed fine. I looked fine. I hadn't eaten all day, and my face always looks better when I'm hungry. More defined and chiseled, right. I like the way I look sometimes. Jesus. Thank God for that. I never have to worry too much about going out and looking a mess. And then I came here. And here we are. And I'm fucking starving. So let's order some food.

Contributors

Adelina Anthony is an interdisciplinary Xicana lesbiana artist—a writer/actor/director/cultural activist. She is cofounder and artistic director of Los Angeles' MACHA Theatre Company, which produces works by lesbians of color. Her op-eds are published by the Progressive Media Project; her poetry has been published in Texas and Germany; and her short stories appear in *Texas Short Stories II, Nerve,* and *Pillow Talk III.*

Francesca Lia Block is the author of numerous books, including three *Los Angeles Times* bestsellers: *Dangerous Angels: The Weetzie Bat Books, Violet and Claire,* and *The Rose and The Beast.* "Mer" is from *Nymph,* her collection of erotica. Her work has been translated into many languages and published around the world. She lives in Los Angeles with her family.

Paula Bomer has an M.A. in creative writing from the City College of New York. Her work has appeared in *Global City Review, Open City, Feed, Ms.,* and other publications.

Debra Boxer is a writer from New Jersey currently living in Seattle. Her work has appeared in *The Best American Erotica 2000, Nerve, Clean Sheets, Moxie, Publishers Weekly,* the *San Francisco Chronicle,* and *The Daily Record of New Jersey.*

Poppy Z. Brite is the author of five novels—*Lost Souls, Drawing Blood, Exquisite Corpse, The Crow: The Lazarus Heart,* and *Plastic Jesus*—as well as two short story collections, *Wormwood* and *Are You Loathsome Tonight?,* and a collection of nonfiction, *Guilty but Insane.*

She lives in New Orleans with her husband, Christopher. Find out more about her at www.poppyzbrite.com.

Jamie Callan's work has been published in *Story, Buzz, American Letters and Commentary,* and *The Missouri Review.* She teaches writing at Yale University, New York University, and Fairfield University. She's recently completed the novel *Hollywood Slave Girl Tells All.*

Nell Carberry is a screenwriter and teacher living in Hoboken, New Jersey, birthplace of the zipper. Her past work has appeared in *Salon, Libido, Bust, Paramour,* and in the anthologies *The Best American Erotica 2000* and *Exhibitions.* She is a passionate advocate of public transportation and can be reached by e-mail at nellcarberry@yahoo.com.

Ernie Conrick is a freelance writer and the former senior editor of *Tricycle: The Buddhist Review.* He lives in Brooklyn where he spends his time raising South American rodents and ingesting CalmPlex, a soothing herbal dietary supplement. His novel, *Safe in Heaven Dead,* written under the name of Richard D. Connerney, is available on Amazon.

Robert Devereaux is the author of *Deadweight, Walking Wounded,* and *Santa Steps Out: A Fairy Tale for Grown-ups.* The last of these, banned in Cincinnati, relates the erotic mishaps of Saint Nicholas, the Tooth Fairy, and the Easter Bunny. Out soon is *Caliban and Other Stories.* Robert's future novels will silence forever our yammering foes in the culture wars.

Maggie Estep has published two books, *Diary of an Emotional Idiot* and *Soft Maniacs: Stories.* Her third, *The Woman Who Ate the Sun*—a crime novel involving Coney Island, horse racing, a stripper, and a pianist—will be published in 2002. Maggie lives in Brooklyn, plays classical piano, and hangs out at racetracks, cheering on long shots. Visit her online at www.maggieestep.com.

Nalo Hopkinson is a science fiction writer from Canada by way of Jamaica, Trinidad, and Guyana. She's published the novels *Brown Girl in the Ring* and *Midnight Robber* as well as a collection of short stories, *Skin Folk.* She's currently working on *Griffonne,* her third novel.

J. T. LeRoy, aka Terminator, caused a minor sensation when, at the age of sixteen, he sold his first novel, *Sarah.* He writes regularly on music for the *New York Press.* He lives in San Francisco, and his new book is *The Heart Is Deceitful Above All Things.*

Shaun Levin lives in London. He has stories in *The Gay Times Book of Short Stories, Quickies 2, Best Gay Erotica 2000,* and *Slow Grind,* as well as in *Mach, Indulge,* and *Harrington Gay Men's Fiction Quarterly.* He runs Gay Men Writing, a creative writing workshop for gay men. His e-mail address is shaunlevin@yahoo.com.

Tsaurah Litzky lives in a Brooklyn waterfront apartment with a view of the Statue of Liberty. This is her fifth appearance in *The Best American Erotica.* Her work has appeared in *Penthouse, Paramour, Pink Pages, Longshot,* and many other publications. She teaches erotic writing and erotic literature at the New School.

Alma Marceau, the author of *Lofting,* is a homemaker and entomologist living in Los Angeles, California. When not on the hunt for very small game in the tropical forests of Mexico and Costa Rica, she may be found tending her backyard Weber (she's partial to a hickory/applewood combination for ribs and brisket) or playing hockey (she's capable on defense, but her stickhandling could use some improvement). *Lofting* is her first work of fiction.

Andi Mathis is the pseudonym of a New York academic. She is single, butch, and wears a leather jacket. Her ambitions include a successful novel, teaching in China, and raising a morally straight son. She likes women, but not cats. Her work has appeared in many lesbian publications.

Stacey Richter is the author of the collection *My Date with Satan.* Her stories have been published in *GQ, Zoetrope, Granta, The Pushcart Prize Anthology XXII* and *XXIV,* and elsewhere. She lives in Tucson, Arizona, and is a licensed cosmetologist.

Gary Rosen is a writer, actor, and filmmaker. His stories and essays have appeared in *Strange Fruit, Cuir Underground, Frontiers, RFD* magazine, and the collection *Tricks and Treats.* His first film, *Totally Confused,* played at festivals around the world, including Independents Night at Lincoln Center and the Berlin International Film Festival. He currently lives in Manhattan.

Simon Sheppard is the author of *Hotter Than Hell and Other Stories,* and is the coeditor, with M. Christian, of *Rough Stuff: Tales of Gay Men, Sex, and Power,* and the forthcoming *Rough Stuff 2.* His work has appeared in more than fifty anthologies, including two previous *Best American Erotica* volumes and nearly every edition of *Best Gay Erotica.* Currently he's hard at work on a nonfiction book, *Kinko-rama.* He lives in San Francisco and is PADI certified.

Laurie Sirois, after nearly a decade in San Francisco, has returned to her home state of Maine. She now enjoys her rural environs, both as lifestyle and inspiration. The majority of Laurie's time is spent telecommuting to a technology company in San Francisco and caring for her dog, Otto.

Jane Smiley is the author of ten works of fiction, including *The Age of Grief, The Greenlanders, Ordinary Love & Good Will, A Thousand Acres* (for which she was awarded the Pulitzer Prize), and *Moo.* She lives in northern California.

Michael Stamp's earliest writing influences were Gordon Merrick and John Preston, so it's not surprising that all Michael's erotica, including his S/M tales, have a decidedly romantic bent. His stories appear in the anthologies *Best Gay Erotica 2001, Casting Couch Confessions, Sex Toy Tales, Strange Bedfellows,* and *Best S/M Erotica.*

Lucy Taylor's work includes the collections *Close to the Bone, Unnatural Acts and Other Stories, Painted in Blood,* and *The Flesh Artist,* as well as the Stoker-winning novel *The Safety of Unknown Cities.* Her latest book is a suspense thriller called *Nailed.* Taylor shares a home with her husband, Don, five cats, and a springer spaniel named Zeb in Mead, Colorado.

Anne Tourney's erotic fiction has appeared in various publications, including *The Best American Erotica* and *Best Women's Erotica* series, the anthologies *Zaftig: Well-Rounded Erotica* and *The Unmade Bed,* and the online magazines *Scarlet Letters* and *Clean Sheets.* Her darker fiction has appeared in *Embraces: Dark Erotica and Dark Regions.*

Pam Ward is a Los Angeles native and graphic designer. She likes to write about all the stuff your mother told you "hush" when you asked her: violence, sex, and road trips on the jacked-up streets of LA. She worked the hash food line in high school, did temp work for two sex maniacs in North Hollywood, and ran amok in corporate America until she was asked very nicely to leave. Her work has been published in *Men We Cherish, Catch the Fire,* and *Calyx, A Journal of Literature for Women.* She has received a California Arts Council Writing Fellowship and a New Letters Award for Poetry. Her self-published chapbook is entitled *Jacked Up.*

Reader's Directory

Arsenal Pulp Press

Arsenal Pulp Press is a leading independent press publishing a wide range of titles, which include *The Bald-Headed Hermit and the Artichoke: An Erotic Thesaurus; Carnal Nation: New Sex Fictions; Exhibitions: Tales of Sex in the City; The Embroidered Couch: An Erotic Novel from China; Quickies: Short Short Fiction on Gay Male Desire,* volumes 1 and 2; and *Hot & Bothered: Short Short Fiction on Lesbian Desire,* volumes 1 and 2. For more information, write to 103–1014 Homer Street, Vancouver, BC, Canada V6B 2W9, or visit www.arsenalpulp.com.

Black Books

Black Books publishes books on underground urban subcultures— erotic short fiction anthologies and nonfiction resource guides that enable fringe groups to network with one another. It also publishes *The San Francisco Authors Series:* fiction by well-known and upcoming authors living around San Francisco, or writing about its underground scenes. For more information, write for a catalog at P.O. Box 31155, San Francisco, CA 94131, or visit www.blackbooks.com.

The Blacklisted Journalist

The Blacklisted Journalist includes fiction and nonfiction contributions from writers all over the world. It also features erotica and includes a poetry section. *The Blacklisted Journalist* is not just an e-zine but a body of work that grows each month with the addition of another column, which is what each issue is called. The contributions range from first-time efforts by fledgling writers to works by established authors. With a growing cult following that now exceeds 100,000 readers, *The Blacklisted Journalist* can be contacted via e-mail at black@bigmagic.com or at Box 964, Elizabeth, NJ 07208-0964; or at www.bigmagic.com/pages/blackj.

Bloomsbury Publishing Plc

Bloomsbury Publishing is the publisher of the bestselling books *Kitchen Confidential* by Anthony Bourdain and *The Tulip* by Anna Pavord; other authors include Ben Cheever, Karen Karbo, and J. T. LeRoy. Bloomsbury discovered J. K. Rowling and is the publisher of the Harry Potter series in the UK. Also on its UK list are Booker Prize winners Margaret Atwood and Michael Ondaatje, as well as John Irving, Joanna Trollope, and the *Encarta World English Dictionary*. Visit their Web site, a fusion of their publishing, a literary magazine, reference library, and bookshop at www.Bloomsbury-Magazine.com.

Circlet Press

Circlet Press has been blending the erotic with the fantastic since 1992. Vampires, cybersex, magic—Circlet's specialty is high-quality erotica with a twist. The contact address is 1770 Massachusetts Avenue, Suite 278, Cambridge, MA 02140, or www.circlet.com.

Clean Sheets

Clean Sheets is a weekly online magazine devoted to encouraging and publishing quality erotic writing, as well as providing the public with honest information and thoughtful commentary on sexuality. A new issue of the magazine—showcasing articles, exotica, fiction, art, poetry, and reviews—is published every Wednesday at www.clean-sheets.com.

Cleis Press

Cleis Press has published provocative books on sex and gender by both women and men for more than twenty years. Notable authors include Gore Vidal, Patrick Califia-Rice, Susie Bright, Annie Sprinkle, Tristan Taormino, and Carol Queen. Titles such as *New Good Vibrations Guide to Sex, The Ultimate Guide to Anal Sex for*

Women, Best Lesbian Erotica, The Whole Lesbian Sex Book, and *Susie Sexpert's Lesbian Sex World* are just a few of its groundbreaking books, as well as *Zaftig: Well Rounded Erotica* (edited by Hanne Blank) and Pat Califia's new nonfiction collection, *Speaking Sex to Power: Politics of Pleasure & Perversity.* Visit www.cleispress.com.

Haworth Press

Haworth Press has been publishing books on human sexuality, especially of interest to the L/G/B/T community, for several decades. Harrington Park Press is an imprint of Haworth Press. Visit its online catalogue at www.haworthpressinc.com.

In Touch For Men

In Touch For Men is a monthly magazine featuring erotic short stories, adult video reviews, and nude photographs of young men in their prime. To obtain submission guidelines, write to *In Touch* magazine, Attn. Michael Jimenez, 13122 Saticoy Street, North Hollywood, CA 91605. Its guidelines can also be viewed online at www.intouchformen.com/edguide.html.

Alfred A. Knopf

Alfred A. Knopf is one of America's foremost book publishers, dedicated to publishing distinguished fiction and nonfiction. Knopf is the flagship imprint of the Knopf Publishing Group, a division of Random House, Inc.

Melcher Media

Melcher Media is an award-winning creator of innovative illustrated books, based in New York City. The hit anthology of erotic short fiction, *Aqua Erotica: 18 Stories for a Steamy Bath,* edited by Mary Anne Mohanraj, was published in 2000 by Three Rivers Press using Melcher Media's patent-pending waterproof format, Dura-Books. Its sequel, *Aqua Erotica: Bodies of Water,* debuts summer 2002. Melcher Media has also created the deluxe photography collection *Voyeur and Peepshow,* a stereoscopic book on 1950s pinup photography, complete with built-in 3D glasses and an introduction by Bunny Yeager. Visit www.melcher.com.

The Missouri Review

The Missouri Review is a nationally acclaimed triannual literary magazine that publishes fiction, poetry, essays, author interviews, and more. In close to twenty-five years of publishing high-quality contemporary literature, it has earned a reputation for discovering new writers of exceptional talent. To subscribe, or for selections from the print journal, a lively literature discussion forum, submission guidelines, and contest rules, visit online at www.missourireview.org.

Nerve

Nerve is a smart sex magazine for men and women. In both its print and online versions, Nerve features exceptional photographs, fiction, and reported articles. For its mix of Pulitzer Prize–winning authors alongside MoMA photographers, *Entertainment Weekly* has dubbed it "the body of *Playboy* with the brain of the *New Yorker.*" *Nerve* has created four books to date: an anthology from its first year, *Nerve: Literate Smut;* a fiction collection, *Full Frontal Fiction;* a photo collection, *Nerve: The New Nude;* and a history of sex in literature, *The Naughty Bits.* Visit www.nerve.com.

New Mouth from the Dirty South

New Mouth from the Dirty South publishes kick-ass fiction and true stories, *Tales of a Punk Rock Nothing* and *Gynomite: Fearless, Feminist Porn* among others. It also runs a subscription service, Factory Direct, that delivers quality, underground, self-published literature to your house every other month. For details, write New Mouth from the Dirty South, P.O. Box 19742, New Orleans, LA 70179-0742; or phone (504) 948-2228; or visit www.newmouthfromthedirtysouth.com.

Noirotica

The *Noirotica* series is an ongoing line of erotic anthologies in the crime-noir genre. *Noirotica* (Rhinoceros Books, 1996) was the first anthology ever to explicitly explore that territory, and *Noirotica 2: Pulp Friction* (Rhinoceros Books, 1997) continued the series. *Noirotica 3: Stolen Kisses* (Black Books, 2001) is the most recent volume. For more information on the *Noirotica* series or to order a copy, write Thomas Roche at P.O. Box 410686, San Francisco, CA 94141-0686, or visit www.thomasroche.com.

Studio Loplop

The novel *Lofting* by Alma Marceau was published by Studio Loplop, an independent press based in the southern reaches of the California Floristic Province. Letters should be addressed to Loplop Publications, 4804 Laurel Canyon Boulevard, Suite 303, Valley Village, CA 91607. Editor in chief April Platinum also maintains the company Web site at www.Studioloplop.com.

Venus or Vixen Press

Venus or Vixen is an independent press publishing fiction and anthologies. It is the publisher of books such as *Viscera* and *Embraces: Dark Erotica.* It is also a free, award-winning online magazine, venusorvixen.com. Editor in chief/publisher is Cara Bruce. For more information, write to PMB #121, 322 Cortland Avenue, San Francisco, CA 94110 or visit www.venusorvixen.com.

Warner Aspect

"Ganger (Ball Lightning)" by Nalo Hopkinson originally appeared in *Dark Matter: A Century of Speculative Fiction from the African Diaspora,* now available in Warner Aspect trade paperback. Fans of Nalo Hopkinson can look to Warner Aspect, an imprint of Time Warner, for her first collection of short fiction, *Skin Folk.* To learn more about their other science fiction/fantasy titles and authors, visit www.twbookmark.com/sciencefiction.

Credits

Reader Survey

1. What are your favorite stories in this year's collection?

_____

_____

2. Have you read previous years' editions of *The Best American Erotica*?

_____

3. If yes, do you have any favorite stories from those previous collections?

_____

_____

4. Do you have any recommendations for *The Best American Erotica 2003*? (Nominated stories must have been published in North America, in any form—book, periodical, Internet—between March 2002 and March 2003.)

_____

_____

_____

5. How did you get this book?

☐   Bookstore
☐   Library
☐   Mail-order company
☐   Web site
☐   Sex/erotica shop
☐   Borrowed it from a friend

6. How old are you? _____

7. Male or female? _____

8. Where do you live?

☐   West Coast
☐   Midwest
☐   South
☐   East Coast
☐   Other

9. What made you interested in *The Best American Erotica 2002*? (Check as many as apply.)

☐   Enjoyed other *Best American Erotica* collections
☐   Editor's reputation
☐   Authors' reputations
☐   Enjoy "Best of"–type anthologies
☐   Enjoy short stories in general
☐   Word-of-mouth recommendation
☐   Read book review
☐   Erotica fan

10. Any other suggestions for the series?

_____

_____

_____

Please return this survey or any other BAE-related correspon-
dence to: Susie Bright, BAE Feedback, P.O. Box 8377, Santa
Cruz, CA 95061, or e-mail Susie at: BAE@susiebright.com.

Thanks so much. Your comments are truly appreciated.